# Are we there yet?

## A GUIDE TO LIFE, LIVING AND DEATH

# Are we there yet?

## A GUIDE TO LIFE, LIVING AND DEATH

DENNIS D HUNT

Matador
9 De Montfort Mews
Leicester LE1 7FW, UK
Tel: (+44) 116 255 9311 / 9312
Email: books@troubador.co.uk
Web: www.troubador.co.uk/matador


ISBN 10: 1 905886-26-8
ISBN 13: 978-1905886-265


Typeset in 12pt Bembo by Troubador Publishing Ltd, Leicester, UK
Printed in the UK by The Cromwell Press Ltd, Trowbridge, Wilts, UK

**Matador** is an imprint of Troubador Publishing Ltd

For Linda who made my life whole

*One must know oneself.*
*If this does not serve to discover truth, it at least serves as a rule of life, and there is nothing better.*

*Thus all our dignity lies in thought.*
*Through it we must raise ourselves, and not through space or time, which we cannot fill.*
*Let us endeavour then, to think well: for this is the meaning of morality.*
*Pascal*

# Contents

Why this book?                                          1
Searching                                              6

*Part I – Life*                                        11

In the beginning - God or what?                        13
Some Metaphysical Answers                              21
Universal Law                                          31
Root Assumptions                                       35
Life Purpose                                           38
Universal Mind  - The Power That Is                    41
Consciousness                                          46
Thought the Creative Power                             55
Destiny                                                63
Our Life  – Our Creation                              67
Spontaneity and the Moment                            77
Thought Watching                                      85
Learned and Cultural Beliefs                          89
The Outer is always the Manifestation
of the Inner                                          94
Time                                                 100
Effecting Change                                     104

*Part II – Living*                          109

Love                                        111
Happiness                                   119
Fear and Worry                              129
Pain                                        143
Guilt                                       152
Health                                      158
Healing                                     169
Symbols                                     177
Miracles                                    185
Action – the Solution                       195
Work and Creativity                         202
Attitude                                    210
Freedom from Attachment                     214
Sex, Drugs, Drink and Spirituality          219
The Nature of Evil                          223
Evil – from Global to Individual            236
Trust, Love and Spontaneity                 247


*Part III – Death*                          251

Preamble                                    253
Death                                       261
Dying                                       265
Life after Death                            278
Reincarnation                               292

Conclusion                                  307

## Why this Book?

While we were enjoying a meal together recently, my wife asked me whether I believed in life after death. After pausing to decide if she knew more about what I had just eaten than I did, I replied that I had no doubt that life continued after death. In fact the question, as such, was no longer a question in my mind. This naturally enough led her to ask me what I believed the form that life after death took. I tried to answer in as few words as possible, not an easy task when dealing with the infinite. But whether I satisfactorily explained what I believed or not, I will never know, for at that moment the waiter arrived and asked if we had finished our meal!

This conversation got me thinking. I have spent all of my adult life trying to find answers to the difficult questions about life, to determine those things about life that I could accept as valid. Thinking further on the subject, I realised that whilst I had found many answers that satisfied me, I had not summarised these in any way. In the past I have written a number of books on related subjects, but I had not produced a definitive work setting out how I believed this thing called life worked. Something that I could place in the hands of my wife or my children and say, this is what I believe. This book is an attempt to fill that gap and leave behind my testimony on this thing called life. In this context the words of the song by 'Mike and the Mechanics' seem somewhat apt:

*Crumpled bits of paper filled with imperfect thought, stilted conversations. I'm afraid that's all we've got...*

Looking back, I wish my father had left me a book like this, something that summed up what he thought about life. Now that he is gone there are still questions that I wished I had asked him. I did not meet him until 1946 when he came home from the War. As a result we were never really close. I was always closer to my mother who died when I was seven years old. There was the generation gap between my father and I that always seemed to make asking certain questions awkward. Perhaps, if for a brief period, we could have conversed as equals, there would have been the opportunity to explore more deeply those things that we shared.

So from a determination that my children should not have a similar void in their lives, this book was born. I do not present it as a definitive work about life, but simply as a book that summarises what I have found that satisfies me. It is literally the result of my lifelong searching. My attempts to make sense of this thing called life that we are all born into, seemingly without choice, to make of it the best that we can. I regard myself as a pragmatic spiritualist; that is I am interested in those things that make greater sense of life in a practical way. That provide answers that work in everyday life. Answers that help lift depression, heal sickness and ill-health, and where this is not possible provide a philosophical framework that makes suffering more bearable. If when reading this book the reader fundamentally disagrees with my findings, then well and good. For in the disagreement will be the formulation and clarification of their own views and this is what is important, for each must follow their own path, must find their own answers to the puzzles and conundrums that life poses for them.

For over a century now scientists and secularists have been predicting the ultimate demise of religion. But if anything religious activity has increased during this period, particularly the fundamentalist versions. It seems to me that one of the main underlying reasons for this is the propensity of science to treat humans beings as accidental elements in the physical world and the universe. Whereas religion inextricably links humans to a personal God and in addressing the spiritual aspect of our psyche provides the reassuring answers that science does not. We are more than mere physical and mental beings. There is within all of us a spiritual dimension that must be recognised if we are to address the wholeness of man, and by spiritual I do not mean religious, for religion has, in many instances, given any idea of God a bad name. People do not want a factual version of how it is. They want to know how it is for them; they want answers to the questions posed to them by their life. Answers that enable them to face the issues and problems that confront them daily.

Whilst psychology and psychiatry have value, science in general is not best suited to deal with people's anxieties, fears and worries; physics in particular does not deal in emotions. Religion thrives because it seeks to provide answers to the fundamental human condition. Science can at best only provide answers to the building-blocks of our world and universe. It can never provide answers to the fundamental questions posed by being human. Indeed what the scientist and researcher are examining they are. A fascinating conundrum indeed.

The book is wide ranging in the subjects it covers. It is the outcome of my searching that continues to this day. For ease of reading I have broken the book down into three main sections, with the intention that each section can stand alone, and can be read as such. The three sections are:

1.  *Life* – An exploration of how we came into being; the essence of being human. This section explores the purposes of life, consciousness and the power of thought and imagination.

2. *Living* – This section takes the form of essays on life, and follows on naturally from the opening section. It covers the important areas of life such as Love, Happiness, Fear and Pain. It explores the nature of Evil together with Health, the fascination of the age.

3. *Death* – and life after death. This aspect of life must be addressed if life is to be seen in all its fullness. Without coming to terms with our mortality, any treatise about life would be incomplete.

I have no doubt that in this book, by its very nature, I risk offending both the religious and the non-religious in equal measure. Be that as it may, I can do no more than state my findings and beliefs as honestly as my literary and grammatical skills allow.

I am neither a scientist nor an academic. I draw my knowledge from a lifetime of exploration of the big questions that face all of us. Of dealing with people on a daily basis in my work; of finding out what actually works in practice, rather than in theory. I do not ask that the reader accepts any conclusion that I have reached – merely that they are able to understand my reasoning.

Viktor Frankl, the Austrian founder of Logotherapy, literally the therapy of meaning, wrote that each person is seeking a meaning in their life which is specific to them. *'Man's search for meaning is the primary motivation in his life.'* Each of us must find answers which are specific to us alone; which have lasting meaning and which can serve as the foundation stones on which we can rest our weight. This book encompasses and explores the answers which are meaningful for me.

As a member of Western society I am concerned about the unhappiness that seems to be endemic today, even though we live in a time of plenty, with all of the aids of technology and modern medicine to assist us. This unhappiness, it seems, is due to the frequency of anxiety, fear, malaise, depression and chronic fatigue from which many people suffer. A recent (2006) Report by the Mental Health Foundation and the World Health Organisation said that mental illness in the UK was growing with:

- 1 in 15 children self-harming.

- 19,000 suicide attempts by teenagers every year.

- 20% of people suffering from genuine mental distress such as anxiety or depression.

- 25,000 people sectioned each year under the Mental Health Act.

Many of those who suffer from mental illness will have their symptoms, in theory at least, eased by the use of drugs. But the statistics are evidence, if evidence were needed, of the basic existential problem which is everywhere present today, which is that life for many people is meaningless and lacking in purpose. If this book helps in some small way to provide answers to some of these fundamental existential problems, then the time spent in writing it will have been time well spent.

Finally, I must express my thanks to John Fitzsimons – or Fitz as he is affectionately known to his family and friends, for the painstaking proofreading that he undertook of the original manuscript. Being an ex-headmaster his comments and corrections were always shown in red pen. On occasion his remarks were similar to those that I received all those years ago in my school reports. I remain forever in his debt.

Dennis D. Hunt
*July 2006*

## Searching

When did my search for answers begin? I don't know. When I began to think for myself I suppose, as opposed to simply reacting to what was happening to me. I have always been fascinated by people, being an avid people-watcher from an early age. I remain so to this day, people in all their shapes and disguises, looks and sizes fascinate me. I want to know who they are, where they come from, what their background is. What they are like as people and what shaped them to become the people they are now.

When I was growing up my brothers and I lived in some old cottages opposite a village green in Linslade – now a suburb of Leighton Buzzard, Bedfordshire. Half a dozen of the cottages were tumbledown and uninhabited. I would often sneak into these to hide and retreat from the working demands my stepmother made upon me to help with the endless chores that made up the business of running our small farm.

In the bedroom of one of these derelict cottages I uncovered a treasure trove of *Picture Post* magazines that went back to 1939 and the commencement of the Second World War. These magazines charted the progress of the War, with stories and colour pictures of all of the campaigns that raged across Europe and the Far East from 1939 to 1945. I would hide away in this old cottage and immerse myself in the magazines, losing all sense of time as I read and mentally explored regions and realms, as yet unknown to me.

I remember being moved to tears by the stories of British and American troops liberating the concentration camps in Europe. The harrowing pictures of skeletal survivors, together with the pictures of piles of emaciated corpses, haunt me to this day. This followed by the return of Japanese prisoners of war who had been held in the notorious death camps of the Far East, only increased my horror of man's inhumanity to man.

Questions formed in my mind; questions without answers as to what was the purpose of it all? Who were these people whose lives and families had been torn apart and destroyed by war, so cruelly and painfully? Was this what life was about? If there was a God, how could 'He' allow such things to happen? How could such evil exist? Why were we here? Were we merely an accident of the Universe? Was there a God that I was hearing about in school and through attendance (forced) at our local Methodist church? And if there was a God, how could 'He' allow such awful things to happen to mankind; 'His' creation? Questions, so many questions, all apparently without answers.

My time at school I tolerated, rather than enjoyed; it was after all some relief from the grinding drudgery of work on our small farm, from feeding the pigs, to mucking out the animals. I remember that my favourite lesson was Religious Affairs. This subject was taught to us at Linslade Leopold Road, Secondary Modern School, by John Aldridge, my favourite teacher. The classes consisted mainly of discussions when we debated, those of us who could be bothered, religious topics from the stories of the Bible to the very existence of God, which I recall most of the class doubted. Time used to fly by as the debates, heated at times, absorbed me. These lessons fed my hunger to know more. Yet when I questioned the Methodist Minister seeking proof of the existence of God, I was told simply to trust. Not to question, but just to accept and trust. To an inquisitive youth who saw everything in black and white terms, a wholly unsatisfactory answer.

As I moved into my teens life became ever more complicated. A painful time of my life that would perhaps be better covered in an autobiography. Memories, however, that pale into insignificance when compared with the suffering of children in Africa, Palestine, India and even Eastern Europe that I read about and see on the television screen today. To me the time was painful and confusing, but with the benefit of hindsight, and in comparison with those children who suffer so today, perhaps not so bad after all. It seemed bad to me, mainly because I compared it with my contempories, who all seemed to be loved and cared for. An illusion perhaps, but one I held at the time. With adulthood I began to find time to pursue my quest to find answers to the deeper questions about life. I have subsequently travelled many miles, met and discussed the subjects covered in this book with many people, and read and devoured many books on the subject. It is not my intent for this book to be autobiographical, so I will keep details of the places I have been to at a minimum. Likewise the many interesting people I have met along the way, except where they are directly relevant to the context.

It is clear to me that the greatest uncertainties of our age are not those concerning the Universe, awesome though it is. Our knowledge of the Universe has expanded enormously over the past century and continues to expand at a pace today. Our greatest uncertainties remain, as they have through the ages – the problem of understanding ourselves – human behaviour and the human mind. Of answering the most fundamental questions about life and living that still remain unanswered. These problems have challenged man throughout recorded history and do so today. This book is my attempt to set out the answers that I have found to these most tantalising questions, and to contribute in some small way to what I consider as the greatest challenge that confronts mankind, for this indeed is the 'last frontier'.

I was reminded frequently throughout my search of the young child who, like all young children starting out on a journey, asks: 'Where are we going?' and then, in the way that any parent will recognise, shortly thereafter asks again: 'Are we there yet?' An apt title that summarises my searching over the years.

# Life

## In the Beginning – God or What?

The first questions to which I sought answers as I commenced my search were: How did we come into being as a species? How did our Universe and our world come about?

As the Darwinist philosopher Michael Ruse, in his book *Can a Darwinian be a Christian?* asked:

> *Why should a bunch of atoms have thinking ability? Why should I, even as I write now, be able to reflect on what I am doing and why should you, even as you read now, be able to ponder my points, agreeing or disagreeing, with pleasure or pain, deciding to refute me, or deciding that I am just not worth the effort? No one, certainly not the Darwinian as such, seems to have any answer to this... The point is that there is no scientific answer.*

Modern-day science tells us that our bodies are composed of complicated atoms of carbon, nitrogen and oxygen, together with many others. Yet these atoms did not come ready-made within the Universe, they were created by nuclear activity within the stars over billions of years. This nuclear activity resulted ultimately in massive explosions that distributed and scattered debris and dust throughout the Universe. It is extraordinary to think that the nucleus of every carbon atom within our bodies has come into being through the birth, growth, death and subsequent deterioration of stars. The very material from which we are made in physical form being the stuff of the Universe.

Emanuel Swedenborg, the Swedish scientist and mystic, writing in the 18<sup>th</sup> century wrote:

> *However obscure our idea may be, yet we shall clearly perceive with a little attention, that the stupendous machine of the animal body could by no means have come together without a positive directing force... Such a directive is not without, but is within...*

The fundamentalist Christian is most likely to point me to 'Genesis', the first Chapter of the Bible for the answer. But does the Christian God of the Bible really exist? Or are the 'Big Bang' theorists right in their belief that the world and all that is in it is simply the result of cosmic and chemical activity and interaction? Could there be an internal world which is spiritual and an external world which is scientific? Are we simply accidents of nature, or more than this? Is there a 'first cause' that answers this most fundamental of questions?

There was a time, not so long ago, when it seemed that astrophysicists could explain to us what the Universe consists of. Recently, however, these explanations have started to unravel. There is, it seems, a lot more to the Universe than meets the eye, for when the known mass of our universe was added together, it was found that it only made up about 4% of the known Universe. The rest of the Universe it seemed, was made of other mysterious substances, which the astrophysicists named, equally mysteriously, 'dark matter' and 'dark energy'.

Two scientists at Princeton University – Professors Peebles and Ostriker – suggested that there was ten times more 'dark matter' in existence than there was ordinary matter. But despite its labelling, 'dark matter' is a substance that remains completely unknown. Nothing that particle physics can come up with comes near to describing it. 'Dark matter' has, as yet, to be detected let alone explained. If 'dark matter' is everywhere present in our galaxy, then it must be present on earth. In fact it must be passing through the earth every day. As it does not interact with ordinary matter it can pass straight through the substance of the earth.

In 1997 Professor Saul Permutter, while looking at the expansion of the Universe, accidentally discovered that not only were all stars and galaxies moving away from each other, they were doing so at an accelerating rate. This meant that 'something' was pushing the stars apart. But what was actually doing the 'pushing' remained a mystery. It was then decided to call this force: 'dark energy'. However, like 'dark matter', 'dark energy', whilst inferred from the movement of the stars and galaxies, has only been named as such in order to give form and shape to our understanding of the Universe and how it works.

Scientists have calculated that the universe is made up of 4% ordinary matter, 21% 'dark matter', and 75% 'dark energy'. This means that there is no physical evidence for the stuff that makes up a whopping 96% of our Universe. To put it at its crudest, this 96% consists only of a theory, or as Professor Mike Disney of Cardiff University, in a recent Horizon programme on television pithily put it. 'Not physics at all, just fairies at the bottom of the garden.'

Way back in 1929, observations of distant galaxies showed that the light from them behaved is if the galaxies were moving away. It appeared to scientists as if the Universe was expanding. If the Universe is expanding, then what did it expand from? The answer to this question led to the 'Big Bang' theory. Using the data available to them, scientists calculated that our Universe is between 15 and 20 billion years old, with our world being around 4.5 billion years old. In human life span terms, a very long time indeed.

According to the 'Big Bang' theory of creation our Universe had a beginning. Prior to this, there was nothing; during and after that moment there was something: our Universe. The Big Bang theory is an attempt to explain what happened at the very beginning of our Universe. There are, however, many misconceptions surrounding the Big Bang theory. For example, we tend to imagine a giant explosion. Experts, however, say that there was no explosion; rather there was an ongoing expansion. Rather than imagining a balloon popping and releasing its contents, we should imagine a balloon expanding: an infinitesimally small balloon expanding to the size of our current Universe.

Any discussion of the Big Bang theory would be incomplete without asking the question: But what then about God? Cosmogony (the study of the origin of the Universe) is the area where science and theology meet. First Creation was, and remains, a supernatural event. That is, it took place outside of the natural laws as we understand them. The fact of the creation naturally leads to the question: Is there anything else which exists outside of the natural realm? Specifically, is, or was there a Master Designer? We know that the Universe had a beginning, but was God the 'First Cause'? God v The Big Bang; Evolution v Creation. Can the void between these diverse views be bridged? Do they all contain truth in their own way?

According to Hongbao Ma of the Department of Medicine at Michigan State University, East Lansing, the Big Bang theory is very vague on the how, when and where the event happened. He asks in his paper 'The Nature of Time and Space':

> *Was it located in space? If so, space has no beginning and space must be absolute. Some scientists consider the big bang to*

*be a rapid expansion of space. If space can expand, then it is in motion, and thus cannot be a dimension that defines motion. If we say the beginning of the universe, we need to ask the beginning of what? According to modern cosmology the concept of time has no meaning before the beginning of the universe. It did not exist then.*

So what existed before the Big Bang? For we know that from nothing can come only nothing. Hongbao Ma goes further and asks:

*If we say the universe is finite, we must ask and answer what is outside of the universe? Although this is an ancient question that nobody can answer reasonably. 'Nothing' is not a satisfactory answer.*

Whether we believe in a God, in whatever form or under whatever name, or whether we believe we are simply the result of cosmology, what cannot be disputed is that our Universe did have a beginning; and further, that whether we want to call it 'dark matter' or 'dark energy', we are immersed in a creative energy, which powers us and all living things.

As I write, reports of a milestone court case in the USA are in the newspapers. In the biggest courtroom case on evolution for 80 years, a Pennsylvania Judge has ruled that schools cannot mention divine intervention in biology classes as an alternative to Darwinian evolution theories. The judge's decision to ban any reference to 'intelligent design' (ID) is, apparently, another blow to Christian hardliners concerned about the marginalisation of their faith in the teaching of biology in schools. ID maintains that life on earth was produced by an unidentified intelligent cause. ID proponents, like Swedenborg before them, argue that biological structures are so complex that they must have been designed by an unidentified intelligent being.

Contrary to most reports, ID is not a religious-based idea, but an evidence-based scientific theory about life's origins. According to Darwinian biologists, such as Richard Dawkins of Oxford University, living systems 'give the appearance of having been designed for a purpose'. ID proponents hold that there are tell-tale features of living systems that are best explained by a designing intelligence. The theory of ID does not challenge the Darwinian basis of evolution as such, but it disputes Darwin's idea that the cause of biological change is wholly blind and undirected. ID, it seems, is not based on religion, but on scientific discoveries and the experience of cause and effect. Unlike creationism, ID is best described as an inference that arises from the study of biological data. Regrettably, ID's association with religion in the minds of many, has led to the automatic rejection of the theory as worthy of consideration by many scientists and modern philosophers.

The Catholic Church commented on ID in the official Vatican newspaper. Professor Fiorenzo Facchini, a specialist in evolutionary theory, at the University of Bologna, is reported to have said recently that: 'Intelligent design is not science, it belongs in the realm of philosophy and religion, but not science.' The Vatican has long tolerated the teaching of evolutionary theories even though it believes, as stated in the Bible, that the world was created by the hand of God. Cardinal Christopher Schonborn, in October 2005, called into question the idea that Catholicism and evolution were at odds. He said: 'I see no difficulty in joining a belief in a Creator with the theory of evolution, but under the prerequisite that the borders of scientific theory are maintained.'

In the 19th century, St George Jackson Mivart, a Catholic critic of Charles Darwin, argued that a given genetic mutation might well appear random or accidental, which in turn might be explained by science as being brought about by a set of physical causes, whilst still possessing another cause entirely. A cause that could be described as descending 'vertically' rather than effecting events in a time-related, or temporal sequence 'horizontally'. He argued that it owed its existence to God who brings it, and all other physical and temporal causes about out of nothing. Thus faith in God, or Providence, need not change the way the Christian thinks about science, in the way that the faith of the creationist in the literal truth of Genesis is supposed to do. It does nevertheless allow for a sense of purpose, a goal directedness as it were, to be observed by science within the physical world.

In the 20th century, the scientist-philosopher Michael Polanyi analysed the phenomenon of life emergence and concluded that evolution and life itself, must have been originated by the action of an orderly innovating principle of a higher order, the action of which is released by random fluctuations and 'sustained' by fortunate environmental conditions.

Darwinism, on which the theory of evolution is based, claims that all living creatures are modified descendants of a common ancestor. That human beings are merely descendents of ape-like ancestors. Darwinism claims that every new species that has appeared on earth can be explained by descent with modifications. Neo-Darwinism claims that these modifications are the result of natural selection acting on random genetic mutations.

Those who question the tenets of Darwinism – eminent scientists among them – argue that Darwinism has become a materialistic philosophy masquerading as empirical science. That the theory has developed to the extent that it has because there is simply no other materialistic explanation for life on earth. Those who have the temerity to question the theory, by for instance propagating ID, by definition, cannot be scientists.

Yet the scientist who led the team that established the first complete map of the human genome – the study of the approximately 20,000–25,000 genes in human DNA - Francis Collins – the director of the United States National Human Genome Research Institute, claimed recently that there is a rational basis for a creator and that scientific discoveries bring man closer to God. In September 2006 his book *The Language of God* was published.

Distinguished atheists, such as Philosopher Antony Flew of the University of Reading, have revised their views on creation as the result of the ID theories prevalent, particularly in the USA. Flew made worldwide news in 2004 when he repudiated a lifelong commitment to atheism and affirmed the reality of some kind of creator. He cited evidence of ID in DNA and the arguments of ID theorists as important reasons for his shift.

In 2002, one of the USA's leading science journalists, John Horgan – a self-proclaimed lapsed Catholic – conceded that scientists have no idea of how the Universe was created, or how inanimate matter on our planet coalesced into living creatures. 'Science,' he said 'You might say, has discovered that our existence is infinitely improbable, and hence a miracle.' The late Biochemist Francis Crick, who shared the Nobel Prize for discovering the molecular structure of DNA, cautiously invoked the same words a few years ago when he said: 'An honest man, armed with all the knowledge available to us now, could only state that in some sense, the origin of life appears at the moment, to be almost a miracle, so many are the conditions which would have had to be satisfied to get it going.'

## Some Metaphysical Answers

Examining the arguments of both sides leads me to conclude that science does not, as yet, have a generally accepted theory of how life began on earth. It seems that people who believe that life emerged naturalistically need as much faith to support their view as those who argue in favour of ID.

Atheists and Christians, Muslims and Hindus all marvel at the power of nature. Puzzle over the knowledge possessed by plant and insect alike as they create and recreate, season after season, each contributing to the wonder of our world. Nowhere amongst thinking people is there a denial of the reality of the creative power evident in nature. Without it the grass would not grow, nor the flowers open their petals to the sun. Since time began, scientists have been trying to discover the source of this creative force every where evident. The religious attribute this power to God; the Atheist does not accept the notion of a creator and therefore favours scientific theories. Neither denies the power, but each seeks to rationalise it in their own way. So, who is right? Is there a God in Heaven pulling the strings, or are the 'Big Bang' theorists correct?

Man (by which term I embrace all of humankind both male and female, child and adult) needs a framework or philosophical rationale to make sense of life. Through the ages the great religions (of which our modern-day science is one) and philosophies have attempted to provide such a framework. Each generation needing to answer the questions posed to it by life. To hold beliefs that sustain them in times of difficulty, pain and stress. To deal with what Victor Frankl (1905–1997), the founder of Logotherapy, called the existential triad of life: Pain, Guilt and Death.

The first glimmer of the metaphysical answer of 'how it is' that made sense to me, was provided in a book written by Dr Ernest Holmes (1887–1960) entitled *The Science of Mind*. In this truly remarkable book Dr Holmes, a practising Christian Minister, describes the energy source he believed underlay all creation. He stated:

> *There is a Universal Mind, Spirit, Intelligence, that is the origin of everything: It is First Cause, It is God. This universal life and energy finds an outlet in and through all that is energised and through everything that lives. There is one life back of everything that lives. There is one energy behind all that is energized. This energy is in everything. There is one Spirit back of all expression. That is the meaning of that mystical saying 'In Him we live, and move and have our being.' (Acts 17:28)*

Later in the book he wrote:

> *We are surrounded by Infinite possibility. It is Goodness, Life, Law and Reason. In expressing itself through us, It becomes more fully conscious of Its own being. Therefore, It wishes to express through us. As It passes into our being, It automatically becomes the Law of our lives.*

The term 'Law' is extremely important here, for it hints at metaphysical 'Universal Laws' that govern human existence. His excellent, though somewhat complex book, goes into great detail of how these laws operate and can be used effectively in life.

At times on my journey it is as if I have been nudged to go in certain directions, or to read particular books as if they were segments of a syllabus I am following. I am reminded at times of the New Testament sayings *'Ask and ye shall be given.'* *'Knock and the door will open.'* *'Seek and you will find.'* One such example of this was when I was in Amsterdam in the early 1980s. As was my wont, I was exploring the small bookshops in the back lanes. Not the large chains, but the small specialist bookshops. In one of them I came across the writings of Jane Roberts (1929–1984). Jane Roberts was a 'Channel', a term used in America for what we in the UK call a 'medium'. She claimed that her books were dictated to her whilst in trance by a non-physical entity named 'Seth'. Her husband Robert Butts recorded all of her trance sessions in longhand. He has also written extensively about the experience. In the USA, Jane Roberts' 'Seth' books have spawned many groups and organisations who devote their time to further explorations of her work.

Now, like most Englishmen of my generation. I am extremely sceptical of anything that could be deemed as 'Spiritual'. The history of spiritualism and mediums is littered with frauds and charlatans. However, my research has led me to explore the works of eminent scientists such as Sir Oliver Lodge (1851–1940) and F.W.H. Myers (1843–1901) who towards the end of the 19th and early 20th centuries conducted extensive scientific-based work in exploring psychic phenomena. In 1882 Myers founded the Society for Psychical Research (SPR), an organisation dedicated to the impartial scientific exploration of psychic phenomena. The SPR continues to function to this day. Aspects of the work of these pioneers satisfied me that there are genuine instances of communication with those who have died. In more recent times I have had direct personal evidence of this. I accept that it may not be possible to convince anyone of the reality of life after death. Each person must reach their own conclusions based on their own experiences. I was therefore prepared to examine the work of Jane Roberts with an open mind. It would either stand scrutiny and make sense, or not.

As I read her books: *The Seth Material* and *Seth Speaks*, I became absorbed and impressed by the clarity of the material. If Jane Roberts was a fraud, then she possessed a very impressive intellect indeed. In *The Seth Material* published in 1970, Seth extensively describes 'God' thus:

> *He is not human in your terms, though he passed through human stages; and here the Buddhist myth comes closest to approximating reality. He is not one individual, but an energy gestalt... You may perhaps dimly perceive the existence of a psychic pyramid of interrelated, ever expanding consciousness that creates, simultaneously and instantaneously, universes and individuals that are given, through the gifts of personal perspective-duration, psychic comprehension, intelligence, and eternal validity.*

> *This absolute, ever-expanding, instantaneous psychic gestalt, which you may call God, or 'All That Is' if you prefer, is so secure in its existence that it can constantly break itself down and rebuild itself.*

Seth goes on to describe the unbelievable energy contained in this energy gestalt stating that:

> *Its energy is so unbelievable that it does indeed form all universes; and because its energy is within and behind all universes, systems, and fields, it is indeed aware of each sparrow that falls, for it is each sparrow that falls.*

The memory of a state of being in which the ability to create was sensed before being realised is, Seth claims, the driving force with which all humanity is imbued. The drive to be creative, to know more, to grow and become more. This drive is present within each minute portion of consciousness and gives a constant impetus toward renewed creativity.

Commenting on the Christian belief of an individual God, Seth stated:

> *There is no personal God-individual in Christian terms, and yet you do have access to a portion of 'All That Is', a portion highly attuned to you. There is a portion of 'All That Is' directed and focused within each individual, residing within each consciousness. Each consciousness is, therefore, cherished and individually protected. This portion of overall consciousness is individualized within you. This portion of 'All That Is' that is aware of itself as you, that is focused within your existence, can be called upon for help when necessary.*

> *This portion is also aware of itself as something more than you. This portion that knows itself as you, and as more than you, is the personal God, you see. Again: this gestalt, this portion of 'All That Is', looks out for your interests and may be called upon in a personal manner.*

> *'Prayer therefore contains its own answer, and if there is no white-haired, kind, old father-God to hear, then there is instead the initial and ever-expanding energy that forms everything that is and of which each human being is a part.*

The definition of a creator set out by Dr Holmes and Seth was corroborated in a more personal form, directly to me at Stonehenge in the autumn of 1988. I had gone there with two American friends, one of whom acted as a channel (or a medium) for an entity (if this isn't a contradiction in terms) called 'Myriad'. I have subsequently had many 'conversations' with Myriad both through other channels and directly. I retain the original tape recording of this message. I apologise in advance for its length, but feel that its validity can only be judged by the reader having an opportunity to read in full the information that I received that autumn day at Stonehenge:

*Millions of centuries ago the earth and all that became a part of it existed as a dream. A dream in the consciousness of a Great Being. A Being we know without name. A being who is not 'All That Is' – but a Being who is a part of 'All That Is'.*

*This Great Being dreamed the existence of your earth. And in the beginning it was only a dream that repeated itself in never ending cycles. For at this time it had not yet awakened, but merely existed in a dream like state; yet it was a dream with great potential.*

*There finally came a time when the dream of your earth began to wake a bit – to experience a great creative urge – an urge to create for itself, rather than to be just the created. To do this it was important that it understood the notion of that which was quite original. To begin to realise its own creative energy. To 'focus' its consciousness – to bring into being portions of itself that would be responsible for maintaining those beliefs that would allow it to continue its form of existence.*

*At the same time it allowed another portion of its being to spin forth its own creative and most original intentions. To do this it organised a process that enabled it to focus and direct the energy that arose from its own being – from itself. There were beings – like yourself – who chose to participate, to be involved in this process. To bring about that which would allow the original expression and development of the dream.*

*This is the pattern followed by all creative energy (all that is created) that it first comes into being as a dream – without shape and focus – an idea, a thought – of a being. It comes into existence first as a dream, which does not know itself as the dreamer but merely that which is dreamed. Then because all beingness is most creative it begins to recognise and become aware of its own unique form. And as it does so energy pushes forth to bring into being the dream itself. Then it spins off its own existence.*

*Now then your planet and your beingness and your world today, has come to that place (and time) where you may begin to realise that that which you choose to dream you have used for your own purposes and intentions, and now you are capable of becoming much more.*

*You are capable of allowing yourself to express yourself as the creator. Of allowing the extension of the dream, of allowing its own consciousness that it may become in a state of becoming. To become the creator and not just the created. This is what you are about. To allow yourself to develop in such a fashion that you will begin to direct the energy and focus it upon a dream that will become its own beingness – express its own uniqueness and in the process enhance the being that you are as well. So we have brought you here today (to Stonehenge) so that you can recognise that which you are. To understand that you have chosen to participate in such a time and process. To understand that you are the creator and not merely the created. And as you begin to understand this – so also will your earth begin to understand this as well. To rid itself of the notion that it is apart – and to allow itself to realise that it is a part of the whole. So then also do you – and as you allow yourself to do this you also allow yourself to dream and quite understand that it is the creation of the image within the dream together with the intention to allow itself to become itself that consciously directs the process of creation.*

Three similar metaphysical expositions of how we came into being and how our Universe is powered, from three separate and distinct sources. All three are beautiful, almost poetic in their description of how our earth and all that is in it came into being.

There is even something here for the scientist, for contained within the Seth exposition are the words 'The psychic energy exploded in a flash of creation.' Perhaps this is the 'Big Bang' much beloved of by our scientists. What struck me about all of the information given was its similarity. The central theme in each was the same, although presented in different terms, at different times and from different sources.

Dr Holmes called the Power 'First Cause'. Seth spoke of 'All That Is', and Myriad 'A Great Being'. All, however, are agreed that this 'Being' is the source of all our energy and that all within our world comes from, and is contained within, this source. Contained, but not confined, for each description speaks of a power that is much more than its creation. That everything that exists is permeated with the presence of a divine reality or energy that powers and sustains all life. But a 'Being' who is not confined by 'His' creation; who is greater than the totality of the physical universe. Could this energy be an aspect of the 'dark energy' spoken of, but as not yet identified by astrophysicists? The possibility that it could is just as feasible as the other arguments put forward to date to explain exactly what 'dark energy' is.

Recently, the Faith Movement in Britain, has been aiming to reconcile the theory of evolution with Catholicism in its own 'new synthesis'. The movement inspired by the late Father Edward Holloway, posits that God works through evolution to bring about an ordered cosmos. In the words of Fr David Barrett to a Faith Theological Symposium in 2003:

> The Mind of God is actively and dynamically knowing and willing the creation as a unity in development, an evolving whole. So the Unity – Law is identified with and through every aspect of the material universe, and is at the same time the relationship of all these parts as a unity to the Mind of God. Control and direction, space and time, meaning and

*purpose are descriptions of how evolving matter is constituted by Divine Mind in one perpetual act of knowing and willing.*

Do the definitions of Dr Holmes, Seth and Myriad define God? Is the 'New Synthesis' of the Faith Movement close to the truth? Each of us must decide based on the evidence of our own searching. What is not in doubt is that there is a 'God sized' hole inside of mankind which each seeks to fill to their own satisfaction. All four, Dr Holmes, Seth, Myriad and the Catholic Faith Movement, describe a creative mind. A Power that creates for us and with us, constantly creating and sustaining our world and bringing into being all that we think, for we are co-creators. Seth in particular states that:

> *All individuals remember their source, and now dream of 'All That Is' as 'All That Is' once dreamed of them. And they yearn toward this immense source..., and yearn to set it free and give it actuality through their own creations. You create for the same reason, and within each of you is the memory of that primal agony – that urge to create and free all probable consciousness into actuality.*

This yearning, this urge, the sense that there is more to the world and life than can be explained by the simply physical external reality, the hunger within that has driven mystics throughout the ages can be better understood by this element of Seth's exposition. 'The urge to create; that as creative beings we know no other way than to create.'

> *You not only draw upon this overall energy but you do so automatically since your existence is dependent upon it.*

Dr Holmes goes further when speaking of the creative force as 'Spirit'; saying that we are surrounded by, immersed in, and are part of creative mind or spirit that knows no other way than to create in accordance with our thoughts and at our direction. It is this creative power that I wrote about in 1985, in my first book *Creative Thought and Personal Growth*. In that book, however, I did not set out, in fact did not know at the time that I wrote the book, of the Universal Laws that Myriad claims govern human behaviour and creation. The laws that must be understood if we are to be able to maximise our use of the enormous power, of which Seth, Myriad and Dr Holmes claim that we are a part.

## Universal Law

John D. Barrow, recent winner of the Templeton Prize for 'expanding human perceptions of divinity' and currently the Research Professor of Mathematical Sciences at Cambridge and Director of the Millennium Mathematics Project, wrote in the *Daily Telegraph*, on the 21st of March 2006, that:

> *We see now how it is possible for a Universe that displays unending complexity and exquisite structure to be governed by a few simple laws – perhaps one law – that are symmetrical and intelligible laws that govern the most remarkable things in our Universe.*

This proposition is interesting in that it follows a theme developed by Myriad when answering questions regarding the process of ongoing creation. I asked: 'If there is a creative power that powers all and which is individualised, how do we maximise our use of this power? Does it control us? Or do we control it?' Myriad answered this question by stating, that to understand the 'how' of life, we must first come to understand and appreciate the operation of Universal Law in life.

There are, Myriad told me, four primary Universal Laws governing all forms of consciousness, and these Universal Laws drive the whole system within which humanity exists. Only by linking these with the purpose of human existence can we come to understand and make sense of what, on the surface, may well appear to be inexplicable happenings within, and throughout life and the physical world. An understanding of the immutable unchanging fact of Universal Law is essential for a full understanding of life. For these Laws are not 'Root Assumptions', accepted just for a specific purpose within physical form. These are the unchanging Laws obeyed by all consciousness, whether in or out of human form.

Myriad claimed that an understanding and acceptance of these Laws by science and medicine, and their incorporation into every scientific and philosophical textbook in the world, would advance mankind's thinking, and aid progress beyond anything thus far known. On first reading, these Laws did not appear as shattering revelations of truth, but as I studied them their value became more evident.

The Four Universal Laws behind all consciousness which were given to me by Myriad are:

1. Consciousness always seeks its highest potential.

2. Energy constantly transforms.

3. Consciousness is of absolute duration; it had no beginning and will have no end.

4. Consciousness always spontaneously seeks the path that leads to its greatest growth or becomingness.

The *First Universal Law* speaks to the constant striving for growth of all living things; for the need for life at all times to be creative; for the ongoing development and evolution everywhere present in nature. Without this First Law, life would be a sterile, static and unchanging thing. As a result of the operation of this Law, all consciousness is in a constant state of 'becoming'. It is the working of this Law that drives Charles Darwin's theory of evolution. It is not then a debate between creationists and evolutionists, for this Law provides a bridge between the two, here both overlap and can be better understood through the working of this the First Universal Law.

The *Second Universal Law* enables the first to be achieved and is an accepted fact of physics. Energy, and consciousness is energy, is never static nor destroyed. It is ever-changing, ever transforming. As man/woman we are born, we grow, we age and we die, yet continue. The only constant being change. Change therefore is evidence of the fact of this Law.

The *Third Universal Law* is the law of energy itself. Energy can never be created nor destroyed, only transformed. Through this Law is the confirmation that whilst we die physically, the intrinsic core of our being will never die. We will transform, we will change; but life/consciousness is of absolute duration. This Law then denies death, it states unequivocally that there is life before life, and life after death. Consciousness cannot be determined. Our life then must be lived against the background knowledge of the fact of our immortality. The frame within which we normally consider life of three score years and ten becomes redundant. This Law is the law of life, and judgements made purely against a perceived human timeframe become invalid as a result

The *Fourth and final Universal Law* states that innately we always seek the path that leads to our greatest growth. This Law then is the servant of the First. It tells us that we are always spontaneously following the correct path for our own personal development. Even when we are failing, or defeated, or rejected; it is not possible to fail. It is only possible to experience, and from this experience to know, to become. We spontaneously always seek the path that provides for us the potential for our greatest eternal good. Whether we consciously utilise it or not is another matter. Through this Law we can find hope for mankind, hope for all, no matter how low of station, disabled or poverty stricken. It confirms that all has purpose; purpose for individuals, purpose for communities and nations, purpose for humanity. It posits that nothing that happens within our life, or within our world, lacks purpose. It is up to us to look within to find this purpose, to view our life and our world on a much larger canvas than before, for this Law brings equality to all irrespective of their status or distance travelled on the path to becoming. The operation of this Law ennobles all suffering and brings purpose to even the meanest of acts.

Myriad was emphatic that these four Universal Laws govern all forms of consciousness. Understanding and accepting them into our life will enable us to perceive the purpose behind every action we take and every disaster that may befall us as individuals, or as a species. They are the driving forces of consciousness, and as such must be set against the reality that if all has consciousness, then there is no such thing as 'dead' matter. This term can have no meaning.

## Root Assumptions

Myriad outlined the seven Root Assumptions which 'he' claimed are the base material over which is laid the genetic patterning of all in human form. They are common to all human existence irrespective of race, religion or colour and around them we have created families of related branch root assumptions.

Each Root Assumption is surrounded by its own grouping of beliefs. Myriad told me that without acceptance of these assumptions, and their accompanying belief or branch groupings as 'truths' about human existence, life in the form and shape that we know it would not exist.

At our current stage of development the removal or negation of any one of the Root Assumptions would be dramatic in its effect, for they act to create nature, balance, harmony, form and all that enables us to make sense of our world. They are the glue of our existence; the whole of our scientific knowledge rests on our acceptance of them as facts about our world. Root Assumptions therefore form the pillars, the foundation stones on which we rest our collective scientific weight.

The seven main Root Assumptions are:

1. Time.
2. Space.

3. Gravity.
4. The Solidity of Matter.
5. The Individualisation of the Personality.
6. The Centredness of Consciousness within the body.
7. The Uniform System of Opposing Forces.

Even though scientists and philosophers will probe and explore each of these assumptions, attempting to understand them better; to determine how our world works, these assumptions will remain constant. Their very constancy making them foundation stones on which scientific endeavour, rigour and experimentation can be based. Yet Myriad argued that it is possible to effect change in our understanding of these assumptions through an inner, more spiritual approach.

Stories of Yogis and other Mystics, who have apparently found ways of temporarily suspending individual aspects of one or other of these assumptions, abound. Our notion of time conflicts directly with the ability to foretell the future. Yet throughout time this ability has been demonstrated by certain gifted individuals. Out-of-body experiences defy the notion of space and gravity, yet there are many well-documented credible accounts of this phenomenon.

Many books have been written setting out how gifted individuals have apparently defied one or other of the basic tenets contained within these assumptions. The ongoing investigation of them by science will undoubtedly lead to a greater understanding of them, and perhaps even to the harnessing of the latent energy contained within them. None of this however will lead to a change of their basic fundamental reality. Whilst we accept the Root Assumptions as such, they will remain the basis for our reality, our physical world.

We can defy gravity through manned flight; however flight is achieved by accepting the force of gravity and by utilising it to achieve flight. We can demonstrate that gravitational pull is not a constant factor through our exploration of space; however we need to create artificial gravity in order to survive for any period outside the earth's atmosphere.

Our acceptance of the Root Assumption which is embodied in gravity, makes this so. Our acceptance of the reality of all Root Assumptions makes it impossible to survive without each being firmly in place in our physical world. We will only be able to move through them, and exist in apparent defiance of them, when we can see them and accept them as assumptions, rather than as laws, and come to live in the knowledge that man is indeed more than mere flesh and bone.

If what Myriad claims is indeed true, the future holds great promise for our development, but not necessarily solely through scientific exploration of the properties of the 'physical laws' that govern human existence. But also simultaneously through conducting explorations of our inner reality, as opposed to only judging our world solely through the outer reality known to us by virtue of our five senses.

Following the four Universal Laws and operating within the seven basic fundamental Root Assumptions, we travel through life. The Root Assumptions form our reality in physical form – . compasses, as it were, that we use to navigate and guide us. They frame our life and our environment upon which we then paint our own particular life picture. They are not the driving force of life, for Myriad claimed that which inexorably drives us on in life is the fundamental operation of the four Universal Laws. It is these Laws which govern human behaviour and explain much of that which is otherwise inexplicable to reason and logic as we understand and accept it.

## Life Purposes

The four Universal Laws that govern all in physical form, operating within the framework of the Root Assumptions, allow the fundamental purposes of life to be defined. Myriad claims that the purposes of life fall into twelve separate, but inter-related segments. The answers to all of humanity's searching, questioning and probing can be answered by these. To achieve each purpose fully will remove the need to return to human form, to graduate, as it were from the University of Life.

Myriad stated unequivocally that the purpose of life is:

1.   to come to understand and accept that we wholly create our reality, every aspect of it.

2.   to learn to bridge the gap that exists between waking and dreaming.

3.   to realise that we are all one, and that 'All That Is' (God), has no divisions; that we are an integral part of the body or being of God.

4.   to come to understand that there is nothing but good in the entire Universe.

5.   to rejoin our sense of oneness with our higher being, our higher selves.

6.  to come to know that joy, love, happiness, abundance and creation are all that is real of our existence; all else we create through choice and the need to grow; to learn, to experience.

7.  to understand that we operate from a oneness in which there is no division, and that expressions of joy, love and abundance are the only lasting healing tools capable of resolving the existential angst that life brings to all.

8.  to perceive the multitudinous organisation of our consciousness, such that we see the 'Root Assumptions' that sustain human existence as merely that, and as such become able to free ourselves from them.

9.  to realise that all has consciousness, and that any abuse of any form of consciousness, people, plants, objects, the earth itself, are violations of our own being.

10.  to understand that to oppose is to support.

11.  through our life to spontaneously express our uniqueness.

12.  in cooperation with all consciousness to joyously experience the fulfilment of our life purpose through an ever- growing awareness of the secrets of life.

In taking part in life, we agree to accept the rules of physical form and the Root Assumptions that form part of these rules. Whilst we remain in human form these do indeed form our reality. The Root Assumptions operate inexorably throughout all life, framing and to some degree restricting us, and will continue to do so until we come to a stage in our development when we see them for what they are, understand that as we create them, so indeed we can change them. At this time it will become possible to experiment with releasing ourselves from them and experiencing life in a very different form. For the time being however, they remain fixed as immutable laws having a clearly defined purpose: to enable us to experience human form, life with all its beauty and all its pain. Using the chosen experiences that make up our life then we are enabled to grow and become.

Myriad explained to me that only when each and every aspect of the twelve purposes of life have been incorporated into our life will we be freed from the need to reincarnate. A concept similar to the Buddhist belief of 'breaking the wheel'. Then we will have grown through the lessons of life and be ready to move on to other planes of existence. An understanding of these purposes, coupled with a desire to meet them in full, will lead us further in our development as whole beings than any religious tenet or practice ever could, for within them is contained the very essence of life itself.

## Universal Mind – The Power That Is

Dr Holmes, Seth and Myriad all state that the energy gestalt –
'The Power That Is', or, as Dr Holmes preferred, 'Universal
Mind' – created our Universe and our world. We were created
from its very substance, for from nothing can come only nothing.
All is indeed one; there is no separation, no 'them and us'.

Seth, in *Seth Speaks* states:

> *Its energy is so unbelievable that it does indeed form all
> universes; and because its energy is within and behind all
> universes, systems, and fields, it is indeed aware of each
> sparrow that falls, for it is each sparrow that falls.*

Seth and Myriad are unequivocal: before this, nothing existed; in
the void there was only the energy gestalt which the religious call
God. It is pointless to ask as some do: 'Then who made God?'
For the answer would be beyond our current ability to
understand. Myriad hints at the answer by stating:

> *A being who is not 'All That Is' – but a being who is a part
> of 'All That Is'.*

In *The Seth Material* Seth asserts:

> *Chemicals themselves will not give rise to consciousness or life.*

*Your scientists will have to face the fact that consciousness comes first and evolves its own form... All the cells in your body have a separate consciousness. There is a conscious cooperation between the cells in all of the organs, and between the organs themselves.*

He continues:

*Spirit is the force which animates all who live in human form, everything in nature and all manifestations of life in the Universe. It is the force, the power, the vibration of life, and because all life is part of the same spirit, it is indestructible.*

*While you live on earth you are on the same wavelength, vibration or frequency as all around you and thus your physical senses perceive your surroundings as real and solid. But science has told you that nothing on earth is real or solid, but in reality open networks of electrical charges whirling around a central nucleus at a frequency that is the same as your own.*

If Seth's explanation of life is correct, the power of creation that powered the formation of our world is within us, is at the very core of us. We too are creators. Without this power, this spirit, we would not exist, we would be sterile, devoid of life and the power to shape life; to create and procreate. Both Seth and Myriad are adamant that from the beginning we were imbued, with a tremendous creative life-giving power. That our life is indeed purposeful. If this is indeed so, we too are creators, creators of our world and our life. Our design in its original form was perfect. At our inception we were provided with all that we would ever need to exist in physical form operating within Universal Law. However, if this is so, such creative power brings with it enormous responsibilities, for what we create we experience, enjoy or endure. It is indeed our life production.

The proposition is that we were created as self-knowing, choosing creatures. From the exercise of this most essential power then we control our lives and our destiny. The source of our Power working as an inbuilt magnet within us. If Seth and Myriad are right, we cannot be separated from this – the source of our being. To suggest otherwise would be nonsensical. It would be like suggesting that the sun would not rise tomorrow of its own volition. That spring may precede summer, or then it may not. The Law is as fundamental as the laws of nature. As choosing beings, whilst we may stray from our source, always we will be drawn back, unable to drift far, before the pull becomes impossible to resist.

Lesley Flint, the famous 20th-century medium, or channel, in his autobiography *Voices in the Dark* records a voice claiming to be the late Archbishop Cosmo Lang as saying:

> *If only I could have seen the golden thread which runs from earliest times through all the great religions and realised that the single thread is the basis for all truth, that all men are of spirit and part of the great plan and that all life no matter what form it takes is indestructible, and that even the lowliest creatures on earth have their place and their purpose not only in your world but also in ours... Spirit is the force which animates all who live in human form, everything in nature and all manifestations of life in the universe. It is the force, the power, the vibration or frequency as all around you.*

This summary supports the notion that the creative force, that created and sustains the world flows through us and all living things. Asking nothing from us, not obedience nor worship, hymns or prayers. The Spirit being universal. If we choose to name this power and worship it, this is our choice. The inexorable operation of Universal Law set into operation at the point of our creation is not dependent upon the acceptance of any religious faith, it will create inexorably irrespective of belief or worship. The Power it seems, is so designed as to inevitably lead us back to our source by choice, by the way that we choose to live our lives, not through coercion, prayer or supplication – 'The Power That Is' or 'All That Is' experiencing itself through its creation, through us, and through every form of physical life. It seems then that like all in the Universe, the wonder of the balance between earth, sun, moon and stars, the system of which we are intrinsically a part is balanced and perfect in every way.

Without doubt an acceptance of the reality of 'The Power That Is' within life can transform it – can be a 'Road to Damascus' moment. An appreciation and acceptance that life does not just happen to us, that we are not just the result of some random chemical action or reaction. That instead of creating automatically and blindly we can instead reach out and take control of our creation, our life. This suggestion that we have more choice and greater power than we might ever have thought possible, if true, is truly awesome.

Seth and Myriad's proposition is that we are equipped with all of the tools that we need to survive, to develop and grow in this world. Whether we choose to open the tool box and use the tools or not is for us to decide. Whether our species has evolved to better use our original mental and physical attributes as our world has changed and transformed is, for me, neither here nor there. This most exciting proposition suggests that we are endowed with all of the faculties needed to enable us to become, to achieve our maximum potential in life, if only we come to accept that this is so.

To accept that we are empowered with the power that created the universe is the start place of change. To understand that we are endowed, as part of this power, with the ability to create our life, to understand that we do indeed create our own reality. That our life, every aspect of it, is our creation. This then can have real meaning and real substance for us to build our life upon.

## Consciousness

*A lifetime gathering baggage. A lifetime believing that in seeking I will find. Find what I already possess.*

*It is time to be me, just me. The essence of me needs no baggage, no layers. So peel away these layers, dump the baggage. Be me, just me. Whatever I am, I am, without description: no need for description. How can you describe what IS? It just IS. To describe is to use comparisons, to use words. When you compare you separate; that which you describe can never be what IS, it can only be an imitation, a show form.*

*I just am — one minute one thing, the next another. I am the consciousness that experiences. I hold nothing, only the memory traces of what was. I can only ever be me. I am the process that chooses — now this, now that. Indefinable me: no labels, no titles, no separation, just me being me. Without pretence or posing, without acting or showing. Without judgement or acclaim, without name. To dump such baggage, what peace ensues. Now I can let go, no need to try, no need to strive, no need to compete or justify.*

*I am alive; I am life. I am consciousness knowing itself. Consciousness aware of itself. Not the observed, just the observer: exploring with curiosity this thing called life,*

*responding to stimulation, responding to life.*
*Responding to intuition and urge, I am life and I*
*respond to me.*

These words are from my book *Infinite Choice*. They were in my head when I awoke one spring morning. Every writer will recognise the urge to write. To record without delay that which is in their mind. So it was with these words. They to some degree answer the question: Who am I? The me that writes these words, that thinks, feels emotes and knows fear and joy.

Not the labels that I carry, but me the person underneath the labels, for the labels are many and various. Depending where I focus I can be a man, brother, father, stepfather, uncle, husband, brother-in-law, businessman, consultant, writer, author, artist, patient, cook, gardener, handyman, bottle washer, cleaner, confidant, friend, consumer – the list goes on. But who am I? Who is the me who lives inside of my skin? Who thinks, dreams, loves, emotes, feels pain and grows old. Who and what is the conscious me? That which enables me to think and ask the question in the first place? A problem philosophers have wrestled with for centuries, but for me no abstract question – instead a very personal one.

I don't go to parties very often these days. But the question I remember being asked most frequently when I did was: 'Who are you?' Whenever this question was asked my mind went into overdrive. My temptation was to reply: 'How long have you got!' But out of politeness I always refrained and replied by introducing myself by my birth name. Invariably the question that would follow was: 'And what do you do?' Answering this question without asking in return – 'When?' – led to me being labelled, compartmentalised and filed away by my questioner. We all love compartmentalising people. Putting them in frames and filing them away. 'That's that one sorted then.'

Many of my older friends complain that since they have retired they have become non-persons. Where once they were teachers, doctors, lawyers, etc. upon retirement they shed their labels and reverted to identifying themselves by saying, 'I used to be a teacher/accountant/manager'. This loss of identity affects many of them severely. They have great difficulty adjusting to their changed, and often perceived by them, reduced status in society. For teachers, doctors, accountants and lawyers are valued by society (although I'm not too sure about the latter!) They have a status and command respect as the result of their training, experience and perceived wisdom... whereas retired people? Where is their status? What do they contribute to society? Aren't they takers rather than givers? Don't they retreat to the shadows of society, there to linger until they die, wasting resources that could be put to better use in supporting the coming generation?

Paul Broks in his excellent book *Into the Silent Land*, envisages a dialogue that takes place after a malfunction has occurred when teleporting his body as a stream of neurons to another planet (think Star Trek). When transportation takes place the atoms that make up his body are disassembled, copied and then delivered and reassembled at his intended destination, with his original body being destroyed. The dialogue he writes of takes place with the controller of the teleporter, when, due to a malfunction of the teleporting process, his body and mind remain intact. As a result of the malfunction two versions of him exist. One on earth, and the other on a far distant planet. When such a malfunction occurs the policy of the 'committee' that oversees such things is that the remaining body be vaporised, to avoid two people who are identical, existing at one time, with all of the confusion that this could bring, particularly to close family and friends.

The original 'He', argues with the controller that he became a different person from his transported persona at the moment the separation of the two occurred. There was then created, himself, and the version of himself that was transported to the far distant planet. The 'He' that was on the planet was not aware of the debate taking place with the controller. 'He' was not aware of the experiences being had by his alternate self on the distant planet. So if 'He' was vaporised, as the 'Committee' decreed, then it would be an act of murder. They would be murdering a sentient being with an individualised memory, much of which was common to his 'other' self, but which was now sufficiently dissimilar, to be considered as a completely separate entity. Paul Broks makes the valid point that he is not his body, but rather the collection of memories that make up his life thus far. In so much as these are individual and personal they provide him with his identity – the 'I' of his being.

Rene Descartes is famous for his assertion 'Cogito ergo sum': I am thinking, therefore I exist. Or as it is more commonly stated: 'I think, therefore I am.' Or as Seth would say: 'What I think, I am!' A survey of philosophical and scientific thought to date shows me the difficult nature of the question that I pose: Who am I?

Science has no generally accepted explanation for the state of consciousness. Over the centuries various theories have emerged and are still emerging today. Consciousness, a combination of seeing, feeling and perceiving cannot be measured, quantified or defined except by the one who sees, feels and experiences. Indeed the 'mysterian' view is that consciousness is simply too complex for human beings to comprehend.

Descartes divided reality into two parts: the material and the mental. The material realm that can be studied, measured and examined. The mental realm, the realm of ideas, thoughts, feelings and sensations that is personal to the individual. Descartes accepted that the two states of being interact causally. It is only by combining the two that we can function in our day to day world.

Later philosophers, such as Berkeley, Hegel and John Stuart Mill rejected Descartes' dualism and argued that all reality is at the most basic level mental. That the world is in some way constructed of ideas. This view is very similar in many respects to that set out in *Seth Speaks*, in which Seth argues that our physical image is the materialisation of our idea of ourselves within the properties of physical matter. He states categorically that without the idea, or held image of our self, our physical being could not exist. It is the initial power and energy of this 'idea' that keeps our image alive.

The modern materialist school of thought such as Wittgenstein and Skinner's has argued that the private world of personal individual thoughts cannot be taken seriously. They argue for a behaviourist concept of the mental state which identifies mental events in terms of their outwardly observable behavioural properties.

Modern physical science has gone further by enormously extending its explanatory range. In particular it has posited a purely physical understanding of a wide range of physiological processes within the human body. The rise of behaviourism and functionalism together with the advances of physiological science has led to little attention being paid to subjective consciousness in the 20th century. Physiologists and philosophers have instead concentrated on identifying the causal roles played by different kinds of mental states. Of dealing more effectively with mental disorders to enable sufferers to live as near normal lives as possible.

Interest in phenomenal consciousness has been revived however in the past twenty to thirty years. The Australian philosopher David Chalmers calls subjectivity the 'hard problem' of consciousness. The 'easy problem', according to Chalmers, is to identify the causal roles played by mental states, and to track down their physiological foundations. But this approach does not tackle the issue of thinking and feeling. This aspect of selfhood remains untouched by this approach. So the debate continues with 'reductionists' who accept the existence of consciousness, but not as something extra to brain activity.

A number of eminent thinkers believe that the answer to the 'consciousness conundrum' lies beyond human comprehension. These so called 'mysterians' suggest that there may be a genuine barrier to human understanding of consciousness. It is possible, they say, that the connection between the conscious mind and brain activity will remain impenetrable to humans.

David Chalmers argues that:

> ...the ultimate goal of a theory of consciousness is (to arrive at) a simple set of elegant fundamental laws, analogous to the laws of physics...

This goal seems at the moment to be far out of reach.

A working human brain is the most complex known object in the Universe. It weaves an average of one million connections every second between its 100 billion nerve cells. It has been estimated that if you connected a Pentium 4 computer containing tens of millions of transistors to every connection on the global internet, the average brain would still be 10 times more powerful. Awesome power indeed.

So what else does Seth say about the question of consciousness, one of the most difficult of questions for humanity? In *Seth Speaks* he speaks of the inner 'I' as our soul, or as he prefers it 'the entity'. This, he says, is not something that we have; it is rather what we are. He goes on:

> The trouble is that you frequently consider the soul or entity as a finished static thing that belongs to you, but is not you. The

*soul or entity – in other words your most intimate powerful inner identity – is, and must be, forever changing. It is alive, responsible, curious. It forms the flesh and the world that you know, and is continually in a state of becoming.*

*…The ego is the exterior self that you think of as yourself. It keeps the physical body operating and maintains communication with the multitudinous stimuli that come from both outside and inside conditions.*

*…the soul is first of all creative, the soul or entity self is itself the most highly motivated, most highly energised and most consciousness unit known in any universe… The soul is not an immortalised ego, your ego is only a small portion of yourself…*

He goes on to claim that our soul, or inner being, is perceiving now with the same methods of perception as we used before our physical birth, and as such will continue to operate after our physical death:

*The inner portion of you will not suddenly change its methods of perception nor its characteristics after physical death.*

We create our own reality. Our physical lifespan is so short when measured against the billions of years that our known Universe has existed. Measured against this our lives are no more than 'footprints in the snow'.

The old saying 'By their actions you shall know them' comes to mind. If we are prepared to look, the evidence of who and what we are is everywhere evident in our lives. Think of the friends you know, you know them by their personality, their life patterns, the way they talk, the way they dress, their interests, sports and hobbies. The books they read, the films they prefer. Their lifestyle, the home they live in, the way they furnish their home. Whether they are neat and tidy, or live in a mess. All of these things come together to make them the person who we know. They create their reality as we create ours. In essence this is who and what they are. The outer is truly the manifestation of the inner. We create our lives from the inside out.

I am reminded, as I write these words, of the children's toy that was all the rage a few years ago. This toy consisted of rows of pins held in a rectangular frame. By pressing your hand or your face against one side of the pins, an image was formed on the reverse, which remained when your removed your hand or face. This image was the 'outer' impression created by the inner fleshy you. Our life is like this toy; the outer aspects of our life are brought into being by the inner impressions of our thoughts and beliefs. If we wish to effect a change in the outer, we first need to work to change the inner. The best work we can do if we wish to change, is not to charge around seeking to make major changes in our external day to day life and activities, but rather to sit in an armchair, examine our thoughts and beliefs, identify those that drive the aspect of our life with which we are unhappy, and commence the process of changing and replacing these beliefs and thought patterns with fresh patterns that will bring into being the change in our life that we are seeking.

I read recently of an excellent technique to use to help effect change in aspects of life with which you may be unhappy. To use this technique you simply see yourself on the screen of your imagination, doing that which represents that which you wish to change in your life. Whatever aspect of your life with which you are dissatisfied. Then, on this screen see in the bottom right-hand corner a small picture of the you that you would be if you could change. Finally, see a windscreen wiper wiping across your screen; with each wipe dragging your small picture up to cover the large picture, whilst you repeat to yourself the word 'wipe' with each sweep of the wiper blade. My addition to this exercise is to say: 'And so it is,' at the end of each session. In effect, 'Amen'. I have no doubt that this exercise carried out for a minimum of five minutes, at least three times a day, for three to four weeks will effect major change. This process works because you are mentally replacing old patterns with new. Old images of you with new images of the you that you wish to become. One final tip: work only on one part of your life at a time. Give the mind clear, simple uncomplicated images to work with, and watch the changes occur.

The real answer to my question: Who am I? Is in one of the four Universal Laws that states: 'Consciousness has no beginning and will have no end.' I am conscious, and as such accept that I am. I am knowing thought, and as such I experience myself through my life which is my creation. Even those areas of my life with which I am unhappy I accept as mine; I am indeed a 'work in progress'. I accept that I, like all who experience human form, are knowing creativity; constantly creating and bringing into form and shape thoughts and beliefs. Through my creation I become better able to understand the creation process, and the enormous powers with which I am endowed. My consciousness in essence is who and what I am.

## Thought – The Creative Power

In my book *Creative Thought and Personal Growth*, I wrote that man is an energy system, existing within an energy system. In effect, that all that exists consists primarily of energy. Matter being energy given shape and form. That human form and all other physical matter is no more than energy vibrating at a particular frequency. This frequency allowing for the density and solidity of form. From this it follows that, in accordance with Universal Law, it is perfectly possible for life before and after death to be a fact and for such life to function in an environment consisting of energy, operating at a higher frequency, a frequency that is more responsive to our thought; an environment where form and density are created differently. To those who scoff at such a proposition, I can only respond by saying that such a concept is no more preposterous, than the concept of 'dark energy', accepted today as a fact by many of the world's leading astrophysicists. Energy that powers the expansion of the Universe, yet which, like its counterpart 'dark matter' is so constituted that it is able to pass through the solid matter of earth without any of our sophisticated measuring devices being able to detect it.

Consciousness is known by our ability as a species to think. Without thought we would not be. We would be as robots, automatons. Thought distinguishes man from the animal. Thought is the conundrum at the heart of the Darwinian creed.

For whilst evolution, the development and adaptation of the species to meet the prevailing environmental circumstances and demands, has logic to it, it does not explain our ability to think. Being able to reason means we can choose and then act. All historical and archaeological records point to the existence of humans as sentient thinking beings. Not gradually developing thinking beings, but beings with the same power and ability to think as we ourselves possess today. There is no evidence of developed or evolved powers of thought. There is no evidence that we are somehow brainier or more intelligent than our forefathers. No archaeological discoveries have demonstrated that the human species has evolved the power of thinking. It seems that as a species we were endowed with this tremendous power at our conception. We are more technically advanced today than our forefathers, but all available evidence points to the fact that humanity, mankind, has always been endowed with the power to think and to reason.

Thought is the essence of us. What we think on a day to day basis; what we store in our minds as memories, make up who and what we are. Whilst many attempts have been made to design and create artificial intelligence, no computer has yet been developed that has been able to demonstrate independent thought, or to be capable of original thought. In fact the suggestion is the stuff of nightmares, and not a few books and films – the 2004 film 'I Robot' starring Will Smith being but one – have been based on it. Original thought is unique to human beings. From it come great works of art and literature, great inventions, medical and scientific advances.

Computers can be programmed to prove that $2 + 2 = 4$. In basic terms, however, they cannot go beyond this. They compute from the data inputted. They are in essence 'Yes/No' machines. Yet humans do not function on this basis. We are endowed with imagination. We can create and design using only thought forms. We can see our creations within our heads; we can describe these thought forms to others using only words as our tools. They in turn can visualise their interpretation of our creation, even though this creation nowhere exists in physical form. Without this innate ability to create in thought form there would be no works of art. No great architectural designs; no Mozart, Beethoven, Bach; none of the great composers would have been able to write their masterpieces without the wonder of imagination. To write music full of emotion and sentiment.

Things do not just happen to us in life – we make them happen – using the tremendous and unique power of our imagination, coupled with reason and thought, combined with physical energy action. Behavioural psychology is based on the concept of cause and effect. If we act in a certain way, then the outcome will be predictable. Yet much of what we experience in life seems to be outside of our conscious control, seems to be determined by the 'fickle finger of fate'.

Now, while it is generally accepted that conscious thought directs our actions, and our actions lead to our accomplishments, small and large, there is no generally accepted school of philosophy that goes beyond this. Indeed, it takes an enormous leap of faith to accept that thought could be more than this. That thought might not only direct our conscious physical actions, but further, could be the process by which we create all of our life. Thought literally bringing to us what we experience as day to day reality. All that we see, touch, feel and interact with being our creation, not just some of it. That we are not in fact set apart from the physical world we inhabit – but are instead co-creators of it. This is the proposition behind all of Jane Roberts' 'Seth' books. This the startling fact about our personal world that Seth posits, that we create our own reality, every single tiny part of it. Both individually and cooperatively with those with whom we share our world.

Seth, when dictating 'his' book *Seth Speaks* stated that:

*Consciousness creates form. It is not the other way round. All personalities are not physical. It is only because you are so busily concerned with daily matters that you do not realize that there is a portion of you who knows that its own powers are far superior to those shown by the ordinary self.*

He goes on…

*If you believe that your consciousness is locked up somewhere inside your skull and is powerless to escape it, if you feel that your consciousness ends at the boundary of your body, then you sell yourself short…*

'Consciousness creates form.' Seth is advancing the proposition that we not only create our body, but further, that we create all that happens to us in life. Such a proposition contradicts so much of that which is inherent in Western thinking. Yet without this being a reality, Universal Law could not be. Universal Law states that: 'Consciousness always spontaneously seeks the path that leads to its greatest growth or becomingness.' This immediately leads to the question: How does consciousness achieve this?

We are brought up to think of ourselves as physical bodies which have within them the power to direct and control our physical actions and thus direct and control our world, our reality, but no more than this. That all else that happens to us is outside of our control. As that awful slogan seen on T-shirts and baseball caps reads 'Shit happens'. We have no say in the matter – it just happens. But Seth is suggesting that this is not the way that it is at all. 'He' states unequivocally that we create every event that happens in our life, that nothing that happens to us is not our creation. That our thought creates all.

Scientists have recently proven that by observing another person's brain activity, it is possible to predict what that person is going to do before he or she is aware that the decision to act has been made by them. That before the action is the thought, either conscious or subconscious, driven by circumstance or learned response. That behind all physical action is mental action. The outer literally being the manifestation of the inner. This brain activity is not visible to an observer, or known by the person concerned. Only through the use of scientific measurement does this brain activity become known.

In *Seth Speaks*, Seth goes further by stating that each thought and emotion exists first as an electromagnetic energy unit that acts as a building-block for physical matter. With the intensity of any thought or emotion determining the degree of energy charge that is imparted, and thus the speed at which the corresponding physical object, condition or event, comes into being in physical form. That thought itself directs creative energy.

We are an extension of the earth's energy and form. The earth operates in an electromagnetic field – we too are electromagnetic systems, an extension of this field. We are not separate from the earth, for we are made and fashioned from the same material. Behind all is Universal Creative Mind. Matter then can best be described as 'decelerated consciousness' directed and shaped by the power of reason and thought, within the framework of accepted Root Assumptions.

The intensity of any feeling, thought or mental image is, according to Seth, the single most important element in bringing the materialisation of an event into reality, into life. We speak of life as having a beginning and an end. Yet Myriad consistently denies this. Universal Law states that: 'Consciousness had no beginning and will have no end.'

Seth's explanation of how matter comes into physical reality forms one of the most fascinating sections of *Seth Speaks* and links closely to Myriad's explanations on the same subject. According to Seth, the soul, that mythical component so beloved by the religious, consists of condensed energy. Energy beyond anything of which we can conceive. From this energy core springs the very essence of our being. This core then is the source of our own individual creation. Seth describes man in physical form simply as an 'energy transformer':

> *Each of you act as transformers, unconsciously, automatically transforming highly sophisticated electromagnetic units into physical objects. You exist in the middle of a 'matter concentrated system'... Each thought and emotion spontaneously exists as a simple or complex electromagnetic unit – unperceived, incidentally as yet by your scientists. ...The intensity determines both the strength and permanence of the physical image into which the thought or emotion will be materialised.*

Physics tells us of the four universally accepted forces: Nuclear, weak and strong, Gravity and Electromagnetic energy. There is however a fifth force awaiting discovery, but it is beyond the measuring devices of today's physicists, and because it exists within the inner dimension of all, it is likely to escape detection by those who explore only physical evidence and external phenomena. This fifth force, referred to often by Seth, is the creative energy, or spirit, that flows through all, and which we use, unconsciously and unknowingly, to create our world. This force is always at our disposal and working at our direction. It is important to realise, however, that it does not choose what is created, the force can only create in the images that we form for it, and flow to those areas of life to which we direct our attention and our emotional energy. The mould is always our thought, both at a conscious and an unconscious level. The direction that we give to our thought then shapes and brings into being all that makes up our life.

The most important tools in our armoury by far are the powers of thought and reason Even without accepting Seth's incredible proposition that we create all of our life, it is generally accepted that what we think of life determines our happiness or our sadness. It is always our choice; as the old saying goes: 'Two men looked through prison bars, one saw mud, the other stars.'

Seth's proposition, however, goes much further. It propounds the idea that we create all that happens to us. That we literally create our life from our thoughts. The 'Power That Is' created the Universe; we create our lives, Seth suggests that it really is that simple. However, for me, the most important part of this proposition is that this power that creates, with which we are imbued, is not selective; we are its directors. This power cannot choose what it brings into being, it can only go forward and create whatever we think into it. It is always our thought which is the controlling director.

My experiences have shown me the truth of Seth and Myriad's proposition of the way that creation is brought about. Over many years I have tested and explored the ideas presented by both Seth and Myriad. I have learnt that it is important to appreciate and understand that *all thought and belief* – beliefs being thought patterns – create. Not just some selected thought and belief. I repeat this, for this is the most important lesson that I have learnt throughout the whole of my searching: *thought creates directly in its likeness.*

What we think is down to us; it is always our choice. The creative power that surrounds us does not reason with us, or select what it brings into our life. It creates directly in the image of the thoughts and beliefs we hold in accordance with Universal Law. The creation process is as natural and integral a part of our being as is our breath. If we deny its existence, it does not cease to create, we simply place ourselves into a state where we create blindly, believing that whatever happens to us in life is down to fate, chance, fortune or misfortune. A belief that is held by many people.

If this all seems too simple, regrettably it is not so. For we are composed of layers of learning through our experiences of life. Patterns of thought based on fundamental beliefs held by us. All of our life we have absorbed teaching from our parents, guardians and tutors. We have grown within a culture steeped in history and entrenched beliefs. We think and move in culturally accepted patterns. To accept and put into practice the ideas presented by Seth is more difficult than it may appear on the surface – even if we can accept them at an intellectual level. For the whole of our experience of life to date will have been predicated on the opposite proposition; founded on the belief that life happens to us. That all that we can do is to make the best job we can with what we have. To suddenly turn around and accept that this is not the way that it is. To grasp the concept that our life is our creation, is difficult indeed. Even where the concept that we create the totality of our life is accepted, it must be understood that the creation process is not something we turn on and off, any more than we can turn on or off the mechanisms that keep our body functioning on a day to day basis without our conscious direction. We are creating our life now; that which we experience tomorrow, we will have created through the thoughts and beliefs about life that we hold today. We create our life every moment of every day. Creation is not something we do in fits and starts. The process of changing from one way of thinking to another will take time. Only through time; through constantly identifying and changing limiting and restricting beliefs and habitual thought patterns that we hold, can we hope to effect lasting change in our life circumstances. Only by singularly and relentlessly policing our thoughts and observing our resultant world will we bring change about. Such a process will enable us to bring into being the reality that we want our life to be, rather than the reality that we experience now.

## Destiny

Destiny suggests a set pattern from which we can not deviate. A pattern laid down before birth which determines our future. This idea, however, could not be further from the truth. Whilst what we experience today is indeed predestined by what we thought and believed yesterday, at any time we can decide to change our thought, work on our underlying beliefs, and take off on a different path entirely.

For we are masters of our destiny in every respect, using the creative energy that springs from our source, we bring into being every aspect of our life and our existence; every single aspect of it. It is important here to refer back to two of the four Universal Laws of life. The first of these Laws states: 'That consciousness, always seeks its highest potential', and the fourth Law: 'That consciousness always spontaneously seeks the path that leads to its greatest becomingness.'

Acting in accordance with these Laws, the direction that we give to our thought at a conscious and subconscious level brings into being our life as we experience it daily. We do indeed create all within our life, but not on a random basis. The four Universal Laws of life govern the ultimate direction our lives take and, as such, help to make sense of the apparently senseless. It is in meeting Universal Law that our life gains overall meaning. It is Universal Law that ensures that every part of our life, no matter how trivial it may appear on the surface, has validity, depth and purpose.

In accordance with Universal Law all has meaning, and through the operation of these Laws no life is without value, no matter how hard, painful or deformed. Only by going down the 'blind alleys' of life do we learn to change, improve and move forward to become more than we are.

At all times we bring into being the circumstances that provide for us the greatest opportunities for our long-term growth and development. At every stage of our life, we are poised at the crossroads that provides to us the greatest opportunity to grow and develop. That give us the option to choose the most beneficial direction in which to travel. It may not always appear that this is so as we look around at a bland boring life that does not seem to have much going for it. But this is always the case, the greater the boredom, the greater the pain, the greater becomes the pressure to change, for this is Universal Law in operation. Nothing is static even when it appears to be so; everything is in a constant state of flux, of potential change. Nothing is for ever, it only seems that way sometimes! Boredom is suppressed energy building inside of us until we are forced by intolerable internal pressure to respond and take action to release ourselves from its grip through creative purposeful activity.

The proposition that we do indeed create, design and plan our own misfortune as well as our own good fortune can be a very hard concept to accept, particularly if we have grown into the habit of blaming destiny, fate, circumstance or others for the life that we experience now. It is indeed much easier to blame others, or circumstances, for the state of our life. To realise and accept that we ourselves have created all the events that we have lived through, and which may at times have caused us considerable pain, takes great courage. To face events that have perhaps scarred us deeply, and recognise that we have been the authors of our own pain and misfortune is a hard task indeed. Yet both Seth and Myriad state categorically that this is indeed so. All must ultimately be judged against the background of Universal Law.

Whilst this could be described as the bad news, the good news is that we can use our knowledge of the operation of Universal Law to reach out and take control over our life. That we can, if we are so determined, learn to more effectively direct our thoughts, and in so doing shape and create events and circumstances which are more beneficial to us. To explore and examine the underlying beliefs that may bring into our life, again and again, experiences that cause us pain and anguish. In so doing we can learn to change and replace damaging beliefs, with beliefs that are beneficial to our long-term growth and development as whole beings.

To come to realise that at all times life has purpose and meaning, no matter how hard or seemingly valueless it may appear on the surface is true wisdom. To use Nietze's dictum: 'He who has a why to live for, can overcome almost any how.' An understanding of Universal Law gives the 'why' to all of life, not just those parts which we judge to have meaning and purpose using the limited yardsticks of our culture and our time.

We are not then after all tossed around on an illogical sea of chance; helpless pre-destined victims of circumstances and events that are out of our control. Our world does have reason and pattern. Such a proposition ennobles all that happens to us in life, no matter how mean, painful or demeaning. Universal Law gives all that happens in life purpose. So that even the most negative circumstances can take on a new dimension both individually and collectively. Both for our life, and for humanity. For we are not separate from the rest of humanity. Our life matters, for what we do with our lives influences the whole of humanity. As dye colours water, so the way we live our life colours the life of all. If we accept that nothing, literally nothing, occurs that does not have meaning and purpose for us and for humanity, then we are able to look beyond the mere surface level of the events that make up our life and the life of our world, and discover a greater meaning. When this meaning is better understood and absorbed, so we grow and become stronger.

## Our Life – Our Creation

Seth and Myriad tell us that we are creative energy beings, living in a creative energy constructed and driven Universe. If Seth and Myriad are correct, then we know of no other way than to create. We may think that we are now active, now idle, but in truth we are constantly active, constantly creating, constantly bringing our lives into being. There is not a moment in our lives when this is not so. This is the wonder of being. Understood and effectively applied it is the secret of the ages. We sustain the very substance of who and what we are through our energised thoughts, belief patterns and the operation of Universal Law.

If you doubt this, forget Seth and Myriad, and simply look around you, everything is changing, nothing is constant. Everything is in a state of growing and becoming, receding and dying. The seasons change daily, almost imperceptibly winter becomes spring, spring summer, summer autumn. We grow, we mature, we age. Even the rocks and the mountains crumble and change with time; only the rate of change marking them out as different. The seas and the rivers are ever changing. Each made up of myriad drops of water, ever moving, never still. The stream we see this minute different from the stream we see the next giving truth to the old saying: 'You never step into the same stream twice.' The oceans evaporate to form clouds, the clouds bring rain. The rain falls where it will, draining to the streams and rivers. The rivers rush to the sea; each replenished by the falling rain. The only constants in both our life and the life of our planet is change, change and constant creation. Growing and becoming, or decaying and replenishing. Why then should we be different?

We were born into a creative energy Universe and, like all living things, infused with an inbuilt drive to create. From the moment our father's sperm fused with our mother's egg, the creative process that became the physical us began. Forming us from the life of the sperm and the egg; continuing life, constant creation. We had no hand in our physical growth or formation; the creative drive coupled with our genetic programming accomplished all; created the physical us.

This same drive within the 'Power That Is', or 'All That Is' created and brought into being the Universe of which we are a part. Set in motion the natural laws that sustain and power our world. Astronomers tell us that the Universe is in a process of constant expansion; evidence of constant creation in action. I am not concerned here though with the Universe, fascinating though it is. I am concerned here with how best to use this marvellous power of creation with which we are endowed.

We know that our bodies are in a constant state of flux. Medical science tells us our bodies completely replicate themselves. That the physical us is no more than ten years of age. Just looking in the mirror or viewing earlier photographs of our self confirms this. Every cell in our bodies is no more than ten years old; an incredible thought. Yet this process of change is not subject to our conscious direction, it is a part of the human process, the process of being. Cells replicate cells using the genetic blueprint with which we were endowed at conception. Like a frequently photocopied sheet, where copy is made of copy, the clarity of the image, the idea of us, gradually blurs and reduces, and so we age.

We accept the wonder of our physical creation. We know that

we create our bodies from the food we eat and the air that we breathe. That our cells are constantly replicating, growing, dividing, dying, a constant process without which we would not be. Yet it is not universally accepted that we also create and recreate our very lives from our thoughts, from our mind and the beliefs and ideas that we hold about life.

So many of our bodily functions are seemingly outside of our conscious control. We can only regulate our breathing by concentration; left to its own devices our body decides on the rate of our breathing, fast or shallow depending entirely on our need for oxygen. Our bodies constantly monitoring the oxygen levels in our blood like every other aspect of our physical system, deciding whether more or less oxygen is required. This translates into our breathing patterns and thus our air intake. Our heart pumps our blood around our circulatory system, bringing with it fresh oxygen and nutrients, taking away our waste to be excreted. In the average lifetime our heart will beat 2.5 billion times. Our kidneys are continually filtering our blood removing toxins and more waste, regulating with exact precision the fluid levels in our body. Draining away excess liquid to our bladder. None of this under our conscious control. Simple examples of the wonderful subconscious control mechanisms with which we are endowed and which we readily accept. Our bodies are a miracle system operating in most cases effortlessly without conscious control or direction.

Yet a recognition that this process of control and automatic creation also extends beyond our body into the creation of every aspect of our daily life is not so easily accepted. A major leap of faith is required before this can be done. Yet an acceptance of this fact will undoubtedly transform our life. An acceptance that we constantly create every aspect of our life as readily and easily as our bodies control our heart rate, and our oxygen levels. Creating through the way we think on a minute to minute basis, within the framework of the beliefs that we hold about our world. This idea may be revolutionary, but it is none the less true.

Now if we want to tune up our bodies; if we have become fat and sluggish and unfit, we can decide to do something about it. We can diet to lose weight, take exercise to regain our fitness. We can develop a programme, and provided we have the will and desire to stick to it, we can achieve our goals. Yet rarely do we adopt the same approach to our life. Rarely do we set out on a planned programme to change any area of our life with which we are unhappy. Yet we can achieve even greater success than any diet or fitness routine can ever do to improve the quality of our lives – every aspect of them.

For our sickness and our health, our happiness and our wealth, our relationships and our work all are directed, created and controlled by us. In a more direct way than most appreciate or accept. For this is not some 'Positive Thinking' life change programme; As Jane Robert's Seth states:

> In a manner of speaking you have been given the gift of the Gods, in that your beliefs become reality. What you believe becomes your experience in life and of life. There is no area of your life to which this does not apply. Understand this and you will take control over every aspect of your life.

This is a pretty awesome stuff. Seth says that whatever we think and believe about our life, about our self, becomes our experience of life and the day to day reality we experience and label as our life. The start place of change then is the recognition and acceptance at a deep level of being that our life is indeed our creation. Every jot and tittle of it. We may blame circumstance, place of birth, race, gender, physical form or disability, for who and what we are. But the plain truth is that we are responsible for who we are today. We bring our lives into being and sustain them on a daily basis. A refusal to understand and accept that this is so will restrict and inhibit any attempt that we may make to change our life for the better. Will consign such attempts ultimately to the dustbin of failed attempts to change who we are. For without changing our thought patterns we quickly return to the old familiar us. Thought creates all; Universal Law states that it cannot be otherwise.

The process of creation is not random, it is indeed highly structured. Operating at all times at our direction, either conscious or subconscious. I have found that many people struggle to conceive of aspects of their mind other than the conscious level of their mind. The concept of the subconscious is impossible for them to picture. So for ease of presentation I will deal here with the three main levels of mind, two of which are the easiest for most people to visualise and work with. The third perhaps more difficult to conceive of, but nevertheless fundamental to our understanding of how the totality of our mind works.

1.   The Conscious mind.
2.   The Subconscious mind.
3.   The Superconscious mind.

Our *Conscious mind* directs and controls our immediate thoughts. It is our immediate interface with the physical world. As such it is the first level of creation. It is the receptor of our five physical senses. Our sight, hearing, touch, etc. Instant, in that it controls our physical actions and reactions to the world around us. Our conscious mind enables us to converse and communicate with others. To react to our surroundings and take decisions. It is the receiver of our senses. It enables us to live in our day to day world. To constantly dip into our memory bank, to compare, analyse, reason and, through recognition and learned response, function in the everyday reality which makes up our life.

Our *Subconscious mind* is the storage chamber of all our memories, habit patterns and beliefs, both individual and cultural. It links with the automatic functioning of our bodies. It holds our beliefs about ourselves and our world. It creates much that we experience, for our belief patterns form our world. What we believe and expect, we go on to create and experience. It operates constantly, both in waking and sleeping states. It is the 'software' of our 'hardware' body.

The *Superconscious mind* is the level of mind ignored by many, and denied by the behaviourists, its very existence questioned. Yet in many ways it is the most important aspect of our mind, for it is the inner core of us that survives physical death. Myriad claims that this is the level of mind with which we unify whilst we sleep. The aspect of our self that plans and directs our overall life in physical form. It is the interface between ourselves and our greater self. That portion of ourselves that straddles the physical and the non-physical. It is here that our life plan is designed, working to achieve the first Universal Law: 'That consciousness always seeks its highest potential.'

Our superconscious mind can, and does, override our other two subordinate conscious states. In seeking to fulfil our quest to reach our highest potential, our greatest becomingness, it creates situations and circumstances that consciously we would not choose to experience. For these are the experiences that test and stretch us. That have the potential within them to cause us pain and suffering; to jerk us out of the comfort zone sought by our ego the 'I' of our being. They are the mental equivalent of our physical gymnasium. Without our superconscious mind we would remain what I call 'plateau people' ever ensconced in the comfort zone. Never tackling the hills and mountains of life. Why would we? For these can be tough and demanding, bringing with them the potentiality for pain and suffering. However, experiences brought into being by our superconscious mind, painful though they may be, can be the most important aspects of our life. It is not the daily round that leads to our growth as beings, it is the births, deaths, accidents, illnesses, coincidences, challenges and other eventful and often extraordinary happenings in our life that carry within them the greatest potential for our growth as eternal beings.

Psychologists tell us that one of the most damaging things we can do is to avoid or suppress our thoughts and emotions. To turn our energy inward upon ourself. To attempt to suppress the energy within leads to increased levels of anxiety, depression and worry. Energy must be utilised and released, not suppressed and contained.

Whatever we give our attention to we give our energy to. The greater the attention the greater the energy. This supports the rule that 'what we resist persists'. Or put another way: 'That which we oppose we support', an apparent contradiction in terms. When we are opposed to something, or try to stop ourselves doing something that we do not want to continue – like overeating, or smoking – whatever we are seeking to resist invariably will persist because of the energy we give to it through our increased attention to it.

Viktor Frankl, the famous psychotherapist and founder of Logotherapy; literally the therapy of meaning, named this law as 'the law of paradoxical intention'. It is the law that brings to us the opposite of what we are trying to achieve. For example, if we stutter we may try to control our stuttering through increased concentration on what we are saying. As a result it is most likely that our stutter will continue and increase in intensity. The technique that Frankl used with his patients in such cases was simple, he encouraged the person who stuttered to try to stutter more, not less.

Invariably they found that the harder they tried to stutter the less they were able to stutter, with their speech often improving markedly as a result. Imagine that you are facing someone and trying to push them over. Likewise they are resisting and trying to push you over. Think what would happen if either of you suddenly stopped pushing, without warning, and stepped to one side. The other person would be impelled forward by their own impetus and most likely fall flat on their face. So to remove the energy from something will lead to it collapsing. Literally – to oppose is to support. It is on the basis of this principle that the throws, performed seemingly so effortlessly in the sport of Judo are based. Judo experts learn to turn their opponents' energy against them, thus minimising the amount of energy that they need to employ to achieve their aims.

Those who wish to stop smoking might like to try this. Rather than fighting their addiction they should force themselves to increase the number of cigarettes they are smoking. To force themselves to smoke even when they do not crave a cigarette. Such action is likely to set up a reaction against cigarettes – with comments like, 'Oh not another one, I just can't face another cigarette.' To continue to force yourself to smoke even when you are sick of the sight of cigarettes will perversely most likely lead to a cessation of smoking.

So it is with our beliefs. We are free to believe whatever we want. But it pays to be selective for those things we choose to believe in we activate within our life. Even when the outcomes are not in our best interests. Those things we focus on exclusively we give our whole lives to. We can – within the confines of physical law – bring into being whatever we choose in life and this then will become our life.

At the root of any of the problems we may be experiencing in life will be the deep rooted beliefs that sustain them. Beliefs about ourself, our world, the part that we play in it, our worth as people, our self image, our culture, our race, our nationality, our entitlements, our rights, our future, the future of our world, our health. The list goes on. To resolve the problems that we encounter daily, that may be causing us pain or discomfort, we must change the core beliefs that we hold about our life which are creating, and recreating, these problems. Until we change the core beliefs that fuel and sustain these problems, the problems will continue to plague us.

The power of belief cannot be underestimated. The religious zealots and fanatics whose activities might appal the majority, fervently believe in the rightness of their cause. To them, their faith and the beliefs on which it is founded is the only thing that matters. Be they evangelical Christians or fundamentalist Muslims. Their belief in their religion and all that it stands for gives them direction, purpose and a reason for living. It fills what Viktor Frankl called life's 'existential vacuum'. It provides the framework around which their life is constructed. Without their religion their lives would be empty and meaningless. Suicide bombers being an extreme example of this. Few of us can imagine the mindset of someone who is prepared to blow themselves into oblivion because of their religious belief. Yet this activity is responsible for the majority of civilian deaths in Iraq and Israel. Reports tell us that today in Iraq there are more would-be suicide bombers than the bomb makers can make bombs for.

We saw an example of this in the UK in 2005 when four otherwise rational and intelligent young men, born and brought up in Britain, blew themselves up, along with many of their fellow citizens in London on July 7th. Fifty-six people were killed and over 700 injured in the explosions. These young men who were on the surface ordinary young Muslims, decided to travel to London carrying backpacks full of explosives for the sole purpose of causing as much damage, and killing as many of their fellow human beings as they were able. Such action defies any form of sane logic, but bear truth to the fact that that which we give our attention to, almost to the exclusion of all else, becomes normal to us. The bombers' behaviour may seem outrageous and beyond the pale to the majority, but to the bombers their behaviour, fuelled by the distorted beliefs they had absorbed, led them to see their behaviour as normal, and the rest of society's behaviour as abnormal. So abnormal that it could only be changed through violence and bloodshed.

To answer the oft asked question: 'If we create all that happens to us in our life why do nasty, painful and unpleasant things happen to us?' we must look to our superconscious. Our superconscious is at all times seeking to fulfil Universal Law. Seeking to enable us to grow to our full potential. If we only created pleasant experiences, we would learn and grow little, if at all. Life above all else is about growth. For growth to occur we need to be stretched, to travel on new paths, to experience new challenges, even when these are painful. For through pain we pay attention. Pain leaves us little choice. It focuses the mind as in no other way. Our world shrinks and we are forced to pay attention to that which we must try to heal in order to regain normal life. We focus our mind on the abnormality of our state of being, of either our mental, or our physical state. We seek treatment, we long to be cured. When in pain, we focus and direct our mind on the need to change, it becomes the most important thing to achieve in our life. It is sad but true; pain effects change in lifestyle faster than any other mechanism known in the physical world. All then does indeed have purpose including pain and suffering. All is created by and through the operation of mind for our growth and the growth of humanity. Through pain and suffering, both individually and collectively, we learn to pay attention to those aspects of life that must be changed in order for the pain to cease. Regrettably, often a great deal of pain and suffering is undergone unnecessarily until this lesson is fully absorbed. Time spent understanding this truism, reflecting on our life and our creation is indeed time well spent.

## Spontaneity and the Moment

An easy subject to write about perhaps? Surely the words will just tumble spontaneously on to the paper. Yet we are born into a world where it is natural to edit, to pause and think before we reply, or determine how to respond to the questions that life poses to us. We are told that only a fool speaks without first thinking through what he is going to say. Yet even this simple statement is not true. For we rarely, if ever, know the ending of any sentence that we start, think through the exact words that we will use in a conversation with another and, if we do, we do not stick to the script. For conversation is not like that, it flows; what we say is almost always conditioned by what others say to us. We trust and believe that once we have started a sentence we will be able to finish it. We trust in our ability to respond without thinking as the conversation progresses.

On occasion we may find ourselves standing a little apart from a conversation, observing both ourselves and the person we are talking to. There may well be two conversations going on, the one that is being heard and the one that is going on inside our heads. For planning, forethought, caution, these we are told are the watch words of the wise, only the fool is truly spontaneous. Only the foolish speak before they think. Or do they?

Our bodies are designed to work naturally, if they were dependent on our conscious direction we would be dead within seconds. Our body is designed to spontaneously create and heal itself, to repair itself, without conscious direction from us. Our hair and nails grow, we blink, cough, sneeze carry out a mass of complex functions without any conscious direction being given by us. Our respiratory and digestive systems perform their vital functions day in and day out. Our attention only being drawn to them when they malfunction. Spontaneity is everywhere evident in the human condition. That is, until we reach the conscious level of mind. All of a sudden our belief in spontaneity, which is the very essence of life, seems to break down.

Both Seth and Myriad state, over and over again, that we create every aspect of our world from the thoughts that we hold, and we do this quite spontaneously. This spontaneous creation happens as naturally as our bodily functions. We create our lives as easily and effortlessly as we breathe. Myriad is quite emphatic on this point. He once laughingly admonished an audience of which I was a part for constantly seeking to know the future from 'him'. Our futures were, he said, created from every thought that we hold. 'He' could only tell us what was going to happen in our future by reading the thoughts in our mind and relaying back to us what they told 'him'. If they were there to be read, then we too could read them. In answer to the inevitable question as to why it was then that so many things happen to us that we would rather not happen, Myriad replied that this was because we had quite got into the habit of ignoring certain thoughts and only recognising others. Of being selective in the thoughts that we chose to pay attention to.

> Your thoughts flit by and you have deliberately lost the trick of observing them. You do not believe that you create your world from your thoughts and so you have not paid attention to what it is that you think. You have switched off this faculty and in order to use it again you must first switch it on. If you were to observe your thoughts you would see that all that happens to you in your world quite spontaneously follows the thoughts

*that you hold, each moment being spontaneously fashioned from the pattern of thoughts as well as the individual thoughts and expectations that you have about life and yourself. Nothing, I repeat nothing, happens to you by chance or unbidden.*

This view of life creation equates with the knowledge that we already have about how our bodies spontaneously regenerate and maintain themselves. We should not then find anything strange or unusual in the suggestion that we spontaneously create our reality both internally and externally. Every minute of every day so many wondrous functions are performed naturally, effortlessly and spontaneously by our bodies. Yet the average person would reject out of hand Myriad's contention, that we create all that happens to us within our lives. The idea that we are completely responsible for every life event that occurs would seem preposterous to most. We are taught that events happen to us, rather than are created by us.

I am reminded here of the story of the wise monk who was asked by a rich man for the secret of a happy life. After pausing the monk replied, 'Attention'. 'Is that it?' asked the wealthy man. 'Surely there must be more to it than that?' 'There is,' said the monk. 'Attention, attention, attention.'

The villain in the piece here is time. The passage of time makes it difficult to pay attention to the moment. The operation of the Root Assumption that is time means that we constantly separate life out into past, present and future. And from such separation, and the power of reasoning, that we depend on in such large measure, comes the process that says that such and such an event happened to us, because of this or that reason. We allow logic, in which we place so much trust, full play here. The thought that this or that reason was itself created by us in order that the life event we are experiencing could come into being is preposterous. Or is it?

Seth in his inimitable style advises his listeners to be spontaneous and trust themselves. The enemy of spontaneity, he says, is reason, for we have been taught to mistrust ourselves. The whole Freudian process is based on the view that we have hidden suppressed desires and that if we take the lid off ourselves these hidden desires will surge out to embarrass us. For to be spontaneous is to be reckless, and to be reckless means to be out of control. We dare not ever be out of control so we keep ourselves under tight rein. We mistrust spontaneity for we mistrust our inner selves. But, Seth asserts, we are never out of control, for our 'Greater Self' is always looking after our best interests; we do not need then to second guess ourselves, or fear that we will ever do other than follow the path that leads to our greater good.

The crucible of creation is the moment, in the moment is all. In the moment is the place where there is no separation, the place where time ceases and a fusing occurs between 'All That Is', or 'The Power That Is', and ourselves. In the moment we can realise our wholeness, our totality. In the crucible of the moment we unify with the whole of creation. It is here that transformation can occur, here that we can literally transform and become part of all, yet retain our individuality our personal identity. Yet how often do we allow ourselves to know the moment? How often do we sink deeply into it and become oblivious to time? Allow ourselves to be released from the grip of the past, present and future?

At the point of death we will know such a moment. Then time will cease to be. The beginning and the end will be encompassed into one ceaseless moment. Then the future will become the present and the past cease to have meaning, as we lose our grip on time. Death then is the crossroads where all realities meet. There is no deception then. No separation, no division. Then we will unify in truth and honesty as so rarely in life.

It is hard, without deliberate effort, to experience such a merging in the midst of a life that is shaped by the Root Assumption of time. For we skip across the moments hurrying onward to meet the next, rarely pausing to enjoy the moment. We confidently move onward with a firm grasp on the past, and a foot hopefully placed in the future. We look back through the facility of memory, and forward with hope, rarely pausing in between and enjoying the present.

To spontaneously experience the moment is difficult for us. For to do so we must cease our onward rush and die temporarily to all that is past and future. To escape from time we must be prepared to withdraw from time, and this we find hard to do. Life for us is continuity, not separation. Separation into moments strung together like pearls on a string; we are never consciously aware of any break in time. So a deliberate act is required to break this appearance of flowing constancy. To pause, to reflect. Only such a deliberate act can enable us to experience the moment and the unification that comes from a merging of all consciousness. Only in such a moment can all become one, and separation cease; no longer the observer and the observed. Spectator and participant; in such a moment we can know the spontaneity of life. And with the spontaneity can come complete honesty, for with total unification there can be no deception, no lies, no distortion. Our response is immediate and in the immediacy there comes complete knowing.

So much of our life is spent editing and determining, watching and censoring. We constantly watch ourselves performing; we are our own audience and our own critic. We observe ourselves and comment on the observation. We judge ourselves against our contempories by measures and norms that our culture and our upbringing have established for us. Measures that have no relevance outside of this time. When we do not fit the preconceived notion of how we should be, we censure ourselves, criticise ourselves, fall into depression and worse.

In our minds there is a constant separation between what is and what we perceive it to be. We fail to taste life in all its fullness: we place filters and layers between us and reality, always looking forward or backward. Dreaming and hoping; deliberately forgetting that which was painful for us and only remembering that which was good. Only in times of great emotion does this separation reduce and we come close to honesty, close to touching what is, rather than what we perceive it to be. Times of great anger and great love. At times such as these we come close to merging with 'All That Is'. We lose ourselves in the moment; then we cease to judge and just become. The strength that can become ours at such times is awesome. We seem to be able to move mountains, we know no fear; we are literally transformed. To experience this is to experience that which can be ours when we merge more fully with the moment. Allow ourselves to sink deeply into the moment without the separation that comes with the concept of time.

Being human means learning to think and talk in time, to look backward and relive or regret, or look forward and plan, hoping or dreading. Yet there is only the moment. The NOW of our existence. We seem to live from moment to moment, yet this cannot be for we are never between moments. There is only and ever a single indivisible moment, and ourselves within it.

To be spontaneous is to live in the moment. To trust impulse and intuition. To respond to life with an immediacy that brooks no fear. To live this way requires great courage and great trust. Courage to overcome the fear of how we will be received if we actually tell people what we are thinking without editing and limiting. If we actually live life the way that we feel it should be lived, irrespective of how far out this is from conventional thinking. Trust in our inner selves to guide our feet and direct our actions. Together however, spontaneity, courage and trust can enable us to experience life more fully and merge more effectively with life.

The fourth and final Universal Law states that consciousness always *spontaneously* seeks the path that leads to its greatest becomingness. This Law means that we can let go and trust and take comfort from the knowledge that we are always in life, exactly where we should be, doing exactly what we intended. No matter how difficult, painful or complex the circumstances appear to be.

It follows that if we create all that happens to us in life, following the path that will lead to our greatest expression of our greater self, then we are always exactly where we have chosen to be at any given moment. When life is hard, when we are in pain and suffering, when there appears to be little purpose and point in going on, therein may be the greatest reason for pressing on, rather than in giving up. To concentrate all of ourselves on the task in hand, whatever that task may be. For it is what we have chosen to do.

Thoughts flit into and out of our mind. In this flitting is the danger of separation. Of a lack of focus. It takes great application and complete trust to focus all on the task in hand, to release all and just be. To trust completely and let go of all fear, all worries all concerns. To enter into this state is to release our powers of healing, to release the energy that is our birthright. The total energy that comes from such unification is awesome. The blending of the physically manifest us with the higher entity us combines to produce creative energy that is abnormal and unusual for us in our present state.

We see such release when we see great musicians perform. They lose themselves in their art and become the instrument and the music at one and the same time. No separation is evident; we forget their humanity, their weaknesses and just wonder at their skill and talent. There is no intensity here, just a refined focus, a naturalness that allows creation to flow through them and takes our breath away.

Meditation can help us to sense our innate power of creativity. To unblock the limitation that we have come to accept as normal. To allow our natural powers free rein. For in meditation we seek to concentrate on the moment, to let go of our focus on time. To hold our thoughts and allow ourselves to transcend the merely physical; to just be. To create within ourselves a stillness that allows us to know our true selves more fully. It is possible to bring such meditative processes into our daily life, to carry this stillness with us throughout our day. To know the peace 'that passes all understanding'.

There is always only ever the moment; only the NOW. And in the now is our greatest Power. In the NOW we free ourselves from the shackles with which time restricts us. Become timeless beings living more honestly and spontaneously in the moment. It is a state of being to be striven for. Yet we cannot earn it or learn it, we can only experience it if our desire is strong enough. If our will and determination are such that we are prepared to die to time. To eliminate the hold that the past and the future have over us. To be truly spontaneous and break out of the hold of linear time and realise that all IS and can only ever be the one moment point.

## Thought Watching

We are our own life laboratory. Through observing ourself in action in life; initiating, responding and reacting to life, we can learn what works for us and what doesn't. What 'presses our buttons'. What turns us on and excites us about life, and more importantly, what turns us off and makes us retreat from life. Wisdom comes through experience and to a large degree this is true. But only where we draw conclusions from our experiences that lead us to change for the better. To become more than we are, in accordance with Universal Law.

If we are really serious about learning about life, then we must learn to watch our thought in action. For all life activity is thought based, both directly and indirectly. Both consciously, and more often subconsciously. We can, if we choose, teach ourself to observe the thoughts that brought into being the life we are experiencing now. We can literally watch thought move.

Our emotions and feelings are an excellent example of this, for these are but thought clothed in energy. Something is seen or thought by us this then gives rise to a state of feeling, or non-feeling, for many thoughts are neutral, they generate feelings that are neither positive nor negative. Others, to a greater or lesser degree give rise to emotion, some positive, some negative. Some so highly charged that we describe them as ecstatic, some so negative that they knock us back or depress us.

Advertisers are only too well aware of the impact that images have on our mental state, for few images are neutral. Imagery is the universal language. It crosses all national and racial boundaries and speaks to all alike. Yet the same image can create vastly different reactions. If I show an image of a large fillet steak cooked to perfection to a meat lover, most likely it will evoke in them feelings of hunger. It will bring to their mind the taste of the steak and all the pleasure that our meat eating observer associates with a perfectly grilled steak. However, if I show the same image to a vegan they are likely to recoil in horror. To them, the image of dead flesh brings to their mind the animal that the steak once was, and it will remind them, and possibly reinforce for them, all of the reasons that led them to their vegan lifestyle. The same image but cloaked in completely opposite emotions and feelings. Same image, different thoughts.

Our feelings are an energy-generated response to internal thoughts evoked by imagined or external images. They can drive us to the depths of despair, or lift us to the heights of ecstasy. They can charge us with energy, or drain our energy away. If we are told of the illness of a loved one, we do not feel a surge of explosive energy. We do not – if we are normal – leap into the air punching the sky. We feel sadness coupled with hope for their recovery. Yet if we are told that we have won a major prize, or gained a favourable exam result, then we are liable to punch the air and shout 'Yes!' We are flooded with energy, we feel alive and exhilarated.

Yet in both states what has moved but thought? Thought and the mental images that have been conjured up by the news we have received. This in turn will have gone on to create our feeling state. Our energy levels will have changed, with us being the transformers.

Remember the last time you were angry, really angry. So angry that you were ready to take action which in your calm state you would have thought of as unacceptable. Rage blots out all restraint. Rage infuses us with overwhelming energy. Our face goes red, we look and feel as if we are about to explode. Often we are ashamed of the things that we do in such a state. We apologise profusely afterwards. Yet where does this energy come from? It is literally thought in action.

Conversely, remember the last time that you were convulsed by the giggles. When you laughed so hard that your stomach ached and you were gasping for breath. Your body filled with energy, it overflowed from you. You could not hold it in no matter how hard you tried. Each of the states, one of anger, the other of extreme pleasure, brings with it overwhelming energy. This demonstrates that thought and energy are inextricably linked one to the other.

One exercise which I often practise is to observe myself as I go about my daily life. Analyse how I feel at particular points in time, and track back to the thought or thoughts, which generated the feeling I am experiencing at the time. If something has annoyed me, I try to identify what was said, or done to me, that created the feeling of annoyance. To track the thought process from act to feeling. To try to uncover the underlying belief that is fuelling the feelings of annoyance I am experiencing. It may be that somebody has said or done something to me that was similar to an event or occurrence that caused me pain years ago. That reminded me of a time when I was perhaps more vulnerable. It may be that the image of myself that I carry around with me has been maligned or challenged. To use the common parlance 'I have been dissed'.

I am reminded here of the old saying that 'Sticks and stones can break your bones, but names will never hurt you.' So unless I am being beaten around the head at the time, in which case I will be too busy defending myself to think rationally, I will have allowed myself to receive from someone, or from some event, action or words, which I have allowed myself to perceive as harmful or damaging to me. It is important to identify then what is harmed? As the mystic Krishnamurti often asked. 'What is hurt?' Often it is merely my perception of myself, or my dignity that has been bruised. This naturally leads to an appraisal of my self-image. Of who and what I think I am − a sobering exercise and one, if properly carried out deflates any ego-driven pomposity.

Watching thought in action can teach us a lot about ourself. Can show us, often in graphic form, what our belief system consists of. What appals us, what frightens us, what disgusts us. What makes us happy. Can identify our underlying beliefs about life, and more importantly beliefs about ourself. The outer is but the manifestation of the inner. It is important to understand and know what fuels and drives us in order to ensure that we are better able to create the reality that we desire, rather than passively accepting what comes to us with resignation, and a belief that there is nothing we can do about it. Such a limiting belief, held by many insecure and damaged people. Where this belief is present, it is always the starting place where work on image and self-belief can bring about the greatest change in the individual concerned.

We are indeed 'works in progress'. We can, through self-observation, ensure that this work is one with which we are more content. We can be more in control of our life than perhaps we realise.

## Learned and Cultural Beliefs

Our earliest beliefs are absorbed from our families and our culture, beliefs about who and what we are. These beliefs become ingrained in us – thought patterns from which we create our world without conscious awareness or direction. Rarely challenged by us they create much of our day to day reality. We in turn become parents and pass on our beliefs to our children, modified by our experience of life, and so the process goes on. Yet becoming an adult must be about questioning the beliefs we hold; validating, and where necessary, changing them.

If we wish to lead balanced, fulfilled and happy lives we must identify and kick out any belief that limits and holds us back. That restricts and distorts our life; beliefs that are based on fear not love. As a wise man once said: 'To end war we must first learn to love peace, for to hate war is to create and perpetuate it'.

Any exploration of our beliefs is by its very nature a personal exercise. It is an exercise in the disciplines of watching and observing ourselves in action. In looking at our life and learning from those things with which we are uncomfortable and which hurt and damage us. It is essential to our well-being and our mental health that we actively and continually review our life and the beliefs on which it is founded. We must learn to reject and kick out those beliefs that we do not want, that are unhealthy and damaging to our happiness or our long-term development.

Beliefs are rarely singular, they are always hierarchical, a fundamental base belief in a lack of worth may, for instance, be expressed in many ways, such as:

- A poor self-image and a resulting lack of confidence.

- Overeating; literally making ourselves fat and unattractive, bringing into physical form the image we hold of ourselves as someone who we believe others find unattractive.

- A belief that we are not entitled to be wealthy, that poverty is our natural state matching our unworthiness.

- An expectation of failure. We are unworthy so how can we expect to succeed in life?

- Shyness and a propensity to be easily embarrassed and humiliated. A reluctance to stand our ground and fight our corner, after all we are inferior people aren't we?

- An underlying feeling of vulnerability and insecurity. This belief making us prone to frequent sickness and ill-health. Such distorted beliefs about ourselves can literally lead to our cells mutating, creating cancerous tumours.

- An unwillingness to take part in life – asthma and other afflictions that narrow our airways may result, for breath is life.

All of this stemming from a fundamental root belief in unworthiness.

Our life and life patterns can be viewed as our own personal laboratory enabling us to observe the power that our beliefs have on the world we experience. Our beliefs are writ large in our life for they have created who and what we are today. To examine our life and come to learn through experience those beliefs that work for us and those that work against us is a very useful exercise. We can, if we choose, take our negative experiences and explore the beliefs that are at the root of them and which, if retained, will continually bring similar experiences into our life. We can then go on to replace them with healthier beliefs and work until these have completely replaced the old damaging beliefs.

One of the earliest books to impress me in the skills of life changing was Norman Vincent Peale's *The Power of Positive Thinking*. This book was a runaway world bestseller for decades and is still in print today.

It taught its followers how to change negative thinking into positive thinking. A powerful book in so many ways. Its one possible flaw, which led to some people rejecting it, was the fact that Norman Vincent Peale was a practising Christian. A minister of religion with a thriving church based in New York. His Christian faith was evident in his books with frequent references to prayer and God. For many, this constant reference to God was a turn off, which was a shame for even without these references his books had the power to change lives for the better.

I agree with much that is written in *The Power of Positive Thinking*. However, simply thinking in a positive manner is not enough. For if we simply think positively because we fear negativity, we are in danger of creating negatively rather than positively. The reason for this is very simple, and is a fundamental truth that must be understood if we are to achieve lasting change. This is the fact that thought does not discriminate between positive and negative images; thought just is, and creates exactly what we think (image) regardless of whether what we think is either positive or negative. So, if I fervently and positively hold a thought that I do not want something to happen or occur in my life, I might just as well think that I want it to happen. For the creative power that is thought simply sees what I image and brings it into being in my life. The natural law of what we resist persisting.

A simple example of this is in my attempt to overcome my tendency to be clumsy. I am forever knocking things over. If I think when setting a glass of water down that I must not knock it over, or spill it, invariably within seconds I will either have knocked the glass over or at the very least spilt some of its contents. If, however, I concentrate on seeing the glass remaining upright with the contents unspilt – hey presto – that is what happens. This reminds me of one of my oft quoted sayings: 'Thought creates – so always think outcomes and not details.'

The danger in positive thinking, if we are not careful, is that often what we are seeking to be positive about is in fact preventing something we are unhappy about occurring. In so doing we actually succeed in bringing the very thing we are unhappy about into being. The solution is always to ensure that we only think or image outcomes. Seeing successfully completed whatever we wish to bring about, nothing more or less. The creative process directed by thought cannot distinguish between positive and negative it just brings into being the thing thought or imaged (imagined).

The present is the created. It is the result of those thoughts and beliefs that we have held about ourself and our life. It is already history and as such unchangeable. What we can change, however, is our future, realising that what we think and believe about ourselves and our life today will bring into being our tomorrows. Only through policing and being aware of what we are accepting into our minds, thinking about and expecting to happen, will we enable us to permanently change our tomorrows.

The power of our mind is little understood by even the greatest of scientists. Some scientists say that the more they discover about the brain, and by implication the human mind, the more they realise what they do not know. The real breakthrough will come when it is accepted by all scientists and doctors alike that thought always creates exactly in its own image. It is this truth that will finally set humanity free. The beliefs we hold about our world are thought patterns that we rarely challenge for they have become essential to our balance and well-being. They enable us to navigate through life, they represent how we see our world. The danger though is in continuing to hold on to beliefs that are unhealthy and which no longer serve our best interests and which have the potential within them to hold back our growth and self-development. All such beliefs must be identified and changed, if we are truly to enjoy all of the blessings that life can bring to us. We should aim to identify and change all those beliefs that are not in our long-term best interests.

## The Outer is Always the Manifestation of the Inner

The following was channelled through me during a trip to Portland Oregon in April 1988. I recall waking up early in my hotel room and having an overwhelming urge to write. As I sat writing at the desk in the room, the words flowed on to the paper without any conscious direction from me. The writing was mine. It was definitely not a case of automatic writing, rather it was as if the words were being channelled through me. I found what was produced most useful to me at that time and reading the words again years later they have lost none of their validity for me. This is what I wrote that early spring morning:

*And if you would see that which is in your heart look at that which is in your life. For the outer is always the manifestation of the inner and in this way you form your life.*

*There is no separation except that which you allow to occur, for in each you shall see the other. Life is not a hidden mystery, neither is it laid out plainly for all to see. Yet you have a vested belief in separation. You look to the parts in a vain attempt to decipher the whole. Yet if you would look to the whole, to the totality of life, there you would see laid before you the greatest mysteries of the ages which once comprehended in their simplicity will enable you to make quantum leaps in your growth as creative beings.*

*That which you have in your life is but the manifestation of your beliefs and if you would look upon these as symbols you would quickly see the beliefs that create and sustain them. For the answer to the question of how creation works? You need look no further than the circumstances and situations that you create, for in each one is the lesson that you must learn.*

*Do not go first to those areas of your life with which you are happy, rather go first to those areas with which you are most unhappy and seek to know those beliefs that have created and which are sustaining the circumstances or situations that cause you such pain. When you allow yourself to see them as merely symbols, signs to you, of your beliefs then you can set about changing them. And in the changing you will glimpse the miracle of creation. For you are choosing beings, and what is the use of choice unless it is coupled with creation?*

*See then not separation and powerlessness, see instead the wholeness of life and in the interweaving and outer play you will see the inner workings. In each shall be seen the other. In all shall be seen the parts. Moving, merging, interweaving, interlinking, each dependent upon the other, each a part of the other.*

*All then are indeed your brothers and sisters, and this world your creation. Where there is sickness and pain and poverty you glimpse these things in yourself. Where there is deprivation and crime and exploitation you see these in yourself. And the fallen are not less than the risen for each is one aspect of the other. In the words of Jesus then 'Judge not less ye be judged' and 'If you do this unto the least of men you do it unto me.'*

*Go now in the peace of God. Think on that which has been presented to you. Use your God-given powers of observation and reason but let not reason separate you from the truth, for reason is of the past and you are creating a new beginning and a new future.*

The outer is always the manifestation of the inner. This fundamental truth, if universally accepted, would significantly change the world for the better. The outer is always the manifestation of the inner in every aspect of life, from physical appearance to health, wealth, relationship, understandings; the list is endless. Every part of physical life shouts and expresses this truth. For as we think and believe individually, culturally and collectively, so we become, this reality is expressed throughout the whole of our world, from our personal world through to our families, communities and our nations. There is no part of our life where this is not so. What we see and experience in physical form is a direct reflection of what we think and the beliefs that we hold.

Emanuel Swedenborg (1688–1777) an eminent scientist, in his work *Arcania Coeletia* (heavenly secrets), wrote that:

> *All natural things represent those which are of the spiritual (inner) things to which they correspond… It has been given to me to know from much experience that in the natural world… There is nothing whatever that does not represent something in the spiritual world, or that has not something there to which it corresponds.*

I am reminded here of the time when I was a young man working on the assembly lines at Vauxhall Motors in Luton. I worked in the trim shop. This area of the factory received painted body shells from the paint shop, and turned them into fully-fitted vehicles by the addition of engines, gearboxes, axles, lighting, carpets, seating, dash panels and other fitments such as door handles, bumpers, glass, etc. By the time vehicles left the trim shop they were ready for final testing and delivery.

The build system worked by breaking each process down into small interlocking actions carried out by teams, or groups of assembly workers. This meant that if you were fitting door handles, you worked as part of a gang of three, thus you would fit door handles to every third vehicle as it approached your work station on the slowly moving track that carried the body shell on its circuit through the trim shop. The other two members of your gang fitted handles to the other two vehicles in their turn. If someone needed a break, then you moved to fitting handles to every other vehicle to relieve your gang member. The work could be incredibly boring, but because of the movement of the various assembly teams, some of whom could be working on one vehicle in four, or five, you were always conducting half a dozen conversations at one time, each interrupted and then resumed as you moved from vehicle to vehicle and from one group of workers to other groups and back again.

One man I worked with was Arthur, a man in his early sixties with grey hair and a kindly manner. Arthur always wore a spotless white line apron and soft fingerless cotton gloves. He seemed gentle almost benign. To my surprise I was told that in his youth he had been quite a tearaway, on one occasion apparently biting a man's ear almost in half during a fight. It seemed strange comparing the old white-haired man with the image of a tearaway who would engage in such vicious street fighting. I spent many hours talking with Arthur as we worked and I still remember, some forty years later, one of the things that he told me.

'Dennis,' he said. 'As people age their faces show their character. They can't hide this, it is a natural part of life and growth. Always look at older people closely, for as they look, so they are.' The inner physically becoming the outer.

As I have grown older I have often thought of Arthur and frequently tested his hypothesis. People who are naturally happy, jolly people always look that way. Laughter and smile lines have creased their faces such that they fall easily and naturally into a smile. Similarly, miserable taciturn folk develop down turned mouths and creases that tell you very quickly what their natural mind set is. This may be an oversimplification, but try it for yourself – I think you will soon find that this first appearance will be a good guide to the type of character that you are dealing with when you meet and work with older people. I call it 'Arthur's law'.

But the fact of the inner becoming the outer goes much further than this. Life as it is experienced in the present is already history; for it is the created, and we its creators. It is so important to understand and accept this fact. What we have today we have created from the thoughts and beliefs that we have held about our world and our life in our yesterdays. We cannot change the past, but we can change the future once we recognise and accept that we create our future from the thoughts that we hold today, this minute, this moment. To effect change in these is to effect change in our future. For we create our life, every single aspect of it.

In physical form there is a gap between creation and manifestation, for this is the purpose of time. Time provides the gap between creation and manifestation. Time gives us the opportunity to observe our creation, for this is its purpose. To enable us to observe, to grow to understand that from our thoughts and beliefs we bring our world into being in physical form. The gap between thought and creation can be measured in seconds, hours, months or years.

As the planting of a seed does not of itself bring forth the flower, the inner workings of the seed nurtured by water and soil over time brings forth the foliage and the flower. When you look at the seed of any plant it is always a leap of faith to accept that contained in the seed is the blueprint of the flower. If indeed you have never seen flowers and I were to show you pictures of one and then tell you that the tiny seed that I held would transform itself into the flower in a relatively short period of time given soil and water, you would struggle to believe me unless you had observed the phenomenon for yourself, for it defies all logic.

Like the seed, the inner us contains the essence of the outer us. What we are today is the result of the bringing into being of our thoughts and beliefs about ourself and our world throughout our life. To effect change in our outer physical world we must first change the core beliefs we hold about our life and ourself. We must examine and understand the inner, and go to work on this to effect the change that we desire in the outer us. My friend Arthur is dead now, yet his insight into human form was right. It took me years of searching to appreciate just how right he was, and to incorporate the truth that he espoused into both my life and my work, for the outer is indeed always the manifestation of the inner.

## Time

Time is a Root Assumption. We need it to plan and organise our lives. To provide markers as we move through life; to help us to coordinate and communicate. Without a universal accepted notion of time we would lead a chaotic uncoordinated existence. As physical beings we think in terms of beginnings and endings, for our lives are governed by this reality; in physical form all living things are born and die. Yet nature knows no clock time, only cycles. Cycles governed by the movements of the planets that influence the length of our days and our seasons.

I write these words in late summer 2005. I am told by scientists that our planet is billions of years old; 2,000 years then is merely a flicker in the lifetime of our planet. Our contemporary history can be measured in hundreds of thousands of years – again a minute fraction of our planet's known lifespan.

Yet the only 'time' I can ever know is the immediacy of the 'now' of my life. I can remember yesterday and think and plan for tomorrow but I can only ever know the now of my existence. Yesterday is gone and tomorrow can only ever be a concept. Seth and Myriad both speak of the 'now' as the 'moment point'; the crossroads of our life, the only time that we can ever know and act upon. In the moment point is all of life. It is the only certain fact in our existence, all else is memory and conjecture.

Both space and time are 'Root Assumptions'. Assumptions that we accept at birth – laws as it were that govern our existence in human form. Time is merely a tool fashioned to enable us to function and work in our physical environment.

Dr Ernest Holmes refers to the description given to time by Dean Inge. In his Glossary *to The Science of Mind* textbook he says:

> For of course time is not a thing of itself. It is simply a measure of experience in eternity. Time does not contradict eternity, but allows it to become expressed in terms of definite experience. Time is necessary because it allows experience to take place within the One, but time is never a thing of itself. It is impossible to measure time; for yesterday is gone and tomorrow has not come. And today is rapidly slipping past. If we were to attempt to put a finger on any period of time, it would be gone before we could point to it. But elusive as time is, it is necessary to experience life.

Apart from the organisational benefits of time what other value does it have for us? And if we can only ever live in the 'now' of life, where are we travelling from and to? Is our movement through life merely a mental concept? Where is the 'I' that existed yesterday? Who is the 'I' that exists today? Where is the 'me' in all of this? Am I merely a collection of memories embedded in physical form as some scientists would have me believe?

Universal Law, as explained by Myriad, states that the underlying purpose of all life is growth; growth in all its manifestations. Growth in the first instance in physical maturity and strength to enable us to procreate and continue our species – that most fundamental of animal instincts. But thereafter growth in becoming as intellectual/spiritual beings is through the choices we make, the disciplines that we impose upon ourselves, the belief systems we maintain. The thoughts we hold about ourselves and our world; all these and more determine the direction and speed of our growth.

Maturity brings with it the wisdom of learning through experiencing life, of what works and what does not. Wisdom enables us from such knowledge to plot and plan our path through the tomorrows of our life. And in theory at any rate to learn from our mistakes. From the past decisions that we have made which have resulted in pain and suffering, we learn what works and what does not.

Without time such observation of life would be impossible. We need to be able to track the sequence of events that make up our life; to observe our journey from where we were to where we are. Of the steps we have taken along the way. Without time we would be in a world of instant creation. Time gives us the facility of comparison. From comparison, judgements can be formed.

A world without time would be a world where we would think and it would be. To live in such a world would be like being dropped into the cockpit of a Formula One racing car travelling at 200mph when we only have the skills to drive a Mini at 70mph. The result would be disastrous – both for us and the car! Only through observation, comparison, learning and development, through the realisation that our world is indeed our creation. Through acceptance of this fact of our reality and through learning how to manipulate and use the natural laws of creation, can we be prepared for an 'out of time' existence.

Time has value for us in that it enables us to observe how we create and bring our life into being. Time allows us to observe, reflect and learn how to manage the business of manipulating and controlling creation – the business of life. To literally see our thoughts in form and action. Without the passage of time this opportunity would not be available to us and we would inhabit a primitive, chaotic, reactive world.

For, as set out in the final section of this book, beyond physical form there is no time; there creation is instant – we think and it is so. Whilst at first glance this may seem an ideal environment, it does not take much imagination to appreciate that unless we have first learned to control and discipline our thoughts the world that we create could indeed be monstrous, created from our fears and our worst nightmares. We could find ourselves at the whim of uncontrolled random thought whisking us hither and thither in a frightening fashion. Only by understanding that our life is indeed our creation can lead us to escape the morass of being trapped in a world of random uncontrolled thought.

By observing our thoughts day by day, and coming to understand that what we think and believe does indeed shape our world, we can learn the disciplines necessary to prepare ourselves for the world beyond the physical. In the process we can substantially improve our day to day world. For our thoughts create, not occasionally, but constantly, and the thoughts and beliefs that we hold about our world today, will without doubt, determine our tomorrows. This then is the lesson and purpose of the 'Root Assumption' that is time.

## Effecting Change

The constant theme, repeated again and again, in this book is that human beings are innately creative. That the whole of our life experience is the result and outcome of our thoughts and our beliefs. That nothing that happens to us is the result of chance, circumstance or coincidence. Belief in these is simply a form of escapism, convenient tools to use to explain away the seemingly inexplicable. Being creative is not something we can decide to be or not to be. We have no more choice as to whether or not we create our life than the seed planted deep in the soil can decide whether or not it should push up towards the light, grow and flower; it knows no other way. Likewise, we constantly create our lives; our creation is literally our life in all its totality. Whether we like it or not, we grow and become that which we constantly think and believe. We cannot decide that we will not create; non- creation is not an option for us. We are innately creative beings. What we think and believe about our life is what we become. Only by understanding and accepting that thought is the creative medium through which we create the whole our life will lead us to greater control over our life circumstances. This is the truth that has escaped man throughout the centuries. To change our life we must first change our thoughts and beliefs, there is no other way.

Bringing about life change is not easy. A knowledge of the 'how of life creation' will not of itself effect any change in our life circumstances. It is just that, 'knowledge'. As Edgar Cayce the 'Sleeping Prophet' once remarked: 'In all your getting get understanding.' We have become used to who and what we are. Our thought patterns have become habitual, our beliefs deep rooted. It takes considerable concentrated effort to change our beliefs about our world, and reinforce any new patterns of behaviour, until they replace the old. In the midst of such change we can become frightened and concerned for we are betwixt and between, neither one thing nor the other. As an friend of mind remarked we must have the courage to breach the 'Terror Barrier'. Better the comfort of the known than the fear of the unknown. To cut ourselves adrift from cherished beliefs about life and embrace new alien thoughts and beliefs is an act of courage, for we must go through the 'Terror Barrier'. And unless we trust and constantly reinforce our desire to change, we will slip back into the comfort zone formed by our old familiar beliefs. Trying to change our underlying beliefs whilst policing our thoughts, will feel unnatural, because it is unnatural. It takes time to replace one thinking groove with another. With perseverance, however, any new belief pattern will take effect and bring into being that which we truly desire.

There are no short cuts to the start place of change. I am reminded here of one of my favourite jokes. It tells the story of the American who was lost whilst touring Southern Ireland. He wanted to get to Dublin but had no idea of which road to take. Seeing a farmhand working in a field he stopped his car and shouted over, 'Can you tell me the way to Dublin?' The farmhand stopped his work and paused for a moment. He then replied in a strong Irish accent, 'If I was you, sir, I wouldn't start from here!'

The fact is that like the tourist, if we want to effect change in our life, we have no choice but to start from here. From where we are right now. The first step we can take is the recognition and acceptance that what we have right now in our life is our creation; we have created every aspect of it, all of it is our responsibility. Change will not be possible without first such a recognition and acceptance. The outer is always a manifestation of the inner. To understand your beliefs and your thoughts simply look at your life; for there they will be writ large.

Look around you. Examine every area of your life. Your relationships, your health, your work, your bank balance, your triumphs, your failures, your hopes and dreams. Look at every aspect of your life that makes you what you are today. This is your creation; you made every part of it. Using your innate powers of creation poured into the moulds of your beliefs about your world, about who and what you are. You brought your world and your life into being. You can remain where you are for as long as you choose; it is after all your life. You must enjoy or endure it, for you have no choice. Until you get so fed up with who and what you are that the desire for change, driven by Universal Law, becomes irresistible. For make no mistake the inexorable working of Universal Law will ultimately bring you to the place where the desire to change, to grow and become more than you are will become too powerful to resist.

It is human nature to resist change. Particularly change that involves effort. We all crave security and love. We long for peace, fulfilment and contentment. These states are not achieved by constant change – the opposite in fact. We resist taking any steps that might disturb the status quo. Yet if we are to achieve our life's purpose there is no alternative but to change, to work to achieve our greatest potential. Universal Law imbues us with the drive to grow and become more than we are. Like a magnet its power draws us on. All attempts to resist it will ultimately fail. For growth is our natural state, and growth will not be denied.

The creative force with which we are imbued is neither positive nor negative, it just is. Thought and belief are the engines of creation. Thought carries within it the mental shapes and images of our beliefs. The moulds as it were that bring into being the events and experiences of our life. I repeat, what we think and believe in and about our life becomes our experience of it. And because this is so it reinforces our beliefs. It becomes an unremitting cycle. We expect to fail, we fail, and our belief in failure is validated.

The equation: Thought + Belief = Expectation. Expectation creates Experience; Experience sustains Belief. So the cycle continues.

Yet we value experience and the lessons we learn from it we label as wisdom, when often it is anything but wisdom. For without care experience simply entrenches false beliefs about our existence, allows them to continue unchanged thus limiting and inhibiting our future. This is where the danger lies. For experience is often no more than a reflection of current beliefs. The creation and recreation of the old rather than the new. For the new to occur we must have new thoughts that challenge self-limiting and defeating beliefs.

Apart from our very basic inbuilt survival instincts, there are two major driving forces in life: Love and Fear. All actions emanate from these two. Examine the activities in daily life and you will realise the truth of this. We work to earn money because of our fear of being without the things that money will provide: food; warmth; comfort; company; security; the satisfaction of working; of feeling useful and purposeful; plus the respect, status and esteem which work brings to us. We fear being valueless and without the status and respect that work brings with it. We love the thought of the comforts and pleasure that the ownership of things bring with them. We crave safety and security.

We fear hunger, cold, discomfort, ill-health, isolation, loneliness, pain, violence and death – self-extinction – the ultimate fear. Regrettably, in our society and our culture the main driving force is fear, not love. Fear of rejection, fear of not conforming, fear of poverty, fear of sickness and disease, fear of violence, fear of war, fear of growing old, fear of death. Fear of non-acceptance by our peers. Our society is riddled with safety features, rules and regulations, concerns for our health, both short and long term, fears of risk to our physical well-being. Ever present is the fear of crime, violence, war, sickness and disease. Our belief in these realities pervades our airways and our thinking. We carry them with us wherever we go; we act to guard ourselves against them. Many believe that our world is a threatening, aggressive fearful place that will turn on them if they relax their guard and cease to be ever vigilant. So we vaccinate, medicate, lock, bar and limit.

We believe our very world is in peril. Global warming is the threat of the age. A failure to act against this perceived threat will lead to catastrophic climate change, floods, cancers and other threats too horrific to contemplate. Caring for our planet and our environment becomes then not an act of love, but one of fear of the consequences if we do not. It is a sad fact that fear sells to a greater degree than love; a fact well known by the drug industry, insurers, politicians and salespeople. Yet because all fears are belief driven they will create and continue to bring into being the very things feared. This is the simple truth of creation that we ignore at our peril.

As Seth said:

> *What we believe becomes our experience in life and of life; there is no area of our life to which this does not apply. To understand this is to take control over life.*

As the next chapter states, only when our beliefs are founded on love. Love for our world, love for our fellow man, love for our planet, our environment and the creatures that we share it with. Love of peace, love of life and the joy of health. Love of sharing without expectation of return. Only then will we effect lasting change, both in ourselves and in our world.

# Living

*Between stimulus and response, there is a space.*
*In that space lies our freedom and our power to choose*
*our response.*
*In our response lies our growth and our happiness.*

## Love

What is this emotion called love, that has fuelled thousands of love songs and poems? That can lead us to ecstasy or anguish in equal measure? A word that is bandied around freely, often without regard to its true meaning. Four letters that encompass such a great emotion.

Is the love I have for my partner a different emotion than the love I have for my dogs? Is the love I have for my family different from the love that I have for my friends? Is my love of beautiful scenery and nature different from my love of good music or literature? Or are they all multifaceted aspects of the same thing? Love it seems can only be when we give ourselves unreservedly to those things and people that we love. Where we seek to merge as completely as we are able with the object of our love. Where a chord is struck within us such that we seek to resonate in harmony. Love lifts, enhances, expands and encompasses our whole being. It is a state of living akin to no other. It is blissful, unmistakable, all encompassing and overwhelming. This is why it is so desired and sought after for it provides highs that exceed those experienced by any known recreational drug, stronger than alcohol, cocaine, ecstasy or heroin.

Love is energy concentrated as in no other way; it is the most powerful force known to man. In love we come close to the essence of 'All That Is' as in no other way. Love is its own evidence for the way that it is, it is overwhelming, all powerful and will ultimately defeat all opposed to it.

> *Today, the term 'love' has become one of the most frequently used and misused words, a word to which we attach quite different meaning.*

So writes Pope Benedict XVI in his first Encyclical letter.

Love today has become a word that encompasses the ultimate consumer 'must have'. Books abound on how to find the perfect partner, what chat-up lines work, books on the rules of love and how to satisfy your partner. 'Love' the commodity used to sell all consumer products. Pope Benedict comments on how we speak of love of country, love of our profession, love between friends, love of work, love between parents and children, love between family members, love of neighbour and love of God. And finally, and especially, love between two people. Against which all other love seems to fade in comparison.

Swedenborg spoke of such idealised love in his writings, 'Conversations with Angels' when he describes what he termed as 'conjugial' (sic) love: the relationship of total union of one man with one woman:

> *Conjugial love in its essence is nothing else but the wish of two to be one, or in other words, a will on their part that their two lives become one life.*

He went on:

> *The states produced by conjugial love are innocence, peace, tranquillity, inmost friendship, complete trust, a mutual desire of the mind and the heart to do the other every good.*

This definition outlines the ideal love between two persons.

What it is not, however, is the transient modern version of love peddled today. Whether Swedenborg's ideal love is realised will depend on whether the state experienced is really true love, or simply one based on lust, desire, or a mutuality of convenience.

Recent studies have shown that the emotional highs experienced when people meet and fall in love last, on average, no longer than two years, before returning to the levels experienced prior to meeting. Whether the relationship lasts after this time depends on a number of factors. Not least compatibility and shared interests. Where the relationship grows through the initial high stage to something deeper and longer lasting is the real test of any relationship. Whether it can become more than the initial attraction is always the ultimate question. Where it was founded on nothing more than desire and lust, then the omens for a lasting relationship are rarely good.

Pope Benedict, in his encyclical, states that true love leads us beyond ourselves. As he puts it:

> *to rise in ecstasy to the divine. Love is a single reality, but with different dimension; at different times one or other dimensions may emerge more clearly.*

It is interesting that this, the first encyclical of a new Pope should be on the subject of love. I cannot, however, write of the Christian version of love without being reminded of Saint Paul's beautiful description of love set out in 1 Corinthians 13:v4–8:

> *Love is patient,*
> *Love is kind.*
> *It does not envy,*
> *It does not boast,*
> *It is not proud,*
> *It is not rude,*
> *It is not self seeking,*

*It is not easily angered,*
*It keeps no record of wrongs.*

*Love does not delight in evil,*
*but rejoices with the truth.*

*It always protects,*
*Always trusts,*
*Always hopes,*
*Always perseveres.*

*Love never fails...*
*And now these three remain: Faith, Hope and Love.*
*But the greatest of these is Love.*

Love is positive; its opposite – hate – is negative. These two are polar extremes. One is constructive and creative, the other destructive and damaging. Love is to be sought, hate is to be understood for what it is, worked through and disposed of, for nothing lasting can be built on a negative foundation. Each create fully in their image, love begets love as hate begets hate. One of the purposes of life set out in the opening section of this book is: 'to come to understand that joy, love, happiness, abundance and creation are all that is of our existence', all else we create from the need to grow, to learn, to experience. If we wish to create pain and suffering, to destroy and tear down, then we will experience the pain that such actions bring to us, to our world and to our loved ones. Until we learn that all is indeed our creation and turn to love, rejecting hate, the learning experience and the pain will continue.

True love is tough. It is about giving to others, without expectation of return. It is in being interested in them, concerned about their well-being, their welfare and their lives. It is about loving those who share life with us. It is not about attachment to things, although people frequently exchange the word enjoy, for love: as in I love my car, my house, etc.

True love can never be conditional with expectation of return, for conditional love is not loving but bargaining. Love that says 'I will love you as long as…' cannot be love. True love comes without conditions attached; it is freely given without expectation of return. This is what makes it so tough. To be so concerned about others that you love them irrespective of their response to you. To be totally committed to their happiness even if this is at the expense of your own, is almost a love beyond reach. Yet if you get right down to it, true love cannot be anything else. All else is simply pleasure and gratification seeking.

I am reminded here of Viktor Frankl's description of his love for his wife recalled from his time in the concentration camps of the Second World War:

> *My mind still clung to the image of my wife. A thought crossed my mind I didn't even know if she were still alive. I knew only one thing – which I had learned well by now: love goes far beyond the physical person of the beloved. It finds its deepest meaning in his spiritual being, his inner self… nothing could touch the strength of my love, my thoughts and the image of my beloved… love is as strong as death.*

Frankl commenting on human sexuality in his book: *Man's Search for Ultimate Meaning* wrote that human sex is more than mere sex. Sex is human if it is a vehicle for love. To make it into a mere means to release tension, or to appease lust is to contradict the humanness of sex.

He wrote in answer to Freud, who had stated that human sex is characterised by three developmental stages: At the most immature level it is only a goal sought, and that goal is tension reduction irrespective of how the goal is achieved; masturbation may do. The mature stage is reached as soon as the sexual instinct centres on normal sexual intercourse. Frankl profoundly disagreed with Freud, he stated that for as long as an individual uses a partner simply for the purpose of reducing sexual tension he is really only 'masturbating on his partner'. To the individual who is really mature, the partner is in no way a means to an end. The mature individual's partnership moves on to a human level, and the human level precludes the mere use of others. It becomes more than an encounter – what takes place then is love. Without love what results is merely promiscuity. And from promiscuity flows chaos. As long as one remains at the level of merely seeking sexual tension resolution, then the sexual instinct may be catered for by pornography or prostitution. This is regression to mere instinctual need for gratification. It is not as Pope Benedict described it 'to rise in ecstasy to the Divine'. Nothing could be further from the true essence of love.

Psychologists generally accept that the two main drives in life are love and fear. Regrettably, most of that which we do in life is fear driven. It can be helpful to explore our relationships with others to determine what the real drive for maintaining the relationship is, fear or love. If it is fear driven, then it cannot be love, for fear and love cannot co-exist.

Bargained love is often a reflection of fear, a lack of self-worth and insecurity; a sense of being unworthy. Fear of losing the love of another because it was not deserved in the first place. A person who has a strong centre, who is whole, has no spaces which must be filled by the adoration of another. Such a one does not say 'I am loved therefore I am.' Rather 'I am, therefore I can love.'

Where one says to their partner 'I will love you as long as…' then there is no love, merely manipulation; playing on another's fears of losing their partner they seek to gain advantage. Where one says 'I love you no matter what.' Then there is true love; true love can never be given in expectation of return.

Acceptance of a creative force within all living things must presuppose a source from which such creation flows. This source can be labelled as 'God', 'Allah', 'The Power That Is', 'All that Is' or whatever we choose. As we love our children and seek the best for them, so does our source love us unconditionally; no matter what. We may not recognise this love nor respond to it, but this does not deny its reality. True love for another is a reflection of divine love. Does indeed allow us 'to rise in ecstasy to the divine.' I am reminded of the sign that I saw outside of a Church in Coventry: 'If God is not in your life – who moved?' A good advertising slogan indeed, but I would argue only an advertising slogan for the core of our being, our very centre is our creative source. We can never be separated from this source any more than our electrical supply can be removed from our generator. An electrical circuit without power is of no value for it lacks the energy to make it work. So too would our world be without its creative energy source.

Whilst I do not call myself a Christian, merely one who believes in a creative (divine) source, I am none the less drawn to the two greatest Commandments given by Christ to his disciples: 'Love your God with all your heart and all your mind, and love your neighbour as yourself.' Both instructions to give to others without reservation. The first Commandment far easier to follow, I find, than the second.

While such Commandments may be difficult to obey, even nigh impossible for us to realise, still we can strive to meet the second of these Commandments as we go about our daily business. For the truth of it is apparent. Fulfilling it would lead to the ending of all wars and conflicts. Would lead to world peace, and a reduction of the poverty and destruction caused by war and armed conflict. A state desired by all right thinking people the world over. Whether Jew, Christian or Muslim, Buddhist or Hindu, Humanist, Atheist or Agnostic. This Commandment can be used as a bench-mark to aim at in our dealings with others.

Can be remembered to sustain and strengthen our resolve when we are tested in our relationships with others.

As my wife says on occasion, when one of our boys tests her patience, 'I may not like you at the moment, but I will always love you.' So, then, should we go about our daily business. Not always liking those we meet and share our world with, but always striving to love them. For as Myriad told me: 'It is love, not money, that really makes the world go round.'

## Happiness

What is happiness? What is this elusive state that we can seek but not find? That comes, often unbidden to sweep over us and provide that 'Ah ha' feeling. Any examination of this pleasurable state shows that happiness and love go hand in hand. When we are with the one we love, we are happy. When we are with family, friends and pets that we love, we are happy. When we are doing the things we love, we are happy. Love and happiness are synonymous. Happiness brings contentment in its wake. When we are happy we know that life is worth living. Happiness can boost our energy and bring healing powers to us that work better for us than any medicine. Happiness then is to be sought by all who wish to improve the quality of their lives.

Yet the state we label as happiness can be elusive to achieve, whilst we may think we know what activities or states lead to it, these are never fail safe formulas. What may make us happy at one time may not have the same effect on us at another; and certainly if we seek to replicate our happiness or pleasure-creating experiences, such as eating our favourite food, or listening to our favourite music too often, they pale and lose their magic for us.

What can science tell us about this elusive feeling that we call 'happiness'? The textbooks tell us that the most immediate recognisable type of happiness involves feelings of pleasure or joy, or a state of contentment with life in general. A judgement made that life is okay and worth living rather than simply implying a brief fleeting joyous and emotional state of well-being.

Surveys have indicated those things that seem to make people happy. Marriage does, pets do (I certainly agree with this), with youth and old age seemingly being the happiest periods of life. Strangely, and contrary to popular opinion, money per se does not make for lasting happiness. In Britain incomes have trebled since the 1950s, but measurable levels of happiness have not increased at all. Studies have also shown that the happiness of lottery winners returns to pre-win levels in as little as one year. Serious accidents and disability seem also to only reduce happiness for the same period. We seem to have been designed with an inbuilt mechanism which enables us to adjust to either very good, or very bad events in our lives, whilst returning to our previous levels, or states of being, within a twelve month period.

American psychologists who studied hundreds of students, concentrating on the top 10%, found that those who socialised most were the happiest. It seems that increasing the number of social contacts we have is one of the best ways that lead to happiness. Behavioural psychologists have also observed that people with problems, who become depressed by them into feeling and believing that they are insoluble, become passive, slower to learn, anxious and worried more easily. Such observations have revolutionised behavioural psychology by suggesting the need to challenge depressed people's beliefs and thought patterns, not just their behaviour. Depressed people often suffer from a sense of victimhood – they are battered by events and the actions of others into believing that they have no control over what happens to them.

Victor Frankl challenged this belief as a result of his experiences in the German concentration camps in the Second World War. He commented that:

> *In the concentration camps one lost everything, all human freedoms except the freedom to choose one's attitude in any given set of circumstances, to choose one's own way.*

Prisoners who allowed themselves to be overwhelmed by despair, who gave up their freedom to choose, often descended into paralytic apathy and depression. The key to helping such people, Frankl learned, was to show them how they could find meaning in their lives even in the face of unimaginable horror. Every prisoner had a moral choice to make, to surrender their inner self to the evil of their Nazi jailors, or to find meaning in their everyday life that would give them the strength to go on. In the final analysis the prisoner's attitude towards their suffering could provide them with the very meaning in their lives necessary for their physical survival. Frankl argued that this philosophy holds good today in dealing with depression; a therapeutic approach that concentrates on the patient's attitude towards their condition, can, when combined with appropriate medication, lead to a lasting resolution of the depression.

Of the six universal emotions, four: anger; fear; disgust; and sadness are negative and only two – love and joy – are positive. Science tells us that the ability to feel negative emotions derives from ancient built-in danger recognition systems formed early in the brain's evolution. The survival instinct, the need to preserve the species understandably imprinting and wiring our brains to seek safety and security before happiness and joy.

One of the problems of the modern world is the tendency to link the search for happiness, contentment and life fulfilment to possessions and image. As the survey of lottery winners shows, most people rapidly adjust to having good things, and then simply want more. It seems that the immediate surge of happiness and pleasure quickly declines. Getting things and improving our image can become addictive, however. I read recently of people who have become addicted to plastic surgery believing that if only they could improve their image, become more beautiful, then they would become happier. In the years 2004–2005 alone cosmetic surgery operations in the UK rose by 50% to around 75,000. Adverts and articles which peddle plastic surgery make-overs promise 'instant happiness' simply by changing people's external appearance. These advertisements hold up the illusion that simply looking better will lead to happiness.

Now it might be that someone who is disfigured, or simply plain ugly as the result of protruding ears or an extremely large nose, may have their lives improved by corrective surgery. But where surgery is undergone simply to improve a person's image, the reasoning behind any such action must be seriously questioned. The outer is always a manifestation of the inner, and those whose inner self is beautiful have no need of plastic surgery, their light will shine out and overcome any perceived physical shortcoming. I find it very hard to believe that the average person is likely to experience any long-term lasting benefits from putting themselves through the pain and suffering that inevitably results from cosmetic surgery. As 'Judge Judy' the television judge so pithily puts it 'Beauty fades – dumb is forever!' The results of any cosmetic surgery will age and deteriorate with the passage of time requiring possibly more extensive surgery. Better to spend our time and money on developing and improving our inner selves, for this will certainly not age, and improvement to the essence of who and what we are, can be of lasting benefit to us in so many ways.

Psychologists call constantly seeking after pleasure from things and image make-overs the 'hedonistic treadmill'. The mechanisms that fuel our desires are it seems insatiable. Once we obtain what at one time seemed the recipe for lasting happiness we desire other things. We move our desires on from one thing to the next 'butterflying' through life. Constantly seeking happiness and pleasure from 'things'. Yet the things that we desire are not necessarily the things that ultimately give us pleasure. There are things that we tire of less easily, like good friends, a loving family, good health, the enjoyment of the natural world, beautiful sunrises and sunsets, etc. These pleasures are 'free' in terms of economics. Apart from the joys of the natural world the rest require working at. Whilst they are freely available to all irrespective of status or wealth, they will not come about without effort. Indeed the happiness factor that scores most heavily in surveys is described as 'a meaningful life' with a commitment to the pursuit of aims and objectives that are greater than oneself.

Psychologists tell us that our personality does not change much after the time we reach 25. Significant change to who and what we are is difficult to achieve after this age. Yet there are many things we can do that will make us happier and more content with our lives. We can train ourselves to be happier, to seek ways to enhance the internal image that we hold of ourselves and to boost our positive emotions. We can work at living more in the present rather than constantly harking back to perceived 'happier times', or looking forward to the elusive time somewhere in the future when we will be happier. We can decide to be happier NOW. To be determined to enjoy what we have at a deeper level rather than seeking newer and fresher stimulation from things and events.

Simply concentrating on the past as is the case in much conventional psychiatric treatment is of limited value. Evidence shows that it is difficult for psychiatrists to find even small effects of childhood events in an adult personality and there is no evidence at all of large effects. The real risk with concentrating on past traumas is that we recreate them in the present. We re-energise and breathe new life into them, rather than allowing the normal passage of time to deprive them of the energy they need to influence our present. Through regressive psychoanalytic therapy we risk breathing new life into the past husks of things that may at one time have been painful for us. For we create the future from the present, NOT the past. We create our future lives from the thoughts and beliefs that we hold in the NOW of our existence for this is the only time that we can inhabit, experience and influence. All else is memory and illusion, looking back and looking forward. To deliberately renew our acquaintance with past painful events in depth through psychoanalysis is to risk giving such events even greater power over our future. At all times that which we think we create; or in this case recreate. This is not to say that painful events and experiences should not be seen for what they are – things that once happened to us – but that it should be recognised and accepted that they are now in the past, over and finished. We should learn to release them and let them go, not continually re-visit and re-energise them.

A new area of therapeutic research which promises much is 'Cognitive Therapy'. Cognitive Therapy, like Logotherapy, places less emphasis on the past. It works by challenging a person's thinking about the present and by setting goals for the future. Another relatively new form of therapy called 'Brief Solution Focused Therapy' discourages talk about problems and instead helps its adherents to identify strengths and resources that they possess that will help them make positive changes to their lives. Also similar to Logotherapy, this type of therapy is an approach to counselling that is, as its name implies, brief in length – usually no more than five sessions in total. Research shows it brings about lasting change in up to 83% of referrals. It is future-focused and works with the strengths of those who come to it by encouraging and enabling them to make the best use of their resources. It claims to be able to bring about lasting change because it aims to build solutions rather than simply seeking to solve problems. Some of the research studies carried out on this type of therapy relate to very serious mental health problems, drug and alcohol abuse, criminal behaviour and domestic violence. It is certainly a therapy that holds much promise for the future happiness of those who discover and utilise it.

Viktor Frankl taught that primarily man does not seek pleasure, instead pleasure – or happiness – is the side-effect of self-transcendence, or rising above the self. Once one has served a cause, or is involved in loving another human being, happiness occurs by itself. Pleasure and happiness are the by-products of meaningful activity or love. As Frankl says: 'Happiness must ensue, it cannot be pursued.' What is clear is that when we choose to serve others, to help unbidden, to contribute to a cause or activity that has positive benefits for others, happiness and increased levels of self-esteem always result.

Happiness is never a constant state, but contentment can be. It is possible through building a meaningful life, engaging in those activities that give meaning to life, to reach a state of balance and contentment. A state where we are able to deal with the normal vicissitudes and petty irritations that confront us daily, free from stress and worry utilising the coping mechanisms that enable us to maintain an even keel as we go about our daily business. Achieving such a level of contentment requires action from us, rarely does it happen automatically.

I am sometimes surprised at the trivial aspects of life that bring happiness. Last week my wife, who is an Interior Designer, asked me to call into a hotel she is working on to take some measurements of a small lounge area, as she was just too busy to do it herself. Having some free time I readily agreed, drove to the hotel, some forty-five minutes from home, and commenced measuring. Only to find, mid-way through the exercise, that I was really enjoying what I was doing and did not want it to end. An analysis of what I was doing provided few clues as to why this was a particularly enjoyable event. Perhaps it was the constructive nature of the exercise. Measuring and recording information in a precise way. Being constructive and engaged in a purposeful activity. I have always enjoyed working with figures and structure and this job combined the two. Perhaps it was that I was carrying out an unpaid act out of love and a desire to help my wife and partner, who knows? But it is an example of what I am writing about here.

At the top of Abraham Maslow's pyramid of needs – defined in his most famous book *Motivation and Personality* – he labelled 'Self Actualisation', or as he further described it: 'Growth Motivation', as the ultimate drive in the human condition. The desire to grow more, be more, which he argued can only come into play when our lower needs have first been met. Our need for food, shelter, safety and security, freedom from pain and suffering, and the fundamental need for companionship and love. Once these basic needs have been met, he believed that human beings require self actualisation, in order to realise complete fulfilment. This conclusion is interesting in that it mirrors directly the first Universal Law: 'that consciousness always seeks its highest potential'.

My Uncle Ernest – one of my father's older brothers, told me when I was quite young that 'if a job is worth doing, it is worth doing well.' This may be in doing seemingly insignificant things like tidying up, or loading and unloading the dishwasher, or cutting the lawn, menial tasks but tasks with clearly observable satisfying end results. I know it sounds trite but I believe happiness can be found in even the lowliest of tasks when once those tasks are seen as meaningful and useful. No one can deny that ensuring that we have clean dishes and tidy lawns and gardens is useful as well as necessary. A life without growth, without purpose, without meaning, is a life that is over, even if the human condition still remains.

Happiness is a by-product of a meaningful and fulfilled life. It is not a state of euphoria that can be achieved in isolation. Rather it comes unbidden when we engage in those things in our life that enable us to feel fulfilled and useful. When we know that our life does indeed have meaning; when we spontaneously pursue those activities that enable us to feel whole and fulfilled then, and only then, will we be happy and content.

In life we face problems and difficulties daily, some large, but most small. Negative events are a part of life's rich pattern. When we find a way of coping with these successfully, of dealing with the daily routines, problems and issues, that life brings to us in a manner that enables us to maintain our mental health and balance, then life will indeed be worth living. This is so important – we should aim to seek balance and happiness every day, not just on special days, birthdays, holidays, etc. Contentment, balance, that feeling of being in control of life are more important than those special, often short lived, 'ah ha' moments.

Medical practitioners tell us that happiness clearly effects our longevity. It seems to defy the old adage that 'only the good die young'. Studies of longevity have shown conclusively that people who are happy with their lives, who are active in their community and who have a good circle of friends, or a close and loving family, are fitter and live, on average, longer than those who do not enjoy these beneficial states. It is a fact that unhappy or depressed people, who live lonely reclusive lives, devoid of friends or active hobbies, tend to suffer higher levels of sickness and disease and die earlier than the national average. Seeking and finding a life pattern that leads to happiness and contentment does indeed have a beneficial effect on our longevity.

Yet none of these ingredients for a happy life simply come about. They take effort; with our families and loved ones, often constant unremitting effort, for the old saying that 'you only get out of life what you put into it' is so true. To make 'happiness withdrawals' you must be prepared to make 'happiness investments'. To love without condition or expectation of return. The same applies to friendships, they must be unconditional, nurtured and cherished, fed regularly and worked at. But these investments are the best that we can ever make in our lives. They are guaranteed to give healthy happy returns. It is not, however, the length of life that is ultimately important, rather it is the quality. If our life is rich and full, if we never have enough time to cram in all of the things that we want to do simply because we are too busy doing the things that we have chosen to do, then our lives will be happy and satisfying irrespective of their length. Grieve not for those who die young and happy; rather grieve for those who die old, unfulfilled and embittered.

In the end the pursuit of happiness in life is our way of trying to feel good about ourselves. Of seeking safety and security, balance and contentment. Abraham Maslow's 'theory of needs' in play. We have to live our lives, every minute, every hour and every day. We can choose to be happy or sad in our life – irrespective we will live it. The attitude we adopt to our life circumstances is ours to choose. But without doubt our mental attitude will be a major determinative factor in whether we are content or discontent with our lot. There are no short cuts between birth and death. None of us – with the exception of the condemned murderer – knows the hour or the day when our physical existence will end. All we can experience is the 'NOW' of our existence. Inner peace truly comes from working to change the things that we can change in our life, and in accepting with good grace those that we cannot. When it comes to choosing between happiness and sadness, between being positive or negative, between being upbeat or feeling depressed, I know which I prefer – how about you? After all it is your life and your choice.

## Fear and Worry

Watching a Paul McKenna television programme on how to lose weight, I was struck by his constant refrain that 'The imagination is stronger than the will.' To underline his message the hypnotist invited a chocoholic on to the stage. This member of the audience claimed that she ate up to four bars of chocolate each day. She desperately wished to rid herself of her chocolate addiction and had tried every technique she knew with every bit of her will power to overcome her obsession with chocolate, yet thus far she had failed. In under ten minutes Paul McKenna had replaced her love of chocolate with loathing. He did this by encouraging her to replace the image she held in her mind of chocolate, with another consisting of jellied eels, which she hated, mixed with hair cuttings and the contents of a spittoon. After imagining swallowing this nauseous mix coupled with chocolate, her desire for chocolate disappeared completely. This graphic demonstration shows that our images are never two dimensional, they are always three dimensional, with the third dimension consisting of the feelings and emotions which we associate with the image being the more powerful.

This is why the imagination is stronger than the will. In my book *Creative Thought and Personal Growth* I described our imagination as our personal design room. The place where we create our world and all that is in it. Thought, powered by emotional energy, creates directly in the images – and all their associations –

that we hold. Mental images fuelled by feeling and emotion bringing our personal daily world into being.

It is important to remember that our imagination goes to work on whatever thoughts we hold, which is why fear and worry are such powerful destructive emotions. They are formed in the same way as the chocoholic's desire for chocolate. The image she held of chocolate was a delicious comfort treat that always made her feel good and lifted her mood. When this image was replaced with a repulsive nauseating one, the craving disappeared. Likewise, when we track down and replace the images that fuel the fear and worry that plague us they too will disappear.

Worry and fear are the plagues of the modern age, driving some to suicide, others to drink, drugs and over medication. For some the fears are little things such as a fear of spiders or heights; I read somewhere that some 80% of the male population of the UK are frightened of spiders, an amazing statistic. For others their fears are massive, dominating every aspect of their lives.

The world is full of things and experiences that have the potential to threaten our well-being, both physical and mental and thus frighten us. The whole experience of this thing called life is enough to frighten some people into a state of ill-health. Constant states of stress and tension are the reality of everyday life for many. Yet our ability to be frightened is, in the scheme of things, good for us. It is a natural emotion experienced in anticipation of pain or danger happening to, or threatening us. It provides us with the awareness that we had better take evasive action to protect our safety and our security. Our 'fight or flight' responses are built-in reactors. Fear, and its kinsman worry, are our acknowledgment of the fact that life can at times be very risky.

Phobias and fear paralyse and debilitate even the strongest. A research of phobias on the net threw up an A to Z of 20 pages of the various types of phobias. From Ablutophobia – a fear of washing or bathing – to Zoophobia – a fear of animals.

The symptoms that fear brings are common enough to those who experience them: a pounding heart; butterflies in the pit of the stomach; increased tension; even momentary paralysis. These physical symptoms being the result of our built-in defence mechanism as we prepare to fight or flee from whatever frightens, or is perceived by us as a threat to our safety and well-being. Our body mechanism gears up to react; our adrenal glands secrete large amounts of adrenaline to give us a temporary boost of power and increased energy. Unless released, this energy will stay with us with potentially harmful results. Causing health problems such as tension headaches, loss of appetite, stomach ulcers, irritable bowel syndrome and much more. Energy must be used at all times, it is non-specific. It can be used to help achieve our aims, which in the short term can be simply to get us out of the situation that threatens us, or if not, it will stay with us and, lacking outward release through action, retain the potential to harm us.

Now the adrenaline rush was fine for our ancestors who daily battled with the elements and wild animals in their battle for survival but, today, these rushes of energy are prone to occur when we are not threatened physically, but perceive ourselves to be threatened by stressful situations and occurrences, such as failure, public humiliation, embarrassment, etc. I have certainly experienced the adrenaline rush when called upon to speak to large audiences. However, the adrenaline rush used carefully can provide us with an added stimulus enabling us to perform above our usual standards on given occasions.

Some poor folk spend their lives frightened and in a constant state of stress and tension. Worried and frightened, they carry a black cloud around with them. Constantly experiencing stress and tension they suffer from headaches and stomach disorders on a regular basis. In an attempt to obtain release they turn to their GPs seeking medication such as pain-killers and tranquilisers. It must be sad indeed to be so restricted by worry and fear. Fear of looking foolish, fear of rejection, criticism, change, illness and sickness, crime, war, loneliness, old age, phobias or compulsive obsessive disorders.

Contrary to the impression of many, statistics tell us that life in the Western world is becoming safer and healthier. Widespread fears about the world descending into war and chaos are actually unfounded. The number of conflicts occurring in the world today are lower than they have been for a decade. In terms of battle deaths, the 1990s was the least violent decade since the end of the Second World War. A recent report – *The Human Security Report October 2005* – details this. What has happened, however, is those conflicts that have occurred have been subject to much greater media scrutiny and reporting than in any previous time in history. So our perception that the number of conflicts has increased has come about.

The same is true of epidemics and sickness. We are currently being assailed with scare stories about bird flu. The Chief Medical Officer Sir Liam Donaldson baldly states that if the virus that causes bird flu transfers to humans, 50,000 Britons could die. At the same time a senior official of the World Health Organisation warned that bird flu could cause 150 million deaths worldwide. Yet the virus that causes bird flu has been prevalent in Asia for over 10 years. With the reported deaths from the rare transfer of bird flu to humans being around 150. This from a world population in excess of six and a half billion people; a miniscule percentage.

The fear generated by news stories about bird flu is evident in the following letter written recently to the *Western Mail*, one of Wales' premier newspapers. The writer, seeking advice from one of the paper's columnists, wrote:

*I have been watching the news and reading all of the papers about the bird flu virus that seems to be creeping closer and closer to affect my family and I am scared stiff. I cannot stop thinking of the danger that my family may be in. I have stopped buying eggs and poultry and I have taken down the bird feeders in the garden. But I am still worried in case my children come into contact with birds or let them spend time with friends in case their parents are not as vigilant as I am. I was worried sick about the Sars virus also.*

The columnist gave the person concerned some very sensible advice regarding their perceived threat of the dangers posed by bird flu. This letter aptly demonstrates how fear can generate abnormal behaviour and a false view of reality.

In 1996, the media were predicting that by now millions would be dying as a result of eating BSE infected beef yet, to date, there have been 157 reported deaths. The 1918 First World War flu epidemic killed some 30 million people worldwide. A large number, yet to get this into perspective more people than this die every day worldwide from infectious diseases. By far the most serious threat posed today is AIDS. During 2004 around five million adults and children became infected with HIV (Human Immunodeficiency Virus) AIDS. By the end of the year, an estimated 39.4 million people worldwide were living with HIV/AIDS. The year also saw more than three million deaths from AIDS, despite the availability of HIV antiretroviral therapy which reduced the number of deaths in high income populations. These facts and similar news reports cause havoc in terms of the fear and worry experienced by those who hear and read about them, without either the information, or knowledge to get them into perspective. Fear is a mutating virus itself. It transforms itself into suspicion, mistrust, anger, hostility, aggression, anxiety, worry and even suicide.

Fear itself is harmful when it prevents us from going about our lives freely and constructively. Rational fears that protect us from reckless or foolhardy behaviour are one thing, irrational fears that are based on false information and erroneous beliefs are another. Healthy fear can improve our choices as we go through life. Unhealthy fears can limit and restrict life in so many different ways.

Fear is the product of our thoughts and beliefs coupled with the power of our imagination. Threats to our physical well-being are easily identified and thus can be guarded against. Non-physical threats are another matter. The old saying 'sticks and stones can break our bones but words can never harm us', is true, but only up to a point. Criticism and rejection can be more damaging and potentially harmful than a broken arm or leg. They stay with us and begin sapping our confidence and our self-esteem for a lot longer than a broken limb. Recognition that we can only be harmed by non-physical acts when we allow ourselves to be, is nearer the mark. If criticism is valid, we must accept it, draw the necessary lessons from it for our future actions or behaviour in similar situations, and then move on. If it is invalid, then we can kick it out of our minds and move on. Rejection can be more harmful and difficult to deal with. But the one essential fact to bear in mind with rejection is that whilst others are free to reject us, as we are them, we must never reject or cease to believe in ourselves, for any such personal rejection will ultimately destroy us.

We need at all times to ensure that the decisions we make in life are not based on fear, but rather on a realistic assessment about what is good, healthy and best for us at any given time. That will promote our long-term growth and well-being and ensure that we are not held back from necessary changes to our life by fears of the unknown.

The perception of risk is usually greater than the reality. Many old people will not venture out after dark because of the stories of violent crime carried regularly in the national newspapers. Still more are haunted by the fear of getting a serious illness or disease. Underlying all of these is the fear of death, a subject today rarely, if ever, discussed in polite society. It is the taboo subject which the growth in secularism and the dwindling church attendances ensure will continue to be shrouded in silence. Yet it is the one certainty in life. All else can be variable but death is not. However difficult, it is important to come to terms with the fact of our mortality. The fear of death, whilst understandable, must be dealt with and overcome if a truly healthy existence is desired.

Shakespeare's Caesar expressed it so well:

> *Cowards die many times before their deaths; The valiant never taste of death but once. Of all the wonders that I yet have heard, it seems to me most strange that man should fear death; seeing that death, a necessary end, will come when it will come.*

The four great drives in the human condition are fear (our desire for safety and security), love, companionship and sex. The last of these being our inbuilt drive to reproduce our species, a drive present in all living creatures. The first two, however, are predominantly human characteristics. By far the greatest driver of humanity is fear, not love. Examine your own life and daily activities; if you are honest you will admit that by far the greater majority of the actions and decisions you take are fear driven.

Our food intake is riddled with fear; the food fads of today bear testimony to this. These fears coupled with the fear of obesity, or simply of getting fat, of cholesterol levels that are too high. We avoid meat, particularly red meat because of the risk of BSE, we fear eggs because of salmonella. Today, we fear poultry in case it is infected with the bird flu virus. White bread is a no no, the same with butter and cream. Hamburgers and chips are the 'kiss of death'. The list goes on driven by the latest health fear or newspaper report. We take vitamins and other supplements to ensure that we do not become deficient in essential nutrients. When we step outside of our doors or go to work the real fun starts, with the hundred and one regulations designed by health and safety and environmental experts to protect us against the perceived threats to life itself. These regulations have been drawn up by those who believe, often supported by 'scientific' evidence, that we are at risk. We are at risk of climate change. Sitting in the sun causes skin cancer. Walking in cities or towns means inhaling fumes and other pollutants. The trees that line our roads are cut down to stop them falling on us. The barking of Police dogs are monitored in case they are above the accepted threshold for 'safe' hearing. Our children cannot play conkers unless they wear goggles and safety helmets. Our children's playgrounds are closed in case a child should fall and hurt themselves. According to the regulators we are at constant risk of disease, accidents illness and death.

Yet if this is true we are at risk from our own world, our planet. The place where, as a species, we have grown and evolved for hundreds of thousands, possibly millions, of years. Through wars, famines, climate changes, environmental catastrophes, ice ages, earthquakes and tsunamis, the human species has survived all of these without the help and protection of the health and safety and environmental zealots who seem to fail to recognise that the natural state of life is coping with danger and risk. It is this which gives us our edge as a species and which has led to our evolutionary development, from being just another life form on our planet to being the most powerful creature – the apex of the animal pyramid.

The cures for fear are not in increased protectionism, however well intended. The keys are in trust and action. 'Trust' an old-fashioned word not much used today. Trust in our Creator, trust in ourselves, in our innate wisdom and ability. We are walking miracles, a marvel of design and evolution. We did not arrive in the world by any conscious action on our part. We were conceived, and developed miraculously in our mother's womb from an egg to a fully formed functioning human being. We grew from babyhood to adult without any conscious decision or action on our part. The innate wisdom within us is beyond our understanding, it is truly awesome. Our leading scientists still do not understand the miracle that is life. Cannot create it, only reproduce or clone it. Given this reality, is not trusting our bodies to know what is best for us common sense? Our body always knows what is best for us – all we have to do is listen. Stop second guessing and treating our body as if it is constantly seeking to betray us and destroy itself.

Myriad once commented that our fears are like balloons – we should take great delight in pricking them! To prick them however requires action on our part. Baby steps in the right direction at first maybe – but once we start to tackle our fears, recognising that they are our fears, the products of our imagination, we can quickly move to giant steps until any fear we are tackling has been overcome. As Henry Ford – 1863–1947 – once said:

> *One of the greatest discoveries a man makes, one of his great surprises, is to find he can do what he was once afraid he couldn't do.*

Our imagination draws to us whatever we visualise. We always get what we expect, not what we deserve, but what we expect. Exactly that and no more. Used correctly, our imagination can bring us amazing things. Yet the opposite is true when our imagination is given free reign to create whatever negatives it wants. We give it free reign and are then surprised or depressed, often in equal measure, when these negatives become realities in our life.

I repeat ad infinitum throughout this book the fact that THOUGHT CREATES. Not just some thought, but all thought at all times. It creates according to the pictures we hold in our mind about ourselves and our world. It is a truism that we live our life inside of our head. Our thoughts are not separate from our life and world. They *are our life and world*. We are at the centre of our world. It emanates from us, surrounds us, embraces and encompasses us. It is not something that happens to us, with us reacting and responding to it. We create the entirety of our world from our thoughts and beliefs within the framework of the Root Assumptions, in accordance with Universal Law. We then react and respond to our own creation. This fact once accepted and acted upon can transform the way that we see life. For with the acceptance of this true reality comes a sense of great power. For if our world is indeed our creation then we are in control of it and thus can change any part of it with which we are unhappy.

This being so, it makes sense to bring our fears out of the recesses of our mind and examine them in the bright light of day, rather than allowing them free reign to fuel our imagination. What is it that we think about? What are our worries and our fears? How real are these threats to our happiness and our sanity? Are our fears valid and sensible or should we be kicking them into touch? What frightens us? What limits and restricts us? What prevents us from growing and being who and what we were destined to be? Those things that we worry about are an excellent guide to our fears, for at the root of all worry is our old enemy fear. Worry is never non-specific. The things we worry about are those things we perceive as being threats to our happiness, our safety, our dreams, goals, aims, our world – and I do not mean the planet – I mean the little individual world we each inhabit.

Phobias are exaggerated worries. Those suffering from compulsive obsessive disorders (COD), such as those who check endlessly that their front door is locked before leaving home, worry that if their front door is left unlocked their homes and possessions will be at risk. They fear the loss of their possessions. Or the person who washes their hands incessantly who fears the germs that they believe constantly threaten their health. The constant hand washing an attempt to prevent themselves from catching the myriad illnesses and diseases which they believe everywhere threatens them.

I knew a man when I was a young, a Company Director, wealthy and powerful, who wore rubber gloves at all times; who would not touch a door handle unless it was with a tissue paper held between his gloved hands and the door handle. Who soaked his hands in disinfectant and scrubbed them until the skin peeled off them. A man who in very other respect was sane and sensible, yet he believed that his very existence was threatened by the germs that were present on all surfaces.

The ritualistic behaviour demonstrated by those suffering from compulsive obsessive disorder start from a base fear, or fears, and then become rituals in their own right. The sufferer believes that unless the ritual or rituals which they perform, such as hand washing, lock checking, etc., are not followed meticulously and in a specific order that which they fear will be brought about. The rituals then become exercises in prevention and thus take on their own validity. 'Cognitive Therapy' (also referred to in the chapter on Happiness) is being used with some success in treating those suffering from COD through demonstrating that their underlying fears are not in fact real.

All phobias are rooted in fear. Each one limiting and restricting in its own way. The fear of flying limiting and restricting travel. The fear of certain foods reducing choice. If we are hypochondriacs, it is because we believe that our life is constantly under threat.

Fears are beliefs, deeply held beliefs. Solidified thought. Thought blocks which we accept to such a degree that they are rarely challenged. In essence, our beliefs make up who and what we are. To say 'I believe' carries so much more weight than 'I think'. Yet both are thought based. One fluid and changing. One set in concrete and rarely changing without conscious effort. Yet where do our beliefs come from? Were we born with them implanted in our brains? Whilst we can accept that some deep rooted instinctual beliefs on which our self-preservation depends are essential to our well-being, how many of our beliefs fall into the self-preservation category? And how many have been absorbed from our parents and teachers as we have grown from childhood to adulthood? If your parents believed that life was basically unhealthy or life threatening, then it will be no surprise if you have grown up with this belief embedded within you. If your parents believed that money was always in short supply, that you needed to scrimp and save to survive, you, are unlikely to have grown up with a wealth abundance mentality.

Beliefs that have not been the subject of rigorous scrutiny are beliefs that can be limiting, restricting and negatively influencing our life and our happiness. Are our beliefs truly ours, or are they simply second-hand beliefs that we have accepted unchallenged from others?

Our behaviour at all times is governed by our beliefs. The way we act towards others, loved ones, family and work colleagues is governed by our beliefs of how we expect them to behave towards us. If we believe that everyone is out for themselves and will take advantage of us at every opportunity, if this is what we truly believe about others, then we will act towards them accordingly. We will be cautious and reluctant to allow people in close to us in case they take advantage of us. As a result we contribute to the creation of the very behaviour we expect from others, so the behavioural circle is complete and our experience of the world continues unchanged.

If we constantly worry about money, it can only be that we believe at a deep level of our being that money is in short supply and that we are not destined to be rich. We fear not having enough money to pay our bills and our mortgage. We fear all of the horrors that will ensue from having no money in our money-oriented society.

Whatever the worry the solution is always to identify the root fear that fuels it. To bring it out into the open and see it for what it is. Be honest about it, don't rationalise or attempt to justify the fear, just identify it. Sometimes just exposing it to the scrutiny of the conscious reasoning mind will be enough to neutralise it. If not, follow the Norman Vincent Peale (NVP) (1898–1993) technique, the author of *The Power of Positive Thinking* to deal with it. This is a process that he recommended, consisting of four simple steps.

*Step 1.* Imagine if your fear became reality what would it mean. If for example your worry is about money and a fear of never having enough, picture the ultimate outcome of the worry. See yourself broke; bankrupt even. Picture the worst outcome of this worry. For worry is hazy, it nags and saps, it rarely has a precise definition. It has no shape – just a general negative outline. So give it shape and substance.

*Step 2.* Next accept this situation as a reality, a fact. Think around it and decide what you are going to do to resolve the situation now it has become a reality. What is your action plan going to be?

*Step 3.* Look at where you are now. The situation and circumstances are always better than your root fear. Give thanks for this.

*Step 4.* Now put a rescue plan into action. Don't wait for your fear to drive you. Rather, reach out and take command of the situation. There is always something you can do. Things are never hopeless or incapable of resolution.

Whatever the worry use the NVP method to take control over

it. Don't let fear drive you. Rather, let action and control be your drivers.

Fear and worry do not need to be an everyday feature in our lives. We can control them if we choose. We will never eliminate them and this is a good thing, for like pain they draw our attention to the beliefs that we should be paying attention to. Fear and worry are the mental equivalent of physical pain and like physical pain can be healed once we take action to identify whatever it is we are frightened of, or worried about. When we explore the base beliefs that underlie our fears and worries – for worries and fears concern things that have not yet happened to us – they remain simply mental creations that are carried in our imagination. When we recognise these mental creations for what they are and proceed to replace them with positive alternative images, using Norman Vincent Peale's proven techniques, then and only then will we be taking steps towards real lasting peace of mind and freedom from the shackles and limitations of fear and worry.

## Pain

Pain, suffering and guilt are endemic in the human condition. I write this chapter two days after the Clapham railway disaster which claimed thirty three lives and injured over forty people, many of them seriously. The papers yesterday and this morning are full of stories of personal tragedy. Over seventy families have had their lives seriously and traumatically affected a week before Christmas.

Last week the news was of a massive earthquake in Armenia; one hundred thousand people are believed to have lost their lives, and ten times this number have lost their homes and their possessions. This in the midst of a severe winter. The victims of the earthquake included thousands of children killed as they sat at their school desks. Such suffering defies the imagination. Both the personal and national suffering will be borne in the memory of the survivors for the remainder of their lives.

We all have stories and memories of personal disasters and losses which, although perhaps not matching the scale of those above, none the less had a significant impact on us and our families as we experienced and lived through them. How can you tell the family of a road accident victim this Christmas that their loss is less than those involved in the Clapham railway disaster because it did not make the national news? Their pain and suffering will be as great, as those involved in any major disaster. Further, it is likely to be experienced alone, rather than against the background of a wave of national sympathy coupled with disaster fund appeals. Theirs will be a personal and lonely suffering. Not a day passes without someone within our immediate locality being touched by loss and tragedy of some kind. How then can we make sense of life, lived as it is against the background of the ever-present reality of pain and suffering?

One of the major themes of this book is that all life has purpose, that not one action within any life lacks purpose. Not illness nor death, disability nor deformity, accident nor disaster; not one instance of pain or suffering. Yet how can such a proposition be maintained in the face of massive suffering such as that experienced in Armenia or other areas of major disaster? Such a suggestion seems an insult to the suffering of the victims. To the millions who suffered in the wars fought in the last century. To the reality of pain and suffering that is a constant and ever-present experience in the everyday lives of countless people.

It seems almost prophetic that we are born through suffering. The intense pain of childbirth impacts subconsciously on both mother and child. Dimly remembered at a deep level of all of us is the memory of the pain of being forced down a narrow restrictive channel into the blinding light of new life. Of being held up by the heels and possibly being smacked into breathing. Hypnotised subjects can be taken back to relive this trauma and without doubt these relived memories outweigh any evidence that we have of the pain of death. Life commences with intense pain, as if we are being prepared for the reality of pain and suffering ever present within life.

As we grow, we experience pain to a greater or lesser degree both physical and mental. In today's world we have the ability to blot out pain with the aid of drugs and tranquillisers. We can soften the impact of our pain considerably, but never completely remove it. Particularly where the pain is mental, caused perhaps by the loss of a loved one, depression, jealousy or mental disorder. What then is the purpose of pain? How can there possibly be a purpose to pain?

Many religions contain within them the belief that pain is sent by God to punish us for wrong doings. Yet if this were the case, only the wicked would suffer, yet we know this not to be the case. The innocent and the guilty suffer alike. Pain does not discriminate. Where physical pain is concerned we accept that one of its functions is to draw our attention to the fact that a part of our body needs attention and possibly medical help. If I had a septic toe and felt no pain, then the infection could spread to the rest of my body without my awareness. This would lead to the risk of major complications arising, perhaps even life-threatening ones. So the fact that I will, through my pain have my attention drawn to my toe can be considered helpful.

That is all well and good, but what about headaches, colds, flu, sore throats and the hundred and one other ailments that are common occurrences that bring with them pain throughout life. How can these be seen as having purpose in the pain and suffering that they bring as their travelling companions? Are they, as the prevailing view propounds, simply scourges of humanity without sense or reason? Or is there purpose even in these the most mundane of afflictions?

Seth and Myriad are unequivocal in stating that all life has purpose, every aspect of it. Further, Universal Law asserts that we always spontaneously seek the path that will lead to our greatest becomingness. The path that provides the potential for our greatest growth and expansion. As we create individually, so also do we create collectively, there is no separation between ourselves and our fellow man. Only in the flesh is individuality expressed. Beneath the surface of the physical all is connected. So we all participate in personal, group, national and international disasters that bring pain, suffering and death, to a greater or lesser degree.

The Sethian view on pain, and particularly death, expressed so eloquently in the many books of Jane Roberts, but particularly in *Seth Speaks*, is that no one dies except at a time of their own choosing. Of course we are not consciously aware of such choices, our ego would be too frightened to participate in decisions about its own destruction. Yet Seth states that we leave the physical plane only when we decide at a subconscious level that we have achieved that which we set out to achieve, or have gone as far towards achieving our life aims as is possible in any particular lifetime. As consciousness never dies and is of absolute duration, our greater self does not fear death, nor see any difference in our existence in or out of physical form. The choice therefore at a deeper level than our conscious awareness of whether to live or die, is not based on love of human life, but simply on the potential that exists within human form for growth and the expressions of creativity that only physical form can provide.

Perhaps those who die in disasters, either local or national have chosen to pass into the world beyond the physical using the means most readily available to them. Their death being all the more significant because it is shared with others. It is those who remain who see their demise as tragic disasters. The prevailing culture sees death as the end of existence. It has a deep rooted belief that the ending of physical life is the termination of consciousness and recognises nothing other than human life and physical form as having life. To die therefore is considered as a tragedy, and a case for mourning. To die in a disaster being a cruel twist of fate.

The deaths of those who die in national disasters always have greater impact than individual deaths. The national and international outcry at any large loss of human life leads to an examination of the causes of the disaster. Leads to a review of the processes designed to protect and preserve life. To improvements in safety, building design, in rescue services, medical aid or information, or in technical awareness. Already in Armenia there are calls for investigation into the poor quality of buildings, and the materials from which they were constructed. Into the web of corruption which lead to sub-standard housing being built. Poor building techniques that caused whole blocks of flats and schools to collapse like packs of cards. There are demands for national emergency teams to be assembled. Not least of all, the eyes of the world are focused on Armenia at a crucial time in its history.

This earthquake was not an isolated incident. The history of this troubled people has been one of tragedy and oppression. The weeks preceding the earthquake were times of considerable national disorder. The territorial disputes with neighbours had been world news that had reported on individual deaths and the destruction of property. Nationalistic fervour abounded and riots and civil disorder had led to the imposition of curfews. The energy that was everywhere present in both individual and national terms was enormous. The transfer of energy from nature to people and back again is not an unknown phenomenon. The tremendous energy here present could easily have resulted in the tipping of the scales of nature, with the earthquake that followed being a very graphic way of releasing the excess energy. Nothing will ever be the same again in Armenia. Whether or not this leads to the resolution of their territorial disputes, or their calls for greater freedom, remains to be seen. But one thing is certain, nothing will ever be the same again for those who lived through this traumatic experience. For with disaster comes change; forced change that would not have come about in any other way. And with change comes greater opportunities for growth and movement. Whether these opportunities lead to better or worse conditions for those affected remains to be seen.

In the same newspapers that reported on the Armenian tragedy I read an article, which although very different, none the less supports the view that I have expressed here regarding the transfer of energy. It was headlined 'Wind a Blow to School Discipline'. The article stated that the wind was being blamed for pupils' bad behaviour by teachers in Cornwall, one of the breezier parts of Britain. A survey by the local branch of the Assistant Masters and Mistresses Association had found that windy weather ranked third as a barometer of classroom discipline. The branch secretary, Mr Green was reported as saying that: 'You get some very bizarre behaviour when the wind blows. Something gets into the kids. They become excitable and difficult, they run round in circles in the playground and it carries on into the classroom. It affects the older children as well.' He went on: 'They get a bit more rowdy and boisterous. On the other hand if it is a nice, calm day they tend to be nicer and calmer too.'

A classic example of an exchange of energy. The wind being pure energy. The children who are less ego structured than adults being more receptive to such energy, and thus able to absorb it more readily into their being. The energy then being expressed in hyperactive, and what teachers see as, unruly and bizarre behaviour. This article contains within it, short though it is, the seeds of the answer to pain and suffering.

When life is running smoothly, when we are healthy and whole, full of the joys of life, when we are balanced and in control of life we are in our most ego focused state in physical form. We feel strong and able to control our life and our environment. We are confident of our ability, we are in a state where we have the least need for spirituality or any assistance from our greater selves or God. At such times we stride forward convinced of our own invulnerability. Then along comes a cold, illness or personal tragedy and all of a sudden we feel more vulnerable, less invincible. All of a sudden we are reminded of our mortality. The term that I use often to describe this state is that 'we become grounded'.

We are grounded in our physicality, we are reminded of our frailty and mortality. Similarly, when we become embroiled in a problem with our loved ones, that has the potential to make us miserable and depressed. When we are moved from a state of extreme confidence and comfort in a relationship to one of misery and uncertainty. Anyone who has ever been in love will know the intensity, the pain that such an event that can bring when things go wrong. Suddenly life is turned upside down. Suddenly the world looks a gloomier darker place and we are reminded of our individuality through our separation from the affection of our loved ones. At such times our self-contained ego focused structured self opens up. With the loss of confidence comes an awareness of our vulnerability and the fragility of the bond between us and another; how delicate the balance. No matter how much we may wish it were otherwise. We become open and much, much more receptive to the spiritual aspects of our existence at these times.

People without number claim to have discovered God or attained a higher level of spirituality through suffering. Some have emerged from prison sentences having been 'reborn' whilst incarcerated. Some have returned from experiences in prison camps claiming that only their rediscovered faith in God sustained them through their ordeals. Others recover from debilitating bouts of sickness with the same message. 'Through my suffering I was forced to re-evaluate my life and discovered God.'

The one aspect which for me reinforces the humanity of Christ, rather than the divinity claimed for Him by his supporters, was His preparedness to undergo suffering. The Bible tells us of His night in the Garden of Gethsemane when He sweated blood from the knowledge of the suffering that awaited Him. Yet from the crucifixion and the resurrection arose Christianity. The symbol of Christianity to this day is the Cross, the symbol of Christ's suffering. It is doubtful, if, without the crucifixion and the resurrection, Christianity would have grown and survived the countless attempts to stamp it out that followed its birth. But the example had been set by the founder of Christianity, and so many early Christians, not unlike the Muslim fundamentalists today, welcomed suffering and martyrdom. They welcomed it because for them it had great spiritual purpose.

It is very difficult in the midst of pain and suffering to lift your head and see purpose in your pain. It would be the most human reaction in the world to be insulted by anyone who were to try to tell you in the midst of your pain, that not only has your pain purpose, but also that you have chosen at a deep level of your psyche to experience it. That it is only in this way that your attention can be drawn to aspects of your life which require addressing. That if only you take the time to seek and understand the purpose, then not only will your suffering be eased, but also ennobled and dignified. Yet this may well be the purpose of pain and suffering. Viktor Frankl argued that one way of finding meaning in life was through the attitude that we adopt towards our pain and suffering. Free-will enables us to determine our attitude at such times, and as such meaning is possible in even the most wretched of circumstances.

Operations that are carried out after we are told by a surgeon or a doctor that they will improve our health and lead to an enhancement in the quality of our lives, are always much easier to prepare for than those which seem to lack such meaning and purpose. Operations such as hip and joint replacements, or heart bypass operations, or any of the hundreds of operations carried out to improve the quality of life of the patient, are always easier to bear because of the hope that they hold out to those who undergo them, than operations for sickness that do not have such a clear intent and promise of a pain-free life. Yet both will be equally painful and life threatening. The difference between the two is the perception of their purpose.

Where there is purpose there is always dignity and illumination. Even in the most wretched of circumstances. If we take the time and the trouble to look back immediately after we have experienced an illness or painful experience, and ask ourselves what the purpose of the experience was for us as individuals, the answer will always come. If we ask the question of ourselves with a clear and certain belief that we will receive the answer, then it will come. It may be that our attention is drawn to certain aspects of our life that are out of balance. It may be that we are being reminded of our humanity and the transitory passing nature of life, being reminded of our mortality and the need to explore, enjoy and better experience this special thing called life.

It may be that our self-centred ego focused concentration is being expanded so that we become more open to the energy that always surrounds us. That we are forced out of our cocooned safe existence back into the reality and fullness of life, being forced to re-evaluate our lives and make judgements about the quality of our life. It may be all or none of these things. The answer will always be unique to the one who asks the question.

Where we can go forward with a conviction that all has purpose. Where we can see beyond suffering, even in the midst of pain. Then we will see hope and a belief in wholeness, rather than separation. Only through seeking within for the answers will we ever make sense of our pain. Through such knowledge we can reach out with love and compassion to those in the midst of personal and national tragedies as in both Clapham and Armenia, and the many disasters which plague and afflict us. We can respect the courage of those whose greater purpose lead them to a preparedness, at a deep level of their being, to experience pain and anguish.

We live in an intensely purposeful world. A world where all has ultimate meaning. A greater understanding of our unique purpose in life can only lead to a deeper understanding of the reason we decided to experience our particular pain and suffering in our life and can help us to ennoble and dignify our pain, and in so doing give us a greater strength to bear it.

## Guilt

Guilt, the final part of the existential triad of pain, death and guilt. All of which are inevitable and inherent in human existence. Guilt, remorse for actions taken, or not taken. Guilt, a uniquely human condition which brings suffering and pain as its companions. Guilt which could not exist without the functioning of our conscience.

Guilt has long roots. It can be experienced years after the event that led to the feeling of guilt, actions, or a lack of action, which may have resulted in harm being caused to others. Things done or said that were destructive, or which caused pain or which damaged our loved ones, or our family or neighbours. Or perhaps which came about because we transgressed against some idealised moral version of what life should be. Drawn from our beliefs of how we should be, as opposed to what we are, or have become. Deep held beliefs which may have fed and reinforced feelings of worthlessness or moral degradation.

The memory of these actions within our conscience leaving behind a residue, like the grit inside the oyster, that grows and forms a callus within our psyche. This callus growing until it becomes too big for us to ignore. The event that caused the callus may have long passed. Indeed, where the action involved another they may themselves have long forgotten it; may at the time it occurred have given it only a passing thought. Yet its impact on us remains in our memory, silently growing, causing us remorse, pain and suffering.

For this is the purpose of guilt, through the working of our conscience it brings to our attention actions that we have taken which may have been detrimental to our inner growth as spiritual beings. At all times acting as a spur drawing to our attention those actions that we have taken which we innately believe are unworthy of us. Influencing our actions in the future by placing markers in our memory, for without memory guilt cannot exist. Guilt reminds us of our fallibility, our humanity; draws to our attention actions which have the potential to impede our growth and development as whole beings. Guilt provides us with the opportunity to change for the better, for we know when we do wrong. Our conscience, our inbuilt moral compass tells us when we have offended against the natural order of things. Perhaps we lost control, lost our temper or lashed out in a thoughtless way. Perhaps we acted in a manner that we would never have done if we had given more thought at the time. Perhaps our action was a deliberate calculated attempt to wound, harm or disadvantage. None the less our internal compass, our conscience has noted what we did, has flagged it up and stored it away in our memory bank.

We draw our moral compass from our conscience, our inbuilt moral guidance system, its influence on us being more powerful than any man-made law. For it is our internal law based on our humanness, our beliefs, both familial, cultural and religious. An unseen indicator telling us when what we are doing is detrimental to our growth as eternal beings. Tells us when we are offending against the natural order of which we are innately aware, acting as our moral guide, signalling to us through our feelings of guilt to withdraw or change the course of action we are pursuing. Guided by our superconscious we know when what we are doing is harmful to the inner, the spiritual us.

Psychiatrists argue that our conscience is no more than the learned response to things we garnered from our parents, guardians and tutors as we grew. That these standards are imbued within us, and that guilt is no more that the inbuilt fear of transgressing against those who taught us; that this forms the basis of our conscience. Yet those who taught us were simply passing on the wisdom of the ages. Wisdom taught to them by their parents; wisdom honed by personal experience that developed their knowledge of right and wrong. They desired to help us, to give us a moral compass to guide us through the vicissitudes of life. To install in us moral standards that would stand us in good stead as we grew into adulthood and became full players in our community and society.

Once again, however, we are reminded to explore our beliefs, for it may be that we are holding on to beliefs that are invalid, or indeed positively harmful to us. Many are those who are tortured by feelings of guilt born out of indoctrinated religious beliefs. Beliefs of unworthiness or innate sin; one of the most damaging being the idea that we are born sinful and that redemption can only be brought about through ritual and rite. Whilst there are undoubtedly deep wells of wisdom to be drawn from in our holy books and teachings, they are after all guide books whose purpose is to help us on our journey through life. We should never allow them to become rule books where we come to believe that transgression can lead to hell and damnation. What we think we create. If we want hell and damnation, then we can have it, but it does not seem a very good career move to me.

Our beliefs should be just that, our beliefs. Not beliefs that we have inherited unchallenged from others. We would be wise to develop our beliefs through constant observation of all that is healthy and good in life; through personal exploration and examination as we learn more, experience more, grow more in maturity and true wisdom. They should become our compass, our moral guide to what is right and what is wrong for us. We should learn to trust in our inner promptings, for we know when what we are doing is wrong and has the potential to harm or retard our growth as whole healthy beings. We are never ever bereft of spiritual guidance. We are never alone when we need help or guidance, all we need to do is ask. As the words of the Bible tell us 'Ask and it shall be given.' 'Knock and the door will open.'

Whatever its source, the fact that we become aware of this thing labelled 'conscience' as we grow is evidence enough of the reality of its existence. For it is only through the recognition in conscience that we have taken a wrong path, a path that is contrary to our moral code, and as such potentially detrimental to our personal and spiritual growth. Have taken a path that may be harmful to ourself or others. Only an honest examination of our actions can lead to true judgement being made. Not the judgement of the external world, but the judgement that comes from our own examination of our actions. This is the judgement that really matters, for only an honest and unflinching judgement that we make can be true and bring with it lasting peace and balance.

To feel guilt however we must first have advanced to a stage where reflection is possible. Reflection, an attribute peculiar to the human state and conscious mind. The ability to pause, and to remember the past in the present, and from this to determine the future. Without this attribute guilt could have no meaning. Without this attribute learning would not be possible. Where the consideration for the feelings of others has grown to a point where it becomes important. Those who appear not to experience the pangs of guilt have not yet reached such a stage in their own personal development. But they will, for this is Universal Law and as such will not be denied. The longer this takes to come about, the greater the burden that must be shed.

This is the basis for the Catholic Church's system of confession.

The need for wrongs to be recognised and the damaging energy therein released through penance and forgiveness. However, confession is only effective where it is accompanied by true remorse. Only through recognising our personal transgressions using our own internal compass can we hope to develop as beings. Guilt then should be welcomed as an aid to lasting growth. When experienced, it is evidence that we have moved to a place where reflection is not only possible, but also has meaning for us, where a desire to make amends has come about. The Church recognises the importance of forgiveness. Indeed its whole creed is based on the forgiveness of sins, or transgressions from the order of things set in motion by the Creator. For through forgiveness we can be freed from the burden we are carrying. Even if we do not share this creed we must understand the importance of forgiving ourselves. Only by working though the issues or incidents that lead to the feeling of guilt in the first place can we come to a place where forgiveness becomes possible. For without forgiveness, the complete release of the stored energy surrounding the memories that produce the feelings of guilt cannot come about.

After death (see the final section), making amends can take the form of reliving such events, and experiencing the pain caused by our actions, or inactions. Each 'wrong' or deviation from the path of growth must be righted. Each pain relived in order that the energy stored therein can be released. The grit, as it were, must be removed from the psyche for the inflammation to subside. So then is true learning brought about. So then is true lasting growth achieved. Not through pious words or deeds, but by inner change brought about by the realisation and appreciation of the effects our actions had upon others and ourself.

Love comes into this healing process, for it is only through truly loving our source, ourself and our fellow man, that we can go forward, aware of our actions and their effects on others. Where our desire is for the welfare and spiritual growth of others, even where such desire requires tough decisions. Then and only then can we demonstrate true love. At such times we must ensure that we do not act in a self-righteousness, 'do gooding' manner. But act simply and quietly from a desire to be of help and assistance. Then we will be about the most creative and self-fulfilling life activity that we can ever be engaged in.

## Health

I live in an alien world, or so I am told. A world that constantly tries to harm me. Through the food I eat and the air I breathe, the sunshine that warms me, the earth beneath my feet and the liquids that I drink. Everywhere I go and whatever I do I am threatened. Viruses and bugs abound, work surfaces are seething with bacteria not to mention toilets and bathrooms. Well, so I am reliably advised by the newspapers and TV advertisements. Health risks abound, from Avian (bird) flu, BSE, MSR, Salmonella, cancer, AIDS and global warming.

Eat this, don't eat that; do this, don't do that. I am bombarded with statistics that tell me what I can expect to suffer from at any given age. That reminds me, I must remember to get my flu jab at my local Doctors' surgery as I fall into the age category for whom this is essential, so the posters in the surgery tell me. All in all I don't know how I've managed to live to 64 – (incidentally I now know the answers to the famous Beatles song – 'When I'm sixty four' but you will have to wait to reach the same age to understand the answers!) If I am lucky, I may be one of those who get the avian flu jab, when it is developed, for I also fall into the risk category to catch this – or does it catch me? I'm never too sure about this.

Yet who can help me guard against these risks to my health and well-being? Can I trust the health profession in general, and doctors in particular? I am a bit doubtful here, for don't they have a vested interest in sickness, disease and death? Isn't their whole background and training based on a fundamental belief in the frailty of the human form? Of its weaknesses and vulnerability? Of course they desire to heal the sick, they would not have entered the medical profession otherwise (unless it was for the pay, pensions and status). But surely to maintain their desire to heal they must first hold a belief in sickness as a reality and a normal human condition. And this really does puzzle me, for isn't the normal human condition one of health rather than sickness? Or have I got this wrong?

Now I write from a background of a great deal of experience in sickness and poor health. Over the last ten years I have come to know the inside of various hospitals – some on the other side of the Atlantic – very well. I am a very experienced patient indeed. But as those who know me will tell you I am anything but patient. One of my favourite sayings is that the only place for patience (sic) is in hospital. I come from an action-oriented base. For me the solution is always in action. Never 'inaction'.

So what is this subject called health, a subject that absorbs acres – or should that be hectares – of newsprint? I have no doubt that whenever newspaper editors have a gap to fill in their papers out come the archived articles on health, fitness, plastic surgery, diets, etc. For editors know that these are topics, above all else, which will attract and hold the attention of their readers. Today the *Daily Mail* centrefold was devoted to obesity and the risk this poses to females over the decades of their adult life. A whole two pages about fat people!

Health, the religion of the age. This topic has surged ahead of conventional religious belief in the minds of the majority of the population of the Western hemisphere. It leaves politics trailing in its wake. In 2004 no less than 8.4% of the GDP (Gross Domestic Product) of the UK went on health care and many believe that this amount is woefully inadequate. Health has spawned massive industries and institutions, drug companies now being some of the wealthiest businesses in the world. There was a time not long ago when drug companies were merely the size of nations, now their size outweighs entire continents. Apparently the combined worth of the world's top five drug companies is twice that of the combined GDP of all sub-Saharan Africa.

Pfizer is the largest and richest drug company in the world. They have been named as the fifth-biggest 'wealth-creator' in America. In 2000, their annual revenue was £20.14bn. Pfizer's main competitors are Merck, Glaxo SmithKline, Novartis, Brystol Myers Squibb and AstraZeneca. Each a massive business in its own right, employing thousands of people and contributing millions of pounds/dollars in tax revenues. In 2001, Pfizer budgeted approximately £3.40 billion for research and development alone, more than any other drug company in the world.

I once thought that if I had but one wish it would be to banish sickness, illness and disease from the world. Looking at the statistics I now realise that I would be pitching hundreds of thousands of people into unemployment, destabilising national governments through the deprivation of taxes and the increased cost of unemployment benefits along the way. Such a wish coming true would have catastrophic effects on our world as we know it today. Imagine for one moment a world without hospitals, doctors, nurses, specialist consultants, surgeons, radiographers, ambulances, drugs companies, pharmacies, chemists. The list goes on and on. Ironically my writing has been interrupted by a telephone call from a lovely lady at my local doctors' surgery with the title of 'Diabetes Nurse'. She was ringing to introduce herself as her predecessor had recently retired. I listened attentively until I realised she just 'wanted to take the p...' or put more succinctly and politely take a sample of my urine to check my sugar levels (apologies for any offence caused). Yet another job to add to the list!

Health, in all its forms is big business. Yet what does this mean for you and me – the little people who fund this turnover that runs into billions. Why are we so obsessed with health? Can we do anything ourselves to improve our health without the professionals and the drug companies? Why do we get sick? How can we prevent this? Can we prevent this? How do we deal with the fear that underlies all our concerns about health – the fear of disability, pain and death?

Death is a topic rarely talked about today; I love statistics and an examination of those covering the past hundred years have some very interesting things to say about the changing pattern of health and death rates in the UK. Today, for instance the death of an infant can, and does on occasion, lead to front page news. One boy here in South Wales died recently of food poisoning – e-coli to be precise. This death understandably devastating for his immediate family, close relatives and friends, spawned innumerable news reports on BBC Wales. It was featured regularly during the period running from the 18th of September through to 1st of November 2005, often being the lead news story. There were demands for a public enquiry into the cause of his death. Schools were closed on the evidence of diarrhoea in unidentified children. Parents were issued with testing kits to determine if their child was infected with e-coli. Would this have been the situation had the death occurred in 1905 rather than 2005?

History shows us how infant mortality rates have dropped significantly over this period. In 1900, the infant mortality rate was 140 deaths per 1000 births. By 1997, this had fallen to 5.8 deaths per 1000 births. A staggering reduction, certainly there would have been few, if any, reports of an infant or child death in 1900 unless the death had been the result of murder. In my father's day every family lost at least one child before adulthood, some two or three. A hundred years ago death was more accepted as a fact of daily life. In the First World War some 752,000 UK citizens perished over the four-year period (1914–1918). Over 20,000 men were killed in one day alone on the 1st of July 1916 the first day of the Battle of the Somme. This was dwarfed by the 20 million people who perished in the influenza epidemic that swept the world after the ending of the First World War. Horrifying statistics. Today, the death of one soldier in Iraq or Afghanistan is a big news story in all of the news bulletins and daily newspapers.

Interestingly, the number of deaths per annum in the UK has remained remarkably similar over the period 1901–1996: in the year 1901 there were 632,000 deaths from a population of 38 million. In the year 1996 there were 647,000 recorded deaths from a population that had grown to 59 million. Whilst the population has increased by 55% the annual number of deaths had increased by only 15,000 or 2.3%. This low change reflecting advances in medical care over the period, improved nutritional and housing provisions, and the resultant generally improved health of the population. The number of deaths relative to the size of population has drastically reduced. Death has been diminished, but so too has our ability to deal with it. Along with the reduction in the rate of deaths has come a reduction in church attendances and a consequent growth in secularism.

Today, death does not seem to figure in the life agenda. It has been replaced by a cult of eternal youth and beauty. Today, we sensationalise and sentimentalise death rather than treat is as the inevitable inexorable conclusion of life. Our obsession with health and youth seemingly driven by our fear of death. It is noticeable that no celebrity, no matter how insignificant simply dies these days; they all die after 'bravely or courageously battling or fighting their illness'. Such public pronouncements amaze me; when you are ill what other choices are there?

The cult of youth and beauty is reflected in the majority of our TV and Press advertising. Given that the population of the UK is growing older (currently the number of people aged 50 and over being in excess of 30% of the population) it seems strange that the majority of advertising continues to be directed at young people. By far the largest majority of the actors shown are young and beautiful. Only a very small percentage of advertisements feature older people. And even then they are seen only as caricatures, or figures of fun. An absorption with health, youth and image prevails.

Now do not think I am writing about health from a history of only enjoying good health and a high level of fitness. In 1996 I underwent a hip replacement operation. In 1997 I entered what the medical profession euphemistically call 'end stage renal failure'. Put more simply, my kidneys stopped working and I was placed on dialysis. An interesting and depressing experience. I was restricted to drinking no more than half a litre of fluid in any twenty-four hour period to prevent me from bloating up like the Michelin man. I lost the ability to urinate. The only fluid I lost was through breathing and perspiring. Any excess fluid I took on board remained with me until I went on dialysis which I did three times a week for four hours at a time. My left arm today has more needle tracks in it than a junkie. My diet was very severely restricted. I carried with me everywhere a list of the foods that I was forbidden to eat – chief among them being orange juice and chocolate. I remained on dialysis for two years before I was well enough to receive a transplant. Then my youngest daughter – bless her heart – gave me one of her kidneys. A gift that literally gave me back my life. Words will never convey how I feel about her enormous sacrifice made as she said: 'To get her Dad back.'

I must take immuno-suppressant drugs for the rest of my days to stop my body's defence mechanism from rejecting what to it is an alien object, namely my transplanted kidney. This, together with blood pressure reducing drugs, again taken to protect the new kidney. The tablets I am on have created some interesting and on occasion painful side-effects, chief among these being gout. I have been hospitalised on numerous occasions since my transplant when the dreaded gout has crippled me, preventing me from walking. I include this information simply to show that, like everybody else, I am subject to the vicissitudes of life and age and all that goes with it. The subject of health being of more than academic interest to me.

However, where I fundamentally part company with conventional modern health wisdom is in my belief that our natural state is one of health and not sickness. It is our obsession with ill-health, sickness, and disease that in many instances actually brings about the very state feared. As Plato observed 'attention to health can be a major hindrance to health'. The Royal College of General Practitioners estimates that 25% of all consultations with GPs relate to psychosomatic or unexplained symptoms. According to figures produced in the USA, more than $20 billion a year is spent on keeping hypochondriacs happy with unnecessary treatments. The internet has further fed this obsession with health – information that was previously only available to doctors can now be accessed by anyone. This 'knowledge' obtained by people self diagnosing causes enormous problems for GPs.

Yet the miracle that is our body is perfectly capable of maintaining our health and well-being when left to its own devices. However, as always it is our servant acting at our direction, according to our thoughts, beliefs and Universal Law – how could it do otherwise? We live in a culture that believes in sickness, ill-health and disease; we have been taught from an early age that we are at risk unless we take specific steps to protect ourselves. What we expect we receive. We have been indoctrinated to believe in the reality of sickness. We take steps to safeguard ourselves against this inevitability. We take pills and potions, vitamins and medicines to protect us from the threats everywhere present to our health. We buy health insurance to indemnify ourselves against the costs we will incur if we seek or need private treatment. Each action evidence confirming our belief in sickness and disease, rather than in health and well-being. We, in effect, 'run scared' from life itself.

In opening this chapter I wrote that I live in an alien culture that constantly — if I accept popular and universal beliefs — seeks to attack me. In addition to this, I am told that my body, given half a chance, will betray me. My cells will mutate causing cancer; I will develop allergies which could kill me; my lungs will close down with asthma. I must be immunised with alien substances to encourage my body to develop antibodies to protect my system against various bugs and viruses. I could go on but I am sure my drift is clear.

Yet Seth and Myriad assure me that we create all that happens to us in our world; every single aspect of it. That the outer is but the manifestation of the inner. That we are the author, director and stage manager of this production called 'our life'. Nothing happens to us that we do not orchestrate in one way or another. If this is so, then sickness, which is an alien and abnormal state, is created by us for a purpose. If we become sick or ill, it is because we have, at another level of our being, decided to be sick or ill. Each illness with its own individual and specific purpose.

Medical science tell us that our body seethes at all times with viruses, bugs and bacteria. We create and destroy these together with numerous cancer cells daily. Why do we not fall prey to these and die? Because these organisms and mutating cells are only activated to harm our physical well-being when we decide at another level of our being to trigger the process that allows this to be so. When we have a reason for so doing. Many things and experiences are created by us in our lives that we would not consciously choose to bring about but which contain within them the potential for us to grow and become as in no other way. So it is with sickness, disease and illness. For no man is ill in isolation. As with the rest of life the event or situation ripples out like the stone thrown into the pond, affecting and influencing our family and friends. Bringing us into contact with people and situations that we would not otherwise meet. Sickness is one of the major agents of change in life, whether we like it or not. Whether we consciously or actively seek it or not. Serious illness or disease cannot be ignored – that's for sure.

To be healthy we must first believe and accept at a deep level of our being that good health is our natural state. We must swim against the cultural tide, for our Western culture believes that sickness and disease are inevitable aspects of life against which we have little or no defence, except those we erect through the use of medical science. We rarely start from the base that good health is the norm and all else an aberration. We believe in the fact and inevitability of bad health. Until we turn that belief around we are not going to improve our health as individuals, or as people. To change any external state we must first understand and, where necessary, change the underlying belief that sustains it.

According to Myriad all illness is psychosomatic in origin. We are mistaken in treating our illnesses as simply physical in origin. Whilst we readily accept the psychosomatic nature of mental illness, rarely do we do so with physical illness. Neither is it enough to talk of holistic medicine until we develop the skills that enable people to explore their own illnesses and identify the meaning that their particular illness has for them. For each person chooses, often with consummate skill, the particular illness or disease that they will suffer from. Whilst it may be possible to compile broad general categories of reasons for particular illnesses, to be truly effective we must go on and refine these in each individual case. For without an understanding of the part that the patient plays in bringing into being their particular illness, true lasting healing will not come about. This does not deny the validity of the illness. It is real in every respect. It is indeed the patient's creation, and as such they must live and experience it to the full if it is to serve the purpose for which they brought it into being.

I remember reading recently of a well-known personality who announced that he had developed a particularly virulent form of cancer and said: 'There was not a day went by that I did not fear getting cancer and now I have got it. Ironic, or what?' Well for me it was not ironic at all, for if you spend time every day thinking about cancer, it is no surprise when cancer comes along. What else could happen? What we think about and expect we create. What we fear we attract. For fear is thought given an added dimension by the emotion (energy) with which we charge it.

All illnesses serve a purpose. Are vehicles in which much can ride. The bugs that cause the common cold are everywhere present. If for example we accept the inevitability of catching a cold, particularly where those around us display typical cold symptoms, then such an expectation will most likely bring about a cold. If there is something coming up at work or home that we may be dreading and wish to avoid, again we may choose to trigger the steps necessary to allow a cold or a similar virus to flourish in our system. We then have an acceptable and ready-made reason for not dealing with the issue concerned. Some people choose illness as a way of getting love and attention, of being different, special in a particular way that is guaranteed to attract sympathy and care to them. Only by asking why we have chosen to allow this virus in, or why we created this symptom will provide the answer as to why we have developed the cold or illness. Yet the mere suggestion that you should ask yourself such a question would be considered as nonsense by most. We don't choose to get colds, we catch them, and the conventional wisdom says that there is nothing we can do about this. The only steps we can take according to the 'cold and flu prevention industry' is to buy their expensive products and constantly dose ourselves up with them.

Behind each illness is a reason, either an individual reason or a collective reason. A collective reason can be triggered by a belief in the inevitability of the spread of the virus or disease concerned. Such an instance might be as a result of the advance publicity given to a strain of a particular virus. Today's bogy virus is Avian flu. Both those responsible for our health at a national level and the media talk of the inevitability of this virus mutating and infecting thousands. What is more, such infection will lead to death and they have even hazarded a guess at how many of these there are likely to be. The ground has been prepared, all we await now is the seed to take root and flourish.

Seth, in the book *The Individual and The Nature of Mass Events* states:

> *Your body mirrors your psychological state powered by the energy of the Universe. Your mind and body come from the same source, from Universal energy. You are powered with vitality, you must seek meaning in your life; when you lose the sense of life's meaning this is reflected in your body.*

As a result, often sickness and illnesses are brought about. So what about healing? What can we do to assist the medical profession by taking greater responsibility for our own health?

## Healing

While we believe that viruses and other infectious diseases are an inevitable fact of life, we will have little or no defence against them and will continue to need to rely upon our doctors to heal and protect us. For we create at all times in accordance with our thoughts and our beliefs, and whilst we operate within an 'inevitability of sickness' belief system so then our life creation will continue to faithfully reflect this.

I am not in any way advocating the abandonment of the medical health system, rather I am advocating that alongside this we take on a greater responsibility for our health and well-being than is commonly accepted as possible. Without doubt, by changing our core beliefs about sickness, illness and disease we can do much to promote our own healing, health and well-being. We can actively seek to gain a better understanding of the beliefs we hold about sickness and health and work to change those that threaten and weaken our body's natural defences. We should be very wary of handing responsibility for our health and welfare over to the medical profession just because we have been brought up to consider those who work in the profession as omnipotent. They are human beings just like us, subject to all of the whims, variations and fallibilities as we. They are also, like us, prisoners of the belief system of the culture and the age.

The well-known 'placebo effect' is a vivid example of what we believe will happen becoming reality. The belief laying the groundwork for and attracting the very thing expected. According to a recently published University of Michigan study in the 'Journal of Neuroscience', patients who believe they are taking pain-killers feel better, even if there is no medication in their dosage. The study referred to involved 14 healthy men from 20 to 30 years of age. Researchers gave the study participants a salt water injection that caused jaw pain. The participants were then told they were being given a pain-killer which was actually a placebo. They were then questioned with their brain activity being constantly monitored and evaluated. It was noted that each of the participants released more natural pain-killing endorphins from their brains after being given the placebo. By monitoring the brain activity after the placebo was given, researchers were able to determine more effectively the bodily mechanism behind the 'placebo effect'.

One patient stood out in the memory of Stephen Straus, M.D. Chief of the Laboratory of Clinical Investigation at the American National Institute of Allergy and Infectious Diseases for her remarkable recovery from chronic fatigue syndrome. The woman, in her 30s, was 'very significantly impaired', says Straus. 'She had no energy, couldn't work, and spent most of her time at home.' But her strength was completely restored during a study to test the effectiveness of an experimental chronic fatigue drug. 'She and her parents were so thrilled with her recovery that they were blessing me and my colleagues,' recalls Straus, the principal investigator on that study.

Like many drug studies, the chronic fatigue medication trial was a 'placebo-controlled' study, meaning that a portion of the patients took the experimental drug, while others took look-alike pills with no active ingredient, with neither researchers nor patients knowing which patients were getting which. It turned out that the woman's quick turnaround from chronic fatigue occurred after taking placebo pills, not the experimental drug. It may be that her desire to be cured, coupled with the need for a treatment to be undergone allowed her to heal herself with justification. What is clear from this trial is that the woman in question healed herself without the active involvement of any medication other than belief in the treatment that she had apparently undergone.

Research has confirmed that a fake treatment, made from an inactive substance like sugar, distilled water, or saline solution, can have a placebo effect, that is, the sham medication can sometimes improve a patient's condition simply because the person has the expectation that it will be helpful. Put simply, the patient believes that they will be healed and as such their belief becomes their reality.

Brain imagery techniques lend support to my belief that thoughts and beliefs not only affect one's psychological state, but also cause the body to undergo actual biological changes. Studies have shown that an average of 32% of patients respond positively to a placebo. A significant percentage indeed. One recently reported Italian study found that when Alzheimers disease robs a patient of the ability to believe that a pain-killer will help them, pain-killers subsequently cease to work effectively for them in relieving their pain.

In one widely reported experiment, patients with knee pain were duped into believing that they had undergone knee surgery, when in fact all that the surgeons had down was to make an incision in the area of the knee and stitch the knee up again. Some of these patients, even though no corrective surgery had been undertaken, were subsequently cured of their knee pain. The knee surgeon concerned now always accompanies any surgery that he carries out by telling his patients that: 'My expectation is that you are going to get better after this surgery.' He believes that such a positive suggestion placed into the patient's mind will significantly improve their recovery rate. It seems that being told by your doctor that you will get well, might be more effective than the actual treatment itself. A method traditionally utilised by those who practise as witchdoctors.

The mind directs and control all that happens to us. Our assessment of our body's condition at all times forms an image that is in line with our conscious beliefs about ourselves. To change our bodily condition we must first change the belief we hold about that condition. Our bodies are recreating themselves daily, they are never static. A state of non-creation cannot exist in physical form, or out of it for that matter. The cells that make up the physical us are constantly growing, dividing and dying. Each following their genetically imprinted pattern, each creating according to the mental image held in mind. Now the beliefs that we hold about ourself and our world are the result of information that has come to us from a myriad of sources. From our parents and our upbringing, from our culture and education, from our friends and colleagues as well as the variety of media and other sources that constantly feed information to us. This stream of information comes together to form the pattern of beliefs that we hold about our body, our health and any particular condition from which we suffer. The prevailing Western belief today is that our world is a threatening and dangerous place. Dangerous not because of the activities we undertake, but because of the threats to our health everywhere present from viruses, infections, diseases and contamination. Little wonder then that we have absorbed this information into our belief system and acted accordingly.

Without doubt, persistent thoughts of illness, whether they be confirmed by the medical profession or not will make us ill. Conversely, persistent thoughts of health will aid in keeping us healthy. In 2004 a pensioner from Wawne in East Yorkshire, England, who was diagnosed with cancer, was given between nine and eighteen months to live by his doctors. The man, Dave

Thorne, was suffering from an aggressive form of bowel cancer which had spread to his lymph glands and his lungs. After a year of chemotherapy Mr Thorne, however, has beaten the disease after a scan showed that no trace of the cancerous tumours remained, much to the astonishment of his doctors. He said in his uncomplicated simple way: 'I never intended to let this thing be the death of me. I just looked inside, told it to hop it and it has. I have always believed that if you are strong in mind anything is possible.'

Until we take full responsibility for our health and well-being; until we accept at a deep level of our being that good health is our natural state and that all else an aberration, we will be denying our birthright. Contrary to popular belief we are not born into an alien landscape that constantly seeks to harm and destroy us. We are a product of our environment. We are formed from the very stuff that everywhere surrounds us, the nuclei of our cells being formed from the very stuff of which the stars in the Universe are made. The food and liquid that sustain us being drawn from the earth; we merge and blend with the earth, nature and Universe. This is our natural habitat, our home, we grew from it and with it. It no more seeks to harm us than we set out to deliberately harm our world. We belong together, we cannot be separated. The physical us came from the earth and will return to it. These facts are indisputable. We live in the habitat and environment for which we were explicitly designed.

If you are sick or ill, perhaps suffering from cancer or heart failure, or any one of the many health problems which can disable and debilitate us, nothing in this chapter is written to invalidate your pain and suffering. Your illness is real; it is your reality. I would not insult you by suggesting otherwise. Like all else in our physical world your illness has great validity. Having experienced serious health problems myself, I share with you your pain and suffering. But take heart; what you are experiencing now has already been created, in a sense it is already history. You are today creating your tomorrows, for you are at all times the creator of your body and your future. You created this painful condition that you suffer from now, and using the same power of creation with which you are imbued you can today start to alleviate the symptoms from which you suffer. I am not promising miracle cures, although these can and do happen. What I am saying is that you have a far greater influence over your pain and suffering than perhaps you realise. Certainly as great as any doctor or medical specialist.

The outer is always the manifestation of the inner. To change the outer we must first work upon the inner. I am a great believer in the effectiveness of visualisation. However, it is important to stress that *what you visualise* is most important. Do not visualise, for instance, your white blood cells as soldiers fighting the invading infection or cancerous cells, as some people do. For in so doing you will merely be giving extra energy to the cancerous cells, for the Universal Law – 'to oppose is to support' – will come into play. Instead, spend time relaxing, say two to three times each day, sitting or laying quietly. During these sessions see yourself in your mind's eye whole, healthy and healed. See the outcome you desire and let the miracle that is your body do the rest. See yourself doing the things that you did when you were fit and active. Remember how you felt then, recreate these feelings as far as you are able. See yourself engaging in normal everyday activities free from pain or discomfort of any kind. As if in your favourite dream see yourself active, hale and healthy. At the end of each session say to yourself the words recommended by Dr Ernest Holmes – the Science of Mind Practitioner – 'And so it is.' In effect, 'It is created'. For your visualisation will go before you giving the creative power that brings all to you a shape, a mould from which to create that which you have visualised. Don't expect instant results, it took time to create the physical you which exists today. It will take time to recreate the new you in your new image. Keep working daily with the healing process safe in the knowledge that you are doing the most constructive thing that you can do to aid your healing, recovery and return to health. Become an active participator in your own healing, do not abandon any medical treatment you are undergoing, instead see yourself supporting and reinforcing this treatment. Together, you and the medical practitioner treating you can bring about a renewed and healthier you.

Remember always to invest in beliefs of health, for to believe in sickness is to create sickness, to believe in health is to be healthy. Even where doctors have pronounced a condition as terminal visualisation can give enormous relief to the pain and suffering experienced and even, in certain circumstances, considerably lengthen the time before death. Nothing is worse, or will hasten death quicker, than feeling helpless in the face of illness and disease and simply abandoning all hope of release from pain and suffering. There is always hope, and if not for a good life, then certainly for a good death.

A report published by the Mayo clinic in Minnesota, USA in August 2002 said that their studies showed that our outlook on life helps us to live longer. It reported on a study that it had carried out on 800 people over a period of 30 years. The study showed that optimists report a higher level of physical and mental functioning than their pessimistic counterparts. Pessimists scored below optimists on quality of life assessments and also scored lower in physical functioning, bodily pain, general health perception, vitality, social functioning, role limitation and emotional and mental health. Dr Toshihto Maruta who headed up the study said, 'How you perceive what goes on around you and how you interpret it has an impact on your longevity and it can effect the quality of your later years.' This report appears to verify the fact that our general outlook on life does effect both our well-being and our longevity.

We believe in the medical profession, the doctors and specialist consultants who have ministered to us throughout our lives. In fact much healing can be put down to this belief. The medical profession are a significant part of our culture. We have much to be grateful to them for; we should continue to trust them and the medicines and solutions which they prescribe. Yet at the same time we should take back responsibility for our own health. We should recognise that what we think and believe on a day to day basis is by far the single most important factor in our own health and well-being.

We do need, however, to radically rethink our attitude to sickness, illness and disease. The medical profession has a responsibility to preach a message of health and well-being. To exude a confidence that infects all who come into contact with them. To encourage us to take greater responsibility for our health in the fullest sense, rather than simply encouraging us to defend ourselves ever more rigorously against the presupposed threats to our well-being. When the reality of the source of all illness is truly understood, then and only then will it become possible for my wish for a world without sickness and ill-health to come true, in the healthiest of ways.

## Symbols

We live in a world of symbols. Objects, things, images to which we give meaning, both universal and individual. Books are symbols – the Bible, the Koran – each copy no more that paper, ink and binding, yet imbued for billions of people worldwide with a symbolism and meaning far outweighing any monetary value. To the illiterate or the atheist both are just books, no more. To the religious they are objects of veneration; insulting the Koran can and does lead to death; prescribed by law in some Arab states, such is the importance placed on this holy book.

Jews worship at the Wailing Wall in Jerusalem, a symbol of their history, their heritage as the chosen people of God. Orthodox Jews are instantly recognisable by their symbolic mode of dress. Christians venerate the Cross, the symbol of the sacrifice made for them by their saviour Jesus Christ. Hindus have their gods and sacred cows, all symbols imbued and vested with meaning.

The whole concept of advertising is symbol orientated. Pictures of blue seas and skies, palm trees and white beaches are used to sell us holidays; to elicit the good feelings that we associate with such images. Delayed flights, lost luggage and stomach upsets are never shown, except to support adverts for insurance or medicine. Food adverts designed to arouse our gastric juices; beautiful women portrayed to sell anything from shampoo to make-up and plastic surgery. People glowing with health sell us vitamins and medication. Car manufacturers target our desire for prestige with their images of beautiful, sleek fast cars. Symbols of wealth, each imbued with meaning, each making a statement. Each aiming to conjure up emotion with image, placing us in the holiday picture, car, state of beauty or improved health.

In the status obsessed world in which we live, even such mundane objects as handbags and watches reek with symbolism. Clothes bear the manufacturer's name emblazoned on the outside enabling the wearer to proclaim to the world: 'Look at me, I can afford Gucci', or whatever 'must have' label is in vogue. The latest must have accessories being literally fought over on occasion. Yet a handbag is just a handbag, a watch just a timepiece, the purpose of clothing is to keep us warm and dry. Yet to their owners these things are status symbols; statements about who and what they believe they are. Those who cannot afford the genuine article make do with copies, anything to maintain the desired image; designer logos ruling all.

Yet how often do the advertisements and promotions create depression in their viewers? Create unhappiness and division by reinforcing the very opposite of what they are selling. Reminding people that they are not young, slim, good looking, wealthy, happy, pain free. etc.; thus breeding resentment and envy as they remind their viewers of the good things in life that are denied to them. For symbols can be both positive and negative. The symbol of the Nazi SS being a classic example. I would imagine that few, if any, Jews of my generation can view this symbol or the Nazi swastika with anything other than loathing; ironic for a symbol that came into being originally as a religious icon but which has, as a result of the holocaust, come to represent totalitarian evil. For always it is what each symbol has come to represent that determines the feeling that it evokes.

Alongside the universal symbols of wealth and status there are personal symbols, items and images with symbolic meaning for individuals alone. Things endowed with hidden meaning singularly peculiar. For instance, shoes for me equate to wealth, why I don't know. Perhaps somewhere buried is the memory of childhood friends playing in bare feet, for shoes then were reserved for school and public outings. Only rich people's children wore shoes all of the time and even owned more than one pair! Watches and clocks symbolise time – heavily symbolic for me. For others, insects, wasps and spiders evoke feelings of terror way beyond any threat posed by the creatures. Each a symbol with deep meaning to those concerned.

In *Seth Speaks*, Seth reinforces this fact of symbolism by stating that:

> *Objects are symbols. You usually think of them simply as realities. You think of thoughts, images and dreams sometimes as symbolic of other things, but the truth is that physical objects are themselves symbolic. They are the exterior symbols that stand for inner experience. The whole nature and structure of physical life as you know it, is a symbolic statement made by groups of entities who choose to work with physical symbolism. So the body is a symbol for what you are, or what you think you are – and these may be two different things indeed.*

> *Any physical ailment is symbolic of an inner reality or statement. Your entire life is a statement in physical terms, written upon time as you understand it.*

> *Once you understand the symbolic nature of physical reality, then you will no longer feel entrapped by it. You have formed the symbols, and therefore you can change them. You must learn of course, what the various symbols mean in your own life and how to translate their meaning.*

> *To do so, you must first of all remind yourself frequently that*

*the physical condition is symbolic – not a permanent condition.*
*Then you must look within yourself for the inner actuality*
*represented by the symbol. This same process can be followed*
*regardless of the nature of the problem, or of your challenge.*

It helps then to become a 'symbol spotter' – to explore life and
determine what is behind the things and objects that we hold in
high esteem or despair. Be they houses, cars, clothes, accessories,
insignia, whatever holds particular meaning for us. Meaning way
beyond their surface use or worth of the things concerned. To
come to understand what 'things' actually represent for us. The
emotions they generate, what they tell us about ourselves. Why we
are so fascinated or obsessed with particular things, activities,
hobbies, etc.

I love words, for me, words are thoughts in action; spoken
words, written words, dictionaries, crosswords, books in general;
they are hugely symbolic. Books contain for me the essence of
their authors' thinking; they tell me about their thoughts and
beliefs. I sense their knowledge and in many cases their wisdom.
I love to learn about the history of the writer, their upbringing,
culture, life experiences, belief system; those things that shaped
them to become the person behind the book. I am surrounded
by books, on occasion, much to my tolerant wife's annoyance,
they spill over from my bookshelves on to any available adjacent
surface. I struggle to comprehend what it would be like to live in
a world without books.

Symbolism extends beyond things and objects into non-tangible
aspects of life such as our relationships with others, the jobs we
do, our hobbies, our likes and dislikes. The problems we
experience in life are hugely symbolic about who and what we
are. From a difficulty in holding down jobs, through to a
shortage of money, marital and relationship breakdowns, etc., the
list is as long as the list of problems that can beset us throughout
our life. Each issue or problem being specifically symbolic to the

sufferer. Relationships in particular are an area of life that is rich with symbolism; relationships with our families and loved ones, with our work colleagues and our associates.

Those who struggle to form relationships, or having entered into them are unable to maintain or sustain them, would be helped by recognising the symbolism that these difficulties represent for them. The beliefs that they hold about themselves that prevents them from finding and bonding with another. For these are aspects of life that can literally shout out for healing. There is no single solution to such problems; our very uniqueness as beings indicates the need for solutions that are specific to the individual problem being experienced. Only by going inward and asking the question as to why the problem or issue has been chosen, what it is symbolic of, can ever elicit the answer that can lead to a lasting resolution of the issue concerned.

Bernie Siegel, the American cancer surgeon, in his two excellent books, *Love, Medicine and Healing* and *Peace, Love and Healing*, writes how his whole professional life has been transformed through coming to understand what his patients' illnesses represent for them. He says that when this is understood and worked upon, miraculous healing can occur. He bemoans the fact that too often conventional medicine works only with the body of the patient, rather than with the body and the mind of the sick person.

Bernie starts his healing from the premise not only that the patient chose to have the particular illness manifest in their lives, but also from the basis that the illness has meaning for them. That it serves a purpose for the patient and is therefore somehow symbolic to them. By helping his patients to come to understand the purpose that their illness represents for them, he is better able to help them to help themselves.

His startling conclusion is that all illnesses are psychosomatic.

That all illnesses are symbolic to the sufferer. That all illnesses have their origin in the mind, rather than the body of the patient. The outer literally becoming the manifestation of the inner. This conclusion is further evidence, if evidence is needed, of the truth of what Seth set out in *Seth Speaks*: that all illness is symbolic. The healing process, he claims, cannot be properly understood, engaged in or utilised, until we learn to interpret the messages contained within the illness or disease from which we may be suffering. Until we understand why we have chosen to experience the illness and what purpose it serves for us.

If Seth and Bernie Siegel are correct in what they state, then even the most trivial of illnesses are imbued with meaning and tell us something that needs to be understood if true lasting healing is to be effected. Perhaps the words of Jesus to the cripple he had healed were nearer the truth than we realise when he instructed him to 'Go and sin no more.' If we reinterpret the word 'sin' to mean deviation from the path to internal growth, then his words indeed support this proposition.

Just imagine the revolution that could be effected in healing, from colds and flu right through to cancer, heart attacks and AIDS, if we as a society were able to accept that all illness is symbolic and specific to the sufferer or the community of which they are a part. Then treatment could take on a whole new meaning. For while the treatment of the symptoms could still be dealt with through medication, work to eliminate the root cause of the illness could also be undertaken. The greatest advances in medical science would then not lie in investing millions of pounds in new hospitals and ever more expensive drugs, but in dealing with the root cause of the affliction. In recognising that to heal the body, the mind of the patient must also be healed, if lasting recovery is to be effected.

It is possible to see illness and disease as symbolic, both on an individual level and as a species. It would be specious and offensive in the extreme to suggest that the millions of AIDS victims in Africa have deliberately brought about their own infection. That children who are born with this awful disease have somehow collaborated in becoming diseased. But if instead of seeing billions of individuals making up humanity we see humanity as a whole, then it could be that certain beings have taken it upon themselves at a superconscious level to suffer on our behalf, to bring to our attention in the most graphic and awful way the evils of poverty, war, exploitation and deprivation. Have become living symbols for humanity as a whole. Symbols that focus the attention of the world in the most graphic way. An extreme 'out of the box' theory I accept, but none the less worthy of consideration. If this were indeed the case, then all who care should work to ensure that the sacrifice of these unfortunate members of our world is not in vain. Should work tirelessly to eradicate the root causes of the evils of poverty, exploitation, starvation malnutrition and preventable diseases wherever they exist.

True healing presupposes complete honesty. For to accept that individually and collectively we create every ailment or problem that besets us takes great courage. Sitting here working, complete with my transplanted kidney and my artificial hip, I can say with certainty that to accept that each of my ailments has been created by me and is symbolic of aspects of my life is indeed difficult to take on board. Yet I accept that my whole life is my creation, even the parts that are painful and difficult. That they represent symbols to me of those areas of my life that I still need to work on.

To see illnesses as symbolic and to accept complete responsibility for them will be most hard for those who hide behind their physical condition, and use their illness and disability as a 'crutch' to help them get through life (no pun intended). For if I am sick and ill, then I can expect sympathy, I can be excused from dealing with the travails that an active life can bring to me. I can demand that society supports me… the list goes on. There can be advantages as well as disadvantages in being ill. In many instances illness and disability can be a very useful tool in avoiding facing up to life; can be a ready-made excuse for not partaking fully in life.

When suffering strikes as a result of accidents, illnesses or other traumatic events seemingly outside of our control, the effects ripple outwards. The saying: 'No man is an island' by the metaphysical poet John Dunne, is certainly true with accidents and illness. The effects ripple outwards through family, friends, colleagues, workmates and community. Like a stone in a pond the ripples can extend far beyond the point of impact. We are all involved and affected by accidents, illnesses and traumatic events to a greater or lesser degree. Such events can have different meaning for each affected by them. Can be individually symbolic in their own way.

Recognising the symbolism ever present in life can help to deal with issues and problems in a practical way. For to see our life laid out before us symbolically can provide us with a picture of our life with which we can work. Like working on any picture, we cannot change our picture all at once, but merely work on one aspect of it at a time, constantly seeking to improve the quality, balance and look of it. As any artist will tell you a picture is never completed, it is only ever abandoned by the artist when their level of skill prevents them from improving their work of art any further, so it is with life. We will never in one lifetime reach perfection, for we can only ever do the best that we can with the qualities within us. But if we do this with a single minded approach in the pursuit of excellence, then we will be fine. As a famous sage commented when advising a disciple: 'Remember, your best is always good enough, as long as it is truly your best.'

## Miracles

The knowledge that we create all that happens to us in life can be scary. For it means that we, and only we, are responsible for what has happened in our life so far. If we have got used to blaming circumstances, parents, infirmities, colour, background, anything but ourselves for who and what we are, then to accept this truth is to drop the crutches that have been supporting us all our life. This is scary stuff indeed.

Now crutches, as I know only too well, can be a great comfort if you are unsteady on your feet. Reaching for them and holding them, even when you are not attempting to walk, can be very comforting. For they confirm that you will have the means to walk when you need. They will help you to get to where you are trying to go, albeit slowly.

During my last stay in hospital, when I was crippled and virtually immobilised with gout in my knees and ankles, I could only make it to the bathroom in the hospital corridor with great difficulty. The physiotherapist loaned me a Zimmer frame in the early days and showed me how to use it safely. A bit different to the BMW that I was used to driving! Leaning on the Zimmer frame gave me great confidence. I would not let it go unless there was something nearby for me to hang on to. Gradually my mobility improved and I graduated to arm crutches, until eventually I could walk again unsupported. Now, like all active and unimpaired people, I rarely think about walking as I go about my daily life. The miracle of walking I take for granted, and it is a miracle, if you doubt this ask anyone who is confined to a wheelchair, or a hospital bed, and they will tell you just how much of a miracle walking is.

Comforting ourselves with thoughts of what we could be, might be, if only… we were not poor or sick, had had better parents, or had been born in a better area or country. If we were taller, better looking, white, black, yellow, athletic, etc., etc. the list can be endless; but it works. It does indeed ease the resentment we may feel at being 'short changed' by life. After all it is not our fault, we are just unlucky; it is all the fault of our circumstances. Why do others get all the luck? What is wrong with us? But operating in the comfort zone of recrimination only guarantees that we will remain exactly where we are right now in life. We will never know the buzz and satisfaction that comes from reaching out and taking greater control over every aspect of life. From being more successful, and achieving our objectives no matter how modest or grand they may be.

The start place of change is the hardest. For it requires that we accept that what we have in our life now is our creation. Every jot and tittle of it. Every wart and imperfection mirrors the inward image and beliefs that we hold of, and about, ourselves. A lack of self-belief and a poor image are the biggest single factor that hold most people back. It is even given merit by some who believe that being humble and self-effacing is 'good'. That this somehow makes them better people. They say things like, 'Oh you go ahead, I've never been very good at – whatever – so you go ahead and enjoy yourself. I am happy staying right here.' When that is anything but the truth. When in fact they are terrified inside, terrified of making a fool of themselves, of being exposed as the person that they believe themselves to be, stupid, ugly, clumsy; the adjectives roll on.

Holding beliefs in our own believed inadequacies is not surprising for we live in an age of perceived perfection. Everywhere we look we see beautiful people gliding effortlessly though life. People who live in grand houses, drive exotic cars, people who always seem to be on holiday or attending this or that top notch event around the world. They gaze out at us from TV screens, billboards, magazines and newspapers. They write (or have written for them) articles that appear in glossy magazines. They are involved in TV programmes built around their fame and public persona. When we compare our lives with these golden ones we are indeed at risk of feeling inadequate. If only we could be like them... I often wonder what these folk look like first thing in the morning, without make-up and airbrushing. When the publicity lights are not shining on them. Few, if any would look very different from you or me. Of course there are personalities, people whose very presence makes impact. Who do not appear to take the media hype and frenzy seriously. Who keep their feet on the ground and remain who and what they are irrespective of the fame and fortune. But, sadly, these folk do seem to be thin on the ground.

This is why the celebrity 'wanabe' shows succeed. These shows that promise instant fame. Big Brother, The 'X' Factor, Pop Idol, etc. Tens of thousands of people apply to be on these shows believing that if only they could be recognised, that instant fame, and all that goes with it would be theirs. Equally, tens of thousands have their hopes of fame and fortune smashed through rejection following auditioning. But the belief holds in the public mind. If I could just get that break... short cuts to fame and fortune.

Many people that I have worked with over the years have had a poor self-image. Even some who appeared on the surface to be comfortable with themselves turned out after discussion to be putting on a front. Others appeared super cool and in control, when in reality they too were merely putting on a front. It is not how we look on the outside that determines our happiness, it is how we feel on the inside that matters. This is why even beautiful people have plastic surgery. Not because of how they look on the outside but how they feel on the inside. If they do not feel good about themselves, then no amount of reassurance from others will change their perception. It is all too easy to believe that if only I could change this or that then my problems would be over.

I am careful how I express, particularly to people who are sick and in pain, that what they are experiencing is wholly their creation. For to tell someone with a painful, debilitating and possibly terminal illness, that their suffering is their creation would be to act extremely insensitively. Far better to talk to them about the steps that they can take to alleviate their symptoms. Explaining how visualisation can bring about lasting healing. Demonstrating to someone who is ill how they can take greater control over their illness can by itself effect miraculous cures. But if a change in thinking does no more than empower a sick person, engenders within them a feeling that they have much greater control over their illness and their day to day life than they may believe, this can by itself bring about significant psychological benefits and as such may be well worthwhile.

I was recently visited by some Jehovah Witnesses. A man, and a woman who was holding a tiny baby in her arms. The man asked me if I believed in miracles. I turned the question around and asked him what he believed. He replied by quoting passages from the New Testament. When he had finished, I asked him why he had to quote from a book when his wife was carrying a miracle in her arms. We may understand how a baby is created physically, but we have no idea how the essence of the baby, their personality and spirit, the special something that will mark them out as unique in their lifetime, comes into being, or at what stage of the pregnancy a baby changes from being merely a foetus to become a person. This debate has exercised the abortionists and the 'pro-lifers' for decades. In short, the creation of each human being from the fusion of egg and sperm into a walking, talking, thinking human being endowed with personality and free-will is nothing short of a miracle.

We live every minute of our lives surrounded by miracles. The very spontaneous nature of our physical being a constant miracle. The way in which we speak, transforming thoughts into words instantaneously. Receive information about our world, sift, sort and react to it. While our bodies at the same time take in air, extract oxygen, pump blood, digest food, remain upright, and walk, talk, hear, feel and respond to stimuli. There are so many wondrous things and happenings on our planet, and in our world, that I do not begin to understand, that I know are beautiful, miraculous and wondrous. I see a rainbow, or a sunset, and while I know the science of how they are brought into being, or think I do, yet I am still awestruck by them. For me they are miracles, a constant reminder of the miracles that ever abound in our world.

When we look at nature – do we see order or chaos? Do we see patterns or random creation? Do the four seasons follow each other without fail every year or does spring on occasion follow autumn? Every where we look in nature we see order, structure and organisation. Organisation woven into the very fabric of nature. Whether we believe in a Creator or simply a creative process matters not. Whether we believe in God or the 'Big Bang' theory we cannot deny the evidence of our own eyes. Cause and effect remorselessly following the rules of nature.

Whilst accepting that we are all programmed to grow from babyhood to adulthood, that we will all mature, age and die without any active intervention on our part, many believe that the rest of life is the result of random creation. Believe in the 'fickle finger of fate'. Such people believe that they are either lucky or unlucky. Usually a mixture of both, most of which they believe is outside of their control.

Yet the only difference between human beings and all other living things is in the choices that we are able, through the exercise of free-will, to make. For example I could, if I chose, shut down my word processor right now, grab a bag and my wallet and passport, and head for an airport, any airport, and catch a plane to the other side of the world. Even if I had little money, unless I was destitute these things would be possible for me, they would simply be my choice. Now I do not choose to do that, not today at any rate. I intend to finish this chapter, and this book. It was my decision to write this. I shall be fulfilling one of my personal goals in so doing. What I am doing now is the result of a conscious decision that I have made; it is my choice. Like all in human form I am a choosing creature, for we, above all in the animal kingdom, are endowed with reason and free-will. It is the one aspect of our beingness that distinguishes us from all other living creatures.

Miracles can happen, but before they do we must learn to control the process of creation that is everywhere evident in our life. Just imagine how it would be in your life if you could speak your word knowing that whatever you spoke would instantly come into being. That you could speak your word and that whatever changes that you wanted to happen in your life would come into being. If this were the case, I am sure that you would describe it as nothing short of miraculous. But this is exactly what does happen, naturally without our conscious awareness. What we think and speak we create; it really is that simple, but it is the very simplicity of the way that creation works in life that leads to it being overlooked. For we know better, don't we? Life is a random thing is it not? It sprinkles its favours and misfortunes seemingly without logic. Some get lucky, but most do not. We are born, we grow, we die and there is not a lot that we can do about it in between. Or is there?

What are miracles. They are happenings or events which appear to defy the laws of physics *as we understand them*. Miracles cannot yet be explained by any science of which we are aware. And this is the problem, our lack of knowledge at present prevents us from understanding and accepting the way that the creation process works naturally in and throughout life. If for example I lived in the middle ages and I suddenly conjured up a radio, switched it on and listened to it – it would seem miraculous to all who observed and heard the radio. If I were able, at the same time, to power a light by electricity, again this would be considered a miracle. Both understandable and explainable today with our knowledge of radio waves and the properties of electricity. To us then neither would appear miraculous. The difference between the two situations is simply the degree of knowledge available making the event understandable.

To better understand the miracle of the power of thought look around you. Realise that everything created by man; everything that you are wearing, living in, driving, flying, reading is the product of thought. Each sprang initially from an idea, a creative thought. Each existed first in imagination before it came into form. Thought creates, nothing man-made comes into existence without the operation of thought, consciously or subconsciously. To fully understand the power of thought is indeed to understand how miracles happen. When we speak our thoughts we give sound and shape to them. What others hear are our thoughts and ideas in action. When we write, draw and express ourselves we are giving shape to our thoughts. Shape to who and what we are.

Now, and here is where the big leap of faith is required; to fully understand and utilise the power of thought we must go one step further. We must accept that thought literally creates the events and circumstances that make up our life. What we think and believe from moment to moment goes before us to form and bring into being the events, circumstances and experiences which collectively become our lives. When we speak our word with conviction and belief powered by emotion, we create our future.

One famous historical figure was renowned for his ability to speak his words with complete conviction that the natural law of life would respond positively to them. Would create events exactly in the manner he expected them to. That man was Christ. It is apparent to me that there was no gap between the words that he spoke and what he expected to happen. In all of us, even the most positive, and those who accept and understand that thought creates, there is still a little voice in the back of our mind that doubts. That questions whether we can actually create that which we think. To the degree that we can still this little voice, will our conscious thoughts become our reality.

The records show that when Christ spoke there was in his mind no doubt. For he understood the natural laws of the Universe. Miracles resulted. I quote from the Gospel of John:

> After these things, there was a feast of the Jews, and Jesus went up to Jerusalem. Now in Jerusalem by the sheep gate, there is a pool, which is called in Hebrew, 'Bethesda', having five porches.

> In these lay a great multitude of those who were sick, blind, lame, or paralysed, waiting for the moving of the water; for an angel of the Lord went down at certain times into the pool, and stirred up the water. Whoever stepped in first after the stirring of the water was made whole of whatever disease he had.

> A certain man was there, who had been sick for thirty-eight years. When Jesus saw him lying there, and knew that he had been sick for a long time, he asked him, 'Do you want to be made well?'

> The sick man answered him, 'Sir, I have no one to put me into the pool when the water is stirred up, but while I'm

coming, another steps down before me.' Jesus said to him, 'Arise, take up your mat, and walk.' Immediately, the man was made well, and took up his mat and walked.*

And, again, in the Gospel of Mark:

*He departed from the borders of Tyre and Sidon, and came to the Sea of Galilee, through the midst of the region of Decapolis. They brought to him one who was deaf and had an impediment in his speech. They begged him to lay his hand on him. He took him aside from the multitude, privately, and put his fingers into his ears, and he spat, and touched his tongue. Looking up to Heaven, he sighed, and said to him, 'Ephphatha!' that is, 'Be opened!' Immediately his ears were opened, and the impediment of his tongue was released, and he spoke clearly.*

The first story tells of how a man who had been crippled for thirty eight years was healed and made mobile again by the words of Christ. Jesus said 'Arise, take up your mat, and walk.' Immediately the man was made well and walked.

The second miracle story tells of a man who was deaf and who had a speech impediment who had his hearing restored and was enabled to hear and speak clearly.

If these stories are true, and it is a testament to the life of Christ that his name lives on today, two thousand years after his life and death, something remarkable took place in Palestine two thousand years ago. What possible explanation is there for these and other miracles occurring? The religious put it down to the fact that Jesus was 'the son of God' the 'chosen one'. What, however, if there is a more prosaic reason? What if Jesus in his ultimate wisdom as a developed being understood the power of thought? Understood that if he spoke his word with complete belief that his word, or thought given sound and direction unhindered by doubt, would be immediately carried out. That what he said would happen without fail. The instructions to the stricken leave no room for doubt: 'Arise, take up your mat, and walk.' And the even briefer: 'Be opened.' An understanding of how the power of creation works at our direction makes these miracles understandable. Momentous events still, carried out by a master practitioner, but nonetheless understandable.

When we can learn to speak our word with the same degree of conviction as Christ. When we can say, and more importantly believe, that what we think and believe we create. When we have mastered this power, then we too will be able to perform miracles. For life is about learning about the process of creation. Learning to manipulate and control our world through the creative medium of thought. We live in a time space continuum specifically designed to enable us to create and observe our creation. We could not handle instant creation, it would overpower and swamp us. We must learn little by little, by trial and experiment, what works and what does not, for this is one of the purposes of life. Only when we have truly mastered this intricate skill will we be able to graduate from the university of life; then miracles for us will be commonplace.

## Action – The Solution

Our hearts pound, our knees grow weak, the sweat runs down between our shoulder blades, our stomach churns, fear and anxiety pervades our being. How often have you experienced these feelings? Perhaps when called upon to perform publicly, or when thrust into an unexpected and embarrassing situation? Fight or flight, that is the question we are asking ourselves at such times. This experience is the reality facing many actors immediately before they go on stage. Faced with the prospect of performing in public many actors are literally paralysed with stage fright. Yet once on the stage their fear falls away. They become too busy, too involved in what they are doing to be anxious.

Heroes are often asked: 'Weren't you frightened at the time you carried out your heroic action?' The answer is invariably: 'I was too busy to be frightened, I just did what anyone would have done faced with the same situation. It was only afterwards that I had time to be frightened.'

Fear and its kinsmen worry and depression are the results of an inactive body and an overactive mind. Fear and worry are the result of misapplied energy. Energy turned inwards instead of being expressed outwards. Energy used *against* ourselves rather that *for* ourselves. We are energy systems; our creative energy will not be denied. If we do not apply our energy externally to work to bring to us those things that we hope for and desire, then it has no choice but to stay with us. For energy must create, it can never be static or stored, if left unused it will work on us resulting in upset stomachs, ulcers, diarrhoea and irritable bowel syndrome, tension headaches and stress. All medical conditions resultant from the inadequate release of creative personal energy.

Our lives are lived inside of our heads first, and in the physical world second. Our view of the world comes to us filtered through our beliefs, perceptions (and often misperceptions) conscious thoughts and feelings. Yet these are not universal, they are personal to us. I have a saying that I use when I begin to become fearful or concerned over any aspect of life; that saying is: 'Action is the solution'. For experience has taught me that when I am physically or mentally involved with a demanding task or activity my mood brightens, I don't have time to worry or be depressed. When I release my energy to work on my behalf then solutions and opportunities that were not readily apparent come into view. Even where the action I am taking is wrong and does not lead directly to a solution of the problem or difficulty I am experiencing, it is still of value, for having identified what does not work I am in a better position to identify what does. Further, I am releasing the energy that otherwise would stay with me to fuel my worries and concerns.

The other technique that I use, particularly when I am in a physically painful situation, such as experienced at the dentist or in hospital, is to remind myself that whatever the situation I am in, no matter how painful, it will soon be history. That before I know where I am I will be looking back at the experience and evaluating it for future reference. Nothing lasts for ever, it only seems that way sometimes!

Human beings are a combination of the physiological and the psychological. Neither can operate consciously without the other. What we think affects our emotions, our emotions determine how we feel about ourselves and about our world. We are in control, or should be, of how we think. It follows then that we should be in control of how we feel. A clinical view maybe, but not a bad blueprint to follow if we are aiming to successfully fight worry or depression that can, and does, blight lives and on occasion lead sufferers to take their own life. What I am writing about here is literally the stuff of life and death.

Fear, worry and depression cannot survive physical activity. Theodore Roosevelt, a two time President of the United States, who suffered occasional depression is recorded as saying, 'Black Care rarely sits behind a rider whose pace is fast enough.' This pithily sums up the fact that worry and depression cannot survive action; it is inactivity that fosters and nurtures these unhealthy states. Doctors are now coming to realise that physical activity can be of considerable benefit to those who are depressed. The energy required in physical activity releases endorphins which act upon the brain and the nervous system in a positive and helpful way reducing and, on occasion, eliminating the feeling of depression. For this is what depression is – an all pervading feeling that flattens and demotivates. That makes life a burden and torments us with feelings of vulnerability and inadequacy. Activity works on this state by changing how we feel. It releases our internalised energy to work externally on our behalf.

People who are depressed often have little energy or motivation; they become less active. People with severe depression may have difficulty with even simple things such as getting out of bed and getting dressed in the morning, attending to their personal hygiene, feeding themselves, etc. As a result the depression feeds upon itself and deepens, their immune system is lowered and they become prey to sickness and infection. Simple daily activities such as shopping, gardening, helping others and even simple domestic tasks can be of enormous benefit to a depressed person. Going for a walk, or going to get a newspaper from the local shop, any simple activity is likely to be of benefit.

Physical activity doesn't have to be strenuous to be of help, just simple gentle activity will pay dividends very quickly. As well as the sense of achievement that results from the activity, the physical improvements that follow on behind will soon become apparent. It is well recognised medically that the less you do the worse you feel. This is the reason why hospitals try to get patients out of bed and physically active as quickly as possible. Even if it is only sitting out of bed on an adjacent chair, it is strongly encouraged. This is not just to counter the risk of bed sores developing, but as importantly to get the patient's system moving again. To lift their spirits by starting the steps to return them to the everyday world.

Physical activity refers to any activity that uses energy. Walking, cycling, climbing stairs, housework, shopping all have their advantages. As fitness improves, planned exercise such as longer walks, cycling, aerobics, dance or active hobbies such as gardening and competitive sports will undoubtedly help.

Mental activity involves any activity that involves concentration to the degree that all other thoughts are put to one side. Crosswords, jigsaws, chess, writing, painting, poetry, literally any mental activity that requires concentration to the exclusion of all else will have a beneficial result in lifting depression or reducing worry.

Recent studies have shown that physical activity reduces clinical depression and can be as effective as traditional treatments such as psychotherapy. Regular physical activity can also reduce the risk of depression recurring. Physical activity has been shown to improve psychological well-being in people who are not suffering from mental disorders, but are simply down and feeling low. Hundreds of studies have documented improvements in subjective well-being, mood and emotions, and self-perceptions such as body image, physical self-worth and self-esteem.

David Jones the Chairman of the Next retail chain and Deputy

Chairman of the Morrison's supermarket group suffers from Parkinson's disease. The effects of which cause him considerable physical distress and limitation. Simple things like getting dressed and putting on his tie and his socks are often beyond him. He takes up to forty pills a day in an attempt to keep his symptoms at bay. Yet in spite of this he holds down very demanding business roles. He explained recently that there are two David Jones, one the high-powered business executive who is much admired and respected for his business acumen and record of success, and the other one with Parkinson's disease. Many people with David Jones's range of physical limitations would have retired on disability benefit years ago, yet he demonstrates that action really is the solution, by keeping busy and mentally active he keeps his severe condition at bay – a role model for us all.

Action really can be the solution to problems, worries and difficulties. Inaction that results in focusing on the problems or perceived difficulties only energises, deepens and worsens them and reinforces the sense of helplessness that these states bring in their wake. Similar effects result when we are feeling sick or low. Many famous performers have commented on how, even though they are feeling sick and low before a performance, once they go on to the stage and start their act they become alive. Their symptoms drop away, they literally lose themselves in their work. Elvis Presley once said that even at his lowest moments performing was a miracle drug that healed him instantly; at the later stages of his life he said that the only time he came truly alive was when he was onstage.

I have noticed through my life a similar phenomena when running seminars or when making presentations to clients or prospective clients. When called upon to 'perform', all cares, worries, fears and feelings of ill-health disappear. I move into another mode, my mind becoming focused on my work, I forget my body, any physical pain felt is pushed into the background.

Action truly is the solution, with inaction simply exacerbating any symptoms of illness we may be feeling. Whilst inactive we have nothing to do but focus on our symptoms and how bad we may feel. In so doing we energise these to a greater degree. Starved of energy through action, the symptoms often fade into the background.

Jack Dee the well-known dour, deadpan British comedian was recently reported as saying, 'If I am not busy, I can get low. I need to be physically busy and have lots going on in my life. I don't have a great concentration span but I need to go and see films regularly, I like to have a good book on the go. I don't like to be on a car journey without a newspaper. I like to have some input at all times. I don't like the idea of wasting time.' He needs to spend his energy rather than letting it feed on him.

Viktor Frankl has told of how prisoners in the concentration camps with him who had been judges, doctors and lawyers, who previous to their incarceration had led lives of luxury, lost physical symptoms that had plagued them for years. Some had, previous to their extreme change in circumstances, been fussy eaters, suffering from ulcers and problems with their digestion. The enormous change to their life circumstances brought about by being held in the concentration camps where they were forced to struggle for their very existence, led to their preparedness to eat anything they could lay their hands on without a thought for their digestion systems. Their focus had changed and so had their physical symptoms. They could not afford to be fussy about what they ate, not if they wanted to survive. The rules of the game had changed and they either changed with them or died.

Frankl also speaks of the 'existential vacuum' that is often found in the lives of those suffering from feelings of depression and a lack of self-worth. He coined this term to describe the feeling that depressed people have who feel that nothing in their life has any meaning or value. Who feel that their life is meaningless. Action gives a sense of purpose to life. It can indeed have a very beneficial effect on those who are feeling depressed and low. It can fill any vacuum and provide life with real meaning. For it is very difficult to be busy and depressed at the same time.

This does not mean that we should not continue to seek for a deeper meaning in our lives beyond that of just being busy. That we should not look beyond the superficiality of books, films, television, etc. for meaning in our lives. For these amusements can be but distractions from the real purpose of life to grow and become more than we are; to aim at all times to reach our full potential. But taking action is the way to start to combat feelings of worry and depression. Only when we have reached a stable platform in our life and are on solid ground, can we go further and explore the deeper meanings behind our existence. For this is a journey that all thinking people are compelled to make at some time and that, at its most fundamental level, can only be travelled alone.

So be busy and be happy. Find meaning through your work and in being of service to others and to mankind. Fill your corner of the world with a sense of purpose, and through such activity, add meaning and joy to your life and the lives of those close to you.

## Work and Creativity

Men and women are creative beings. This instinctual desire to be creative must be met if happiness is to ensue, for we are endowed with constructive energy; creativity is our natural state. Where the drive to create is frustrated, or not expended, serious damage can result to our health and well-being. As the old saying goes: 'The Devil makes work for idle hands'. Energy, and life in its most basic form is energy, will not be denied. It must be effectively utilised and discharged. Energy seeks shape and form; it creates constantly, it knows no other way. Undirected, or misdirected energy, does not cease to create – it just creates destructively. Boredom is a state of internally directed energy to be avoided at all costs if we are seriously concerned about our short and our long-term health. For energy that is not directed externally will go to work internally and can result in illness and poor health.

Universal Law instils in us an internal drive to strive at all times to attain our highest potential. This Law drives us to seek meaning in our life. As Viktor Frankl wrote:

> Man's search for meaning is the primary motivation in his life and not a 'secondary rationalisation' of instinctual drives. This meaning is unique and specific in that it must and can be fulfilled by him alone.

The first way in which Frankl believed that people find meaning is through creative work. He argued that the true meaning of life is to be discovered in the world, rather than within man. Being truly human, Frankl argued, means being directed to something, or someone other than oneself, a meaning to fulfil, or another person to encounter. Interacting with others in the world of work enables this aspect of life meaning to be achieved most readily. As Abraham Maslow, who developed the concept known as 'Maslow's theory of needs' wrote:

> *the business of self actualisation can best be carried out via a commitment to an important job.*

Many people find their identity through their work with their self-image being rooted in their working identity. When this is lost through retirement, redundancy, sickness or any other life changing catastrophe they can quickly spiral down into depression which, on occasion, leads to suicide. For with work comes self-esteem and self-worth. Status in the family and the community. Income, independence and self-respect. With a loss of work all of these are at risk.

Work; purposeful activity, meets the internal drives identified by Frankl as the 'will to meaning'; the 'will to power', and the 'will to money' are met all at one and the same time. These internal drives are present in all. But what is meant by creative work? For not all work can be deemed as pleasurable. Indeed much of it can be mind numbingly boring and tedious. For work includes chores and daily routine slog, as well as satisfying potentially self-enhancing activities.

My Uncle Ernest constantly told me when I was young, that the art of happiness in life was 'through turning chores into pleasure'. For chores, like taxes, are with us always. Life doesn't only consist of the highs that come from achieving those things that have the potential to bring with them acclaim, recognition and fortune. These can be described as the peak of the pyramid, the base more often consists of daily and weekly repetitive chores. The dishes must be washed, the house cleaned, the washing done and ironed. The dog must be walked and the children delivered to and collected from school, the rubbish taken out regularly. Food must be purchased to replenish the fridge and the larder. The job of chauffeuring becomes a regular feature of any parent's life, and seems to go on for years. Even the artist must gather together the implements and tools of his trade. Must purchase paint and paper before he can commence his masterpiece. The brushes must be cleaned after each session and the excess paint removed from wherever it has fallen. All of life's activities involve constant ongoing routine daily chores without which the highs of life would not be possible.

What changes chores into pleasure is through importing into them meaning. When chores become imbued with meaning they can become purposeful. For the artist, the work put into the effective preparation of the work can make the difference between a masterpiece and an ordinary piece of art. Between something which dazzles and captures all who view it rather than simply becoming differently patterned wallpaper. The preparation for painting has been described by many respected artists as the most important part of any painting. When chores gain meaning, they gain purpose. Without meaning they remain just unrelieved slog.

How then can meaning be given to the mundane? It is all very well for those involved in creative, self-satisfying activities to talk of job satisfaction. But what of the boring, the dirty and the mundane. Frankl points the way with one of his stories of helping people through his clinical work. He told of counselling an old woman who lived alone, a woman who was close to the end of her life. She was overwhelmed by a feeling that her life had been wasted and without purpose. She had not married, had no children or grandchildren. She was as she saw it unwanted; her life had been of no value, it was, as she saw it, devoid of meaning. These thoughts depressed and overwhelmed her.

On questioning her, Frankl discovered, that she had spent her life in the service of others. She had been a live-in nanny, and in this capacity had worked for three families. In her working life she had brought a total of fifteen children from infancy to adulthood. Frankl asked her whether all of the children were now functioning normally in the world. She answered affirmatively, and with some pride that all were prospering, and that many were themselves bringing up families. He then asked the woman if any of the children kept in touch with her, she replied that they did. That they remembered her at Christmas and she was often invited to christenings and other family events.

Frankl told her that her life, far from lacking meaning, had instead been very meaningful. She had contributed significantly to the development of all of the children who had been in her charge. Whilst most parents raised three or four children she had raised fifteen. A very significant contribution to society. Frankl told her that the fact that she was invited to social gatherings involving her late charges showed that far from seeing her as an old family retainer, these children, who had now grown to adulthood, were clearly fond of her and valued the influence that she had given to their lives. Instead of lacking meaning, her life had been full of meaning and purpose. This knowledge, once fully accepted by the woman, resolved her depression and enabled her to live out her remaining years with a sense of satisfaction and pride in her life's work.

Without the chores of life, the highs of life would not be possible. The pleasure of a well-tended summer garden would not be possible without much back-aching work. A good meal requires preparation; the pleasure a cook receives from watching guests enjoying the resultant meal can make the work involved in preparing and cooking it well worthwhile. The satisfaction felt often in direct proportion to the effort expended. A pride can be taken in work however mundane the task, and this sense of pride will translate into increased satisfaction. When my eldest son told me that he intended to be a 'Bum'. I replied that he should aim to be the best 'Bum' in the world! Not just any ordinary 'Bum', but one that others would aspire to.

We can not always choose our work; economic pressures and demands often choose it for us, we can, however, always choose our attitude towards our work. We can either give it our full attention and our energy, or withhold it. I remember that when recruiting staff the key ingredient I was looking for was not qualifications, it was a good attitude. Candidates whose personal attitude was positive, who were enthusiastic and keen to grow, these qualities would mark them out above even the highest qualified candidates. For I had learnt through many years in business that if the attitude was right then I could add the other skills I needed for them to be successful in their work. But if their attitude was poor, then no amount of training would change it.

Only we can give meaning to our daily activities. Can take pride in what we do, however mundane. Such meaning can be had by the setting of life objectives and personal goals. When chores are seen as necessary steps on the path to achieving a worthwhile goal, then meaning automatically flows to them. However, only we can establish the goals that are important and meaningful to us. For it is our overall life objectives that are important. If we aim to be the best at whatever we do. If we aim to ensure that every task we undertake is undertaken in a manner determined to achieve the most successful outcome, then the results will always give us satisfaction. We cannot all be surgeons, lawyers, barristers, successful business executives, etc.; the majority of us will not have the opportunity or even intellectual ability to reach the heights of society. And this perhaps is just as well, for without the base of the pyramid, the foundation on which all is anchored, the peak would not be supported.

Those who drive the lorries that supply our daily need for food and energy. Those who repair and clean our roads, our public places, our hospitals and our schools. These are the unsung heroes of our society for they ensure that the very fabric of society is maintained and preserved. If they should cease to function, then we would be in a pretty pickle. We can survive without accountants, and lawyers and many other specialists. We would, however, quickly feel the pain if the water did not flow from our taps, or our power supply failed, or our supermarket shelves were empty. Regrettably we often fail to give the respect and recognition due to those who ensure that the myriad mundane tasks needed to ensure that 'the wheels of our world' turn smoothly, actually happen.

It is all too easy for management to fail to recognise that people have different objectives for working. Some are driven by career objectives, others work for purely economic reasons. Some for the company of others, for the social aspect of work, still others for 'pin' money. I once employed a very able and talented ex-headmaster who told me that he did not want any managerial responsibility in his new job. He did not want to be a 'key holder' or have responsibility for other staff. He was content to fill a routine administrative role which he did very successfully until his retirement. He had had his fill of being responsible for the management of an establishment, for the direction and motivation of staff. In the modern argot: 'He had been there, done that and earned the T-shirt.'

When I ran my own business, I quickly recognised that a sales person did not go out to achieve the sales targets that I set for them – to meet sales targets derived from my budgets. They achieved sales to meet their own personal life goals. It was important therefore for me to understand what these goals were. For unless their personal goals matched my business goals, there was going to be a gap in sales achievement. Staff did not sell for me, they sold for themselves and their families and in order to meet their own aspirations. Some were happy to tick over, seemingly content simply to meet their regular economic outgoings. Others desired to make enough money to send their children to better schools, or buy a bigger house, or take expensive holidays. This latter group were easy to motivate through bonus and commission schemes. The former were a much more challenging proposition. For unless I could get them to lift their horizons, they would not lift their sales. Management then became an exercise in motivation, and sometimes the motivation was not financial, it was in perceived status, or company-wide recognition. Different motivation for different people.

Where work meets personal objectives then, ultimately, it will be satisfying. Where work is simply a means to meet Maslow's famous hierarchy of needs: food, shelter, warmth, etc. then there needs to be some other area of life that will fill the creative need with which each is imbued. For unless this is so, unhappiness and boredom will result. For those who undertake mundane work, activities outside of work often feed their creative urge. Hobbies, sports and other satisfying pastimes can, and do fill the innate urge to be creative and fulfilled thus enabling self actualisation.

When I look back on my working career, I see that the times when I was energised most was when I was following my inner intuition. My gut feel; my internal compass. When I was striving to fill my goals as an individual. Striving to reach my maximum potential. Not goals set by society or family, but rather those which resonated with the 'inner me'. At such times I would work whatever hours were necessary to meet them. The clock and calendar became irrelevant. I worked with a single-minded intensity that recognised space only for food and sleep. Some contemporaries described me then, and still do today, as a 'workaholic'. I did not try to convince them that the whole meaning of my life at this time was achieved through my work. I do not seek to compare myself with others who have been so described. But we all know those who work to becoming the best that they can in be in their chosen field. Whether they be heart transplant surgeons, scientists, business executives, or who hold less exalted positions in society. It is their single-minded pursuit of their goals that marks them out as special. Their desire to be the best that they can be in their field. Who so focus their energy on their work that they achieve remarkable things.

Work gives us our opportunity to fulfil the creative drive within us. Where such opportunity is frustrated or denied, then serious life challenging issues can result. For unless we channel our energy constructively; unless we find ways in which our life can be made meaningful, then existential angst results. The operation of Universal Law, our need to strive to achieve our highest potential in our life is a fundamental need. Many, many illnesses and diseases, both mental and physical respond to work in a manner far superior to medication. Those who lead purposeful, fulfilled lives, live healthier lives than those whose choices have led them in the opposite direction. For with work comes satisfaction, personal pride and the elevation of self-esteem. Outcomes which no psychiatrist or doctor would deny do other than improve health and sense of well-being.

## Attitude

Attitude – the big 'A'. Victor Frankl, writing in *The Doctor and the Soul*, stated that adopting the right attitude is the most important step that any individual can take in facing up to a lack of meaning in their life. In dealing with the 'existential vacuum' which is at the heart of many psychological problems. A feeling that life is meaningless, of little value, lacks worth and purpose.

Frankl's whole therapeutic approach was based on the fundamental need to find meaning in life. He claimed this 'will to meaning', as the major instinctual drive in humans, which if not fulfilled led inevitably to significant personal life issues arising. I equate this drive to the first Universal Law that states that at all times we seek to achieve our maximum potential.

To attain balance in life we must learn to develop coping mechanisms to deal with the 'existential triad' that is part and parcel of being human, namely: suffering, guilt, and death. Frankl argued that these can only effectively be dealt with by finding meaning in life, a reason to live. People can find such meaning in life in three distinct ways. The first is through creative work, work which enables them to give to the world, such as through vocation, career, etc. The second way outlined by Frankl, is meaning obtained experientially, meaning obtained from the world through art, beauty and by the values experienced in nature, culture and love. The third way being through the attitude that is adopted to personal circumstances and life.

Of these three categories of meaning Frankl stresses the third, attitude, as being the most important because it is the one which most addresses all of life circumstances, no matter what these may be. We cannot always choose our life circumstances, sometimes it appears as if we have no control over the events and happenings in our life, as if we are tossed hither and thither by events over which we have no direct control. At such times, whilst we may feel helpless to direct and control these events, we can always control and determine our attitude towards them. Our attitude is always individually ours to choose. We can decide to be happy or sad; to be open or closed in our dealings with others. To be positive or negative; to complain, or get up and do something about that which we are complaining.

Any employer or teacher will tell you that the thing that marks an employee, or student, out as special from all others is their attitude. Not intellectual ability or skill level, but attitude. I would suggest that the major factor that makes for success in life is adopting the right attitude. The person who approaches life in a positive, cheerful and helpful manner, no matter what they are engaged in or doing, irrespective of their circumstances, will be the type of person employers want in their businesses and teachers in their classrooms.

We can determine our attitude towards our life at all times. Whether we are performing brain surgery or wiping somebody's bottom. Whether we are a captain of industry, or a bottle washer. Whether we are healthy, or confined to a hospital bed or a wheelchair. The attitude we adopt towards our work, calling or personal circumstances is always ours to choose. As such, it will always be the major factor influencing our happiness or misery.

I am reminded here of the time when I was working as the

Personnel Manager in a major truck manufacturing plant in Dunstable, Bedfordshire. We were experiencing a period of difficult industrial relations with production being interrupted daily by strikes and other forms of industrial action. I was at the time spending the major portion of my working days in meetings with Union Representatives, trying to resolve the many grievances and problems that were preventing the smooth running of the assembly lines.

As I walked through the Trim Shop one day, I was confronted by one of the Union Representatives. He was wearing filthy overalls covered in what appeared to be a black tarry substance. Around his neck were goggles similarly splashed and on his head was a dirty skull cap. The man asked me if I would come with him to view his working area. My heart sank as I presumed that I was about to be met with a litany of complaints about working conditions, or similar problems. I could not have been farther from the truth. Leading me to an area where the assembly track took the partly-assembled vehicles above head height exposing the underside of the vehicle, he explained that this was where he worked, and indeed had done so for the past ten years. His job it seemed, consisted of spraying the underside of the vehicles with the black tarry substance that covered him, in order to seal the underside of the vehicle thus protecting it from the exposure it would receive from the weather, road salt, etc.

It became apparent that far from complaining about his work or working conditions, the man was showing me this filthy dirty job with a sense of pride. He explained that few other workers were prepared to undertake the task. The majority avoided it like the plague – not surprisingly – but he went out of his way to ensure that he remained doing this work, even resisting transfers to other more congenial working areas. His job satisfaction and pride in his work came from carrying out a job that most shied away from. From being prepared to spend his days doing work that most people found objectionable. The attitude that he displayed towards his job was remarkable and was an object lesson to me in the fact that even the most menial and grim tasks can give pleasure, where the attitude adopted by those who carry them out is positive and constructive.

The importance of instructing young people in the skills necessary to give their life meaning cannot be over emphasised. Parents, guardians, teachers, all should ensure that this most essential part of their charges' education is not missed. Should strive to ensure that the importance of undertaking constructive, creative work that is of service to others, coupled with an appreciation of good books, music, art and an appreciation of nature is understood. By good books and music I do not necessarily mean the classics, it can be popular and stimulating magazines and music. Nature as experienced through local wild life, travel and holidays. Whatever appeals to the age and the culture of the moment. But the importance of adopting and perfecting an attitude of positive openness and enthusiasm is by far the most important attribute that they should strive to influence and encourage in their charges through teaching and mentoring. For the right attitude, when adopted, can and will make the difference between a life fulfilled and a life spent depressed and in seeming futility. Once we have succeeded in this task we can truly 'let go of the bicycle saddle' and let those for whom we are responsible, ride off into their own life, to become fulfilled and happy adults, capable of managing the vicissitudes that life will inevitably bring to them, for attitude does indeed govern all.

## Freedom from Attachment

Attachment is fear in operation. Fear that unless we hold on tight we will lose what we have. A belief in lack, limitation and poverty; such beliefs limit, shackle and imprison.

Ridding ourselves of attachment does not mean giving things up and becoming a wandering yogi, far from it. Rather, it means continuing to enjoy them but with a recognition of the reality that we never really possess anything or anyone, we just have their use or company for a while. For as we came naked and alone into the world, naked and alone we will leave it. An acceptance of the law that states that: in order to acquire something we must first learn to let it go – is very difficult to learn and practise, but essential if we are to enjoy all of the riches that life has to offer. For in seeking to retain, to hold on to that which we have, however little this may be, we are demonstrating our belief in lack and limitation, and thus inhabiting the free flow of creativity, to us and through us.

In late summer 2005, hurricane Katrina devastated the southern states of America and made inhabitable the city of New Orleans. A city I remember with affection for it was there that Linda and I were married in 1990. This ferocious hurricane with winds exceeding 150mph breached the levées which held back the waters surrounding the city. Once these were breached, the flood waters poured in and caused extensive destruction and loss of life.

As I write, the final tally of deaths is yet to be known, although estimates vary from as few as 250 deaths to as high as 10,000, this latter figure being considered widely unrealistic.

When I surveyed the graphic images on television, I was moved by the harrowing stories of those who had lost everything, homes, cars, possessions, even jobs where workplaces had been destroyed. The natural world was, apart from a few trees that had been blown down, intact. Nature would within a relatively short time replace these. I would have been less than human if I had not imagined how I would react to such a disaster in my life.

The major destruction was to man-made structures and possessions. The devastated victims understandably had difficulty seeing past their immediate loss. Their immediate needs reinforcing Maslow's 'theory of needs'. The need for supplies of fresh food and water, medication, clothing, shelter, warmth and security was paramount. Like all humans, their external lives in physical form depending so much on those things which make life comfortable, safe and secure. Until these fundamentals were met little else mattered.

This disaster made me realise that those things the victims had lost they would ultimately lose, for no man takes his possessions with him after death. And that these material things, whilst essential for civilised life, have purpose only in so much as they enable us to live comfortably in physical form. Abraham Maslow's theory of needs postulates that once our basic needs, which could be further described as our animal needs are satisfied, we move on to seek to fulfil our higher needs. The need to be loved, to have companionship, self-esteem, etc. He believed that the final needs that human beings must fill if they are to be fully satisfied in life are their real growth needs.

These needs Maslow called 'Self Actualising' needs. This, he claimed, is the instinctual need of all human beings to make the most of their unique abilities. He described this need as follows:

> *A musician must make music, the artist must paint, the poet must write, if he is to be ultimately at peace with himself. What a man can be he must be. For this is self actualisation.*

Complete satisfaction and contentment in life, Maslow argued, can only be achieved through each filling their own unique purpose. Where this need is not met there is the risk that the resulting vacuum will create what he described as 'Metapathologies'. These are in effect the opposite in many ways to those things that bring about self actualisation. They form attitudes that lead to feelings of bleakness and depression, hatred and distrust, selfishness and the breakdown of the natural moral order. Many symptoms which can be recognised as evident realities in our world today. Nature abhors a vacuum and, unless the needs of self actualisation are met, the human condition deteriorates to a greater or lesser degrees irrespective of the possession of things.

Victor Frankl in his excellent book *The Will to Meaning* speaks of those he worked with who society would consider successful. Doctors, surgeons lawyers, bankers, successful people yet who saw little or no meaning in their lives. People who were successful by every conventional measure, yet who were in despair because their lives seemed hollow and empty without depth or meaning. Frankl believed that finding meaning in life irrespective of external circumstances was the only path to true fulfilment and 'happiness'. Finding meaning in even the lowliest of tasks and occupations; finding meaning even from failure. Our attitudinal values are what count in the long run. Our response to the circumstances and reality of our life. This, he argued, would give true meaning to life. Greater meaning than could ever be achieved by the ownership of things.

These attributes were everlasting and would survive even the fiercest hurricane or natural disaster. For from these attributes a new world could be built; a world worth bequeathing to our children. The absence of these attributes, Frankl argued, would lead to the growth of a world full of problems, wars and criminal activity.

In *The Barbanell Report*, referred to in the final section of this book, which sets out the communications that purported to come from Maurice Barbanell after his death, he describes his passage in the world beyond:

> *Personal relationships and attachment to things hold us back from advancement. We must learn to let go if we are to grow and become more in the world of spirit.*

In essence we must love and enjoy, but not cling. We must seek detachment, rather than attachment.

Achieving a state of detachment as opposed to attachment, comes through developing an unquestioning belief in the natural law of supply. This law states that whatever we need will be given to us in exactly the right measure for our specific and particular needs, exactly when we need it. Attachment comes from fear and insecurity, from a belief in lack and limitation. Attachment is holding on to the known in a belief that this is all that there is. It does not allow for the flow and fluidity of life, the passing of the old and the coming into being of the new. It creates barriers, for beliefs create directly in their image. Put simply, it demonstrates a belief in lack, limitation and poverty and thus creates a poverty consciousness. A poverty consciousness can only create lack and limitation for this is Universal Law in action.

Through working to develop a 'plenty' attitude and a meaningful self actualising life, we deny any belief in lack, limitation and a meaningless Universe. We affirm our belief in the benefice of the

Universe, in our value as individual expressions of the creator of all. We validate the natural laws of creativity and supply. We demonstrate our belief in the endless creativity of the Universe that seeks always our growth, development and well-being. We eliminate the need for attachment for we come to realise that we already possess all that we shall ever need in this life or beyond. This then is real and lasting self actualisation. Freedom from attachment is an essential goal for those who truly wish to grow and become more than they are.

## Sex, Drugs, Drink and Spirituality

Sex, drugs, drink and spirituality, an odd combination, yet each in its own way used to seek to create an elusive state where the cares and worries of the world can be replaced by ecstasy, bliss and the blotting out of reality. A loss of self, an escape from the reality and pressures of day to day life.

The ways that people behave sexually is infinite. Vast swathes of books have been written on the subject. Films and documentaries abound where the main topic is sex and the myriad experiences which spin out around it. To many, the sex act it is a natural part of sharing and bonding with no intent to procreate; an act of pleasure and intimacy, a casual pleasure to be indulged in without commitment. To others, it is an exercise in power, ownership, personal gratification and selfishness. To some, a commodity to be bought and sold.

Where the sexual act is an integral part of a loving relationship, it undoubtedly strengthens the bond between the partners by giving a greater expression to their love. The intimacy of the physical experience providing an opportunity to express the intensity of their love for one another; an intense interpersonal explosive moment when two can become one. The sexual bonding and the magic moment of orgasm eliminating separation. In such moments the sense of self is lost in the intensity of orgasm The experience mirroring our innate yearning for the loss of self that reunion with the source of our being will bring.

Even the client of the prostitute, who merely seeks to use another to release their sexual frustration, is mirroring the need to experience the momentary loss of self that orgasm brings. Sexual activity takes many forms. Some perverse; but behind them all is an inner yearning to experience pleasure and the loss of self that sexual union and sexual acts bring with them. Society judges sexual activity according to its cultural standards. But the seeking to experience the highs of sexual pleasure are part and parcel of the yearning to reach beyond the mundane and experience the height of physical transcendence.

Sex serves many needs; the crescendo experience that is felt at the moment of orgasm can be considered as the top of the pinnacle. Yet it is not necessary to climb to the top each time, nor to be disappointed if you do not get there. There are many lovely experiences to be had along the way. Some offering comfort, some warmth and understanding; some just giving love through intimacy and sharing; each valid in its own way.

Sexual union provides the opportunity to come together with another as in no other way. It has been described as: 'the biological gateway to the truth'. The ways of approaching this gateway are many – the purposes for coming to the gate are multitudinous. But once at the gateway those who perceive will realise that at this time there is a blending of the inner and the outer aspects of life. To pass through the gateway is to unify – to transcend the physical, albeit briefly, through the sexual experience.

Many seek mystical, out-of-body experiences through taking mind-altering drugs and substances. From cocaine and ecstasy to heroin and its derivatives. Seek the highs that these chemicals will bring; the loss of inhibition, the temporary removal from day to day problems and reality through entering drug induced states. The physical risks involved being ignored. There is no doubt that much petty crime is the result of people seeking to feed their addictive drug habit. Drug-taking and criminal activity seem to go hand in hand with many lives being destroyed by the invasive and pernicious effects of using these alien addictive chemicals.

Then there is our old friend alcohol. Present throughout recorded history. Few tales of debauchery and excess are not linked to consumption of this most addictive of substances. Taken in moderation, an undoubted pleasure enhancer. Taken in excess, as destructive as any chemical drug-taking. The disease of alcoholism destroying families, marriages and lives. With only complete abstinence providing release from its tentacles of addiction. Many an alcoholic has described how alcohol provided a crutch that got them through the day. Blotted out their fears and pain. Fed their confidence and released their inhibitions with the highs of drunkenness providing them brief solace from their worries and woes. Drunkenness providing escape from the cares of the world. Escape from reality into the haze that excess consumption of alcohol brings.

Strangely also others seek to lose themselves in their religion. Seeking to enrich their life with meaning through spiritual involvement. Many sects encouraging dancing, swaying, chanting, speaking in tongues and other trance states in order to achieve the resultant highs that can be experienced. Sex, drugs, alcohol and the excesses of spirituality being used to achieve moments of physical transcendence. Seeking to go beyond the physicality of daily life, reaching for more, however achieved.

The separation from the source of our being as set out in Genesis, the first chapter of the Bible, has left a constant yearning behind; a hunger for moving beyond the physical and reunifying with the source of our being. As the adult remembers the womb and the warm embrace of their mother so this yearning to return to our source can lead the seeker down strange paths. It is hard to see the drug addict and the alcoholic bracketed with the sex addict and the spiritualist as such seekers. Yet in a perverse way this is what is happening. Each seeking to immerse themselves in the all too brief oblivion of ecstasy and the separation from self that results; each seeking to re-experience that lost, yet yearned for, unity with the source of their being.

This yearning to return to our source is buried deep within the psyche of us all. Like a magnet it constantly draws us to back. Like the yearning for the womb; no matter how we may try to disguise it or avoid it, seeking to alleviate its constant pull; it remains. It will not; cannot, be satisfied in any other way than through our ultimate return. Through lifetime after lifetime; through pleasure seeking, addictions and power – whatever route we take, all will ultimately disappoint us. For this is the way that it is; our destiny being to search until we satisfy the root of our longing and return ultimately from whence we came.

What matters time? What matters centuries? What matter aeons? There are no measures in eternity. No matter how long we wander; how far our search; whether it be into the outer reaches of space or into the depths of our oceans we shall never find satisfaction, for ultimate satisfaction can only be found through reunification with our source. The foundation of all life; the source of universal energy.

## The Nature of Evil

Accepting that we create all within our world for experiential and growth purposes, obeying the first law of being, which is that consciousness always seeks its greatest potential, can help us to look at all behaviour, no matter how erratic or bizarre. However, it immediately brings with it certain problems. What, for instance, is the purpose of evil? Indeed, what is evil?

C.S. Lewis in his excellent book *Mere Christianity* explores the concept of evil through a number of well-reasoned arguments. The contents of this book were first delivered on the radio by him through the period 1941–1943, in the midst of the Second World War. He asks:'If God made the world why has it gone wrong?' Lewis's argument against God was that the Universe seemed so cruel and unjust. But he asks:

> *How had I got this idea of just and unjust? A man does not call a line crooked unless he has some idea of a straight line. What was I comparing this Universe with when I called it unjust?*

He concludes this part of his argument by saying:

> *If there were no light in the Universe and therefore no creatures with eyes, we should never know it was dark. 'Dark' would be a word without meaning.*

So the very idea of evil must spring from an innate – and in Lewis's eyes, God-given – concept of right and wrong, good and bad.

Even without this inbuilt idea of right and wrong I think we can go further and say that any behaviour which is outside of what is considered normal, or to put it another way tribally acceptable, arouses in us strong feelings as it threatens the status quo that we (society at large) have collectively established and individually accepted. As a result an objective unbiased analysis of bizarre and unusual behaviour becomes difficult to conduct because of the strong feelings such behaviour arouses within us. It can, however, be of value to explore all behaviour, no matter how unusual or unsavoury, to obtain a better understanding of it. In particular, the complex and seemingly imponderable question of the nature and purpose of evil. If the assertion that we create all has validity, then we are led inexorably to the conclusion that all that occurs in our world has purpose, including evil. A further examination of this possibility is not then without merit. The words of Charles Bernard Renouvier come to mind here: 'Life can concern a thinker only as he seeks to resolve the problem of evil.'

One example of what could, using the norms of our society, be described as evil can be judged by the outrage that arises following the discovery that a father has sexually abused his children, indeed paedophilia in general. We recoil in horror from the thought of such an abuse of parental power of adult trust and responsibility. We demand the maximum punishment for such people. Should the man (and it is nearly always a man) concerned be imprisoned, and we are outraged if he is not, then almost certainly he will spend the majority of his sentence in solitary confinement because of the real risk of assault that exists from other prisoners. A paedophile has gone beyond what even the criminal world believes is acceptable behaviour. No laws are required here, the norms of social behaviour have been breached and these have a higher standing in the eyes of all citizens, including those who have been imprisoned, than the laws of the land.

History shows that these norms of social behaviour, however, can change radically from culture to culture: for instance among the Trobianders of New Guinea and the Nama Hottentots of Southern Africa it was the practice for sexual relationships between adults and children to be actively encouraged. In these cultures older men occasionally copulated with girls as young as eight years of age. The Keriaki of New Guinea practised sodomy as a part of their puberty rites, firmly believing that sodomising young boys was a healthy and necessary part of their maturation. Whilst these ancient cultures represent a minority of all cultures they show how beliefs can make 'normal', behaviour that would be considered as 'evil' in other societies.

In these minority cultures a child sexually inducted into the norms of the culture would not have been considered to have been psychologically scarred for life by such sexual practices. Indeed, it was believed by the prevailing culture that a failure to act towards children in this way would have been a gross dereliction of duty. Yet within Western culture any child treated in accordance with the 'norms' of these historical minority cultures would be described as psychologically damaged as the result of such sexual usage. And the cultural beliefs, having been accepted by the child, would inevitably lead to such mental scarring. The belief then creating its mental counterpart in physical form.

In certain minority cultures it was accepted that it was a father's responsibility to instruct his daughter in sexual matters. Such instruction would include full and frequent sexual intercourse. A father who failed to carry out such training would by his society's standards be considered to have failed in his responsibility as a parent. The inhabitants of these cultures would have had very real difficulties in understanding the thinking of a civilisation or society that condemned such behaviour. There would have been much puzzlement and scratching of heads at the thought that our standards, or norms, were the correct ones, and theirs were evil.

The thought provoking book entitled *Unknown Man* by Yatri, describes man as a humanoid living only through past programming and feeling comfortable only in the 'non existential'. In living through memory tapes which are repeatable and not subject to change. As a humanoid 'he' is a perfectionist, 'he' wants things to conform exactly to 'his' programme. Anything which threatens this programming must be eradicated. From such programming it is easy to see how the determination of what passes for 'evil' can arise. It will be any behaviour that wilfully flies in the face of the predominant accepted behavioural norms of the culture concerned. It is true that in most cultures that have been studied, from the most primitive to the most advanced, there are understandings about what passes for wrongful behaviour that seem to bridge all cultural divides. Violence against the person, unless prescribed by law, theft or damage to another's property or possessions, and so on.

Yet if we see all in a state of becoming: if we see all as a part of an integrated whole, which above all has purpose, both individually and collectively, then our perception of behaviour that is non-conformist, that can be considered as 'evil' undergoes profound change. We learn through experiencing, therefore, we must have the potential to experience all if we are to know all. If pain has a purpose, then it has a purpose both for society as a whole, as well as for the individual. Generally speaking, evil is considered as actions that cause pain, harm or suffering to another, and which thereby threatens the safety and security of all members of society, even the perpetrators of the evil acts should the occurrences happen to them.

Further study shows that evil is usually a perversion of that which is deemed by society as 'good'. Sexual union between a man and a woman is recognised as good by society. The drive behind sexual activity is the pleasure that it provides to the participants coupled with the need to procreate, a basic instinctual need inbuilt into all creatures, including humans. Yet this seeking after sexual pleasure can also lead to perverted sexual practices. To paedophilia, to rape, to bestiality, to necrophilia, to incest. Practices which are perverted because they deviate from normal sexual activity and further because of the immense harm which they cause to their victims. But the perversion – which would be deemed by all right minded people as 'wrong' or evil, is derived originally from the 'good' sexual drive to procreate. An exploration of many evil activities and actions leads us down the same path – with the evil act being merely a perversion of a fundamental good.

We accept sickness and disease as a reality within life. We try to keep healthy, we back medical research which seeks to uncover the root causes of diseases which we do not understand. We strive to maintain a healthy balance recognising that the intrusion of harmful viruses or abnormal cellular changes can radically affect our health at any time. Many disabling diseases occur because of errant cellular behaviour, cancer being the most notable of these. If we look at humanity as a whole, and see communities and nationalities distinguished only by their national traits and behaviour patterns, if we eradicate the notion of individuality, it becomes possible to view crime, or 'evil', or other anti-social behaviour, as aberrant cellular behaviour within the body of society. Groups or individual cells within the body which are attacking the health of the whole. When this happens the body is forced by pain to recognise that it is under attack and to fight to combat this. When we fail in this we become sick, the degree of sickness dependent on the extent of cellular disorder or viral impact.

The easiest sickness to understand is that caused by invading viruses. We are under attack from external forces. Our bodies' defence mechanisms spring into action and our white blood cells attack the invader until it is overcome. Similar to attacks being launched on a nation by an invader. Occasionally we lose the battle and are invaded and taken over leading to the 'death' of the individual concerned. More often than not the invader is repelled and we survive. Far harder to understand and decide to deal with, however, is the behaviour of our own cells when they begin to malfunction. When they are triggered by causes that medical science can, in many instances, still only guess at into mutating or malfunctioning, as is the case with cancerous cells.

Similarly, it is far harder when society has to deal with crimes and hidden aberrant behaviour of its own apparently law abiding citizens. Citizens who are prepared to destroy their fellow citizens in pursuit of their own aims which they perceive as good. Terrorism and in particular suicide bombings being the most notable example of this. The individuals who partake in such crimes against their fellows as the planting of bombs or indiscriminate killing may well appear normal most of the time – indeed they would consider their own behaviour as normal when viewed through the prism of their beliefs of what constitutes good and bad. Yet society would consider such hidden behaviour as far from normal.

Yet is not most of our behaviour hidden from the view of our friends and neighbours? We can only know the inner thoughts of another by their behaviour, and most of us have become skilled at ensuring that our behaviour appears normal even when within we are having what would be considered as decidedly anti-social thoughts if they were to become known to our fellows. I believe that it was for this reason that Christ said that if a man thinks adultery, he is as guilty as the man who actually commits adultery. For we are made up of the sum total of our thoughts, even if on the surface our behaviour appears to meet the sociological and cultural norms of our group in every way.

A healthy body is one in which there is no trace of disease. Medical science tells us that this is impossible to achieve, for even a healthy body creates cancerous cells and carries with it viruses. This is a normal state for the body. The healthy body can, however, deal with such cells, and viruses, control and eliminate them. Similarly, a healthy society will have its hidden criminal element, hidden in all of us is the potential for criminality. The checks and balances in place within the community and the society, however, keep this under control in most of us. Just as with our health checks, the policing and the judiciary system are there to regulate and control such behaviour.

If we consider our society as our communal body, then criminal behaviour can be viewed as 'normal' as opposed to 'abnormal'. It would be hard to envisage a body that was always healthy and that did not at some time in its life require the services of the medical profession, so then a society that did not require policing could also be considered as abnormal.

Coming to terms with criminal behaviour in this way can help us to get such behaviour into a clearer perspective. None of us likes to be struck down by sickness or disease, particularly when we are hospitalised or disabled as a result. Likewise, none of us likes to be the victim of burglary or assault, particularly one that leads to us being injured or seriously hurt. Yet both sickness and assault can have the same effect. But we consider sickness of the body normal although inevitable; yet crime within society is not considered to be normal.

We do not put parts of our body on trial for crimes against the remainder of the body when we fall sick, our attitude is one of at worse annoyed tolerance. Yet it would be rare indeed to see such an attitude displayed toward criminal behaviour. Shock, horror, outrage is more likely to be the response.

We do not accept ill-health as something that we can do nothing about. If we are serious about combating ill-health, we will follow all of the guidelines issued by the medical profession. We will exercise and try to keep fit, we may diet to try to attain what we are told is our ideal weight. We will do all that we can to try to be and stay healthy. We can and should adopt a similar approach to criminal behaviour within our society and community. We should do all that is possible to educate, to understand, to persuade the criminal to forego their anti-social behaviour. Where we fail we should isolate the individuals concerned and follow intensified remedial regimes. But at the same time we should appreciate that it makes little sense to moralise about crime.

Every living person, every living thing is changing all of the time. The second Universal law is that energy, and consciousness is energy, is ever transforming. We are never as humans static in our behaviour patterns. We are ever transforming. No matter how hard we try we cannot live simply through past programming. New events, and new challenges are constantly being thrust upon us through the working of Universal Law: are in fact created by us for the purpose of obeying the first Universal Law that states that consciousness always seeks its greatest expression, its greatest potential.

Dr Bernie Rosen, Chief psychiatrist at the famous Guys Hospital, a good friend of mine, wrote to me recently in response to an article that I had written. He told me that almost all family and marital problems can be traced to some change point in the organisation of the group. He believes that family organisations have a natural lifecycle, which demand repeated adaptations by its members. So often he has seen apparently troubled and sick people who were bearing the difficulties of a whole group, scapegoated because the group as a whole was unable to accept change in one of its members or in its circumstances. The crucial factor, he wrote, is that all groups are in a constant state of flux seeking stability. What Bernie was saying, is that the individual patients that he treats have often demonstrated the symptoms of the group's interaction; they have not necessarily been the cause of it.

One of the reasons that we feel so strongly about criminal behaviour is not only because of the obvious threat that such behaviour poses to our own security and well-being, but also because we recognise that within each one of us lies the seeds of similar behaviour. The threat then is not only to our own security and safety, it is also insidiously challenging our own balance and ability to conform to the norms of our society. The criminal then is threatened and punished like the group member because they bear the repressed guilt and fear of the whole group.

The threat that individual criminal behaviour poses is that in threatening the status quo the criminal is forcing us to face the potential for change that we would rather not face. Our search for safety and security, for a world without fear, is grounded in our seeking for a world without change. We know inwardly that such a world can never be and so criminal behaviour, particularly if it is directed at, or threatens us, reminds us of this reality because it brings with it upheaval and change. It is this, together with the accompanying fear of violence with which we associate criminal behaviour, that we fear most of all.

If we can get through life free from threats and actual happenings that are unpleasant, then we are content. We might be bored, but we are also content. All change threatens our ability to maintain our status quo. Externally imposed change forced on us by another, particularly if it is unpleasant, as is the case with criminal behaviour, threatens our very ability to control our personal world and as such must be resisted and fought against.

As we attack viruses within our body, as we seek to maintain our individual good health, so also do we attack criminal behaviour because of the threat that it poses to us. A world without sickness would be a world without challenge and change, a sterile place. Equally, a world without criminal behaviour would be one in which we did not have to face up to the innate criminality within ourselves, would not have to face the potential for evil and destruction that lies within us all. Criminal behaviour forces us to confront these things and, thus, the reality of evil as it affects and threatens us, and as it affects our society. We can hardly ignore it when it threatens the very fabric of society and our own status quo.

This then is the underlying purpose of evil. All behaviour, all circumstance has multi-dimensional purpose. On them and through them ride the potential for becoming, for both the individual and the group. Evil is like pain, through its effects it draws our attention to the fact, to the reality, that it is harmful to us. Harmful to both the individual, irrespective of the apparent short-term gain, and harmful to the group. We do not live in isolation, we are each a part of the other. My behaviour affects my neighbour, his affects mine.

Evil then has great purpose, we live in a world of opposites, through the extremes of human behaviour we see models that help us to mould and direct our lives. The goodness of Mother Teresa on the one hand, and the evil of Hitler on the other. Each marks out for us extremes of human behaviour. An awareness of our potential for such behaviour and the judgements that we make upon it enables us subconsciously to choose. Each unknowingly instructing us through their lives. One a saint, the other a monster. Whilst these are extreme examples there is an infinite range of behaviour patterns and outcomes confronting us each day, each one adding to our instruction, each one adding to our awareness of action and consequence. Some we are directly involved in, some we are spectators to, some we merely read about or hear about through our newspapers or televisions. Each, however, influences us directly or indirectly, each then has purpose.

Purpose for the criminals who are forced to live with the awareness that their behaviour offends the majority of the population. That he or she may at any time be forced to face the consequences of his or her actions. This weight has on many occasions become too great to bear, and has led to criminals giving themselves up to the authorities to be punished for their wrong doings, in order that they can clear their consciences.

Of course there will be exceptions to this rule. Cases without number where we see criminals flaunting the benefits of their activities in front of their fellow citizens, examples that tell us apparently that crime does pay. We are frequently confronted with the spectacle of criminals boasting about their ability to live from the proceeds of their crimes.

Even here there is a working out taking place, all has purpose, and one of the purposes of this behaviour being constantly made known to us will without doubt be symbolic. Criminal behaviour represents evil to society, draws our attention to the presence and the outcomes of evil and from this awareness flows much that can, correctly used, be beneficial for us all.

All criminal behaviour is sensory driven, be it by power, lust, or greed. It is carried out to satisfy sensory urges. Even revenge attacks and other similarly motivated behaviour falls into this pattern. No matter how righteous we may feel in carrying out such revenge, we are satisfying our desire for 'satisfaction' and thus feeding an underlying sensory drive.

In facing up to such behaviour then we would be well advised to heed Christ's words: 'Let he among you who is without sin cast the first stone.' This does not condone the behaviour of the criminal but it does advise us to avoid dealing with it in a hypocritical manner. Each of us in our own way has hurt others, has on occasions carried out acts we would be ashamed to admit to.

It is impossible to go through life without knowingly or unknowingly hurting others. Are we entitled to hide under a cloak of righteousness simply because we have been undetected or because our 'crimes' were minor in nature? Or because we were unaware or them? Is the size of the 'crime' the important issue here? The criminal deserves our compassion as well as the justice of our society. Punishment may be required to correct or instruct a criminal and make him or her aware of the feelings of society as a whole about their activities. But it should never be motivated by a desire for revenge, or from a stance of superiority.

I wince when I hear calls for revenge in the name of the law. What right have any of us to seek to placate our urge to hurt another by invoking punishment in the name of justice and the law? Are we any better than those we seek to punish when we act in this way? Or are we seeking only to carry out 'legalised' criminal behaviour. Is it right for society to condemn another for murder and yet carry out the same act itself in the name of justice? How can it possibly be right to convict an individual for murder and collectively in the name of the law, execute the individual ourselves?

Of course it is right that we protect ourselves from the anti-social activities of the criminal, no matter how severe or petty, but always using as our yardstick the norms of behaviour we would have those we punish follow. It is not just a question of 'there but for the grace of God go I'. It is a recognition that through our response to such activities we have real opportunity to be aware, really aware, of the effects that such behaviour can have upon civilised society, the damage that it can do. Also, we have in controlling and fighting against criminal behaviour a chance to demonstrate the standards that we would wish to see operate throughout society. We have the chance to grow, to develop, to become.

Evil then has purpose, for it provides us with the opportunity to observe the outcomes of harmful action. Provides us with opportunities to observe the effects of such actions, such activities. The choices that we make in determining the path that we will follow through life are better directed because of an awareness of evil. Evil is the sickness of the body of mankind, we can choose whether we seek to have a healthy body or a sick one. Religious meditation has no better expression of this than the passage from Saint Augustine's 'City of God':

*When the will abandons the higher, and turns to what is lower, then it becomes evil – not because that is evil to what it turns, but because the turning itself is perverse.*

It is our choice, we can establish ground rules of behaviour, that we will observe, and that we will seek to persuade our fellows through the example that we set by our lives, that we would have them observe. The presence of evil in no way invalidates the fundamental reality that all has purpose. It does not, as some have argued, support the notion that we live in a world of random chance and chaotic activity. Rather, it sets out for us guide posts and examples without number and provides opportunities for us to become whole as individuals and as a society. This then is its underlying purpose and its validation.

## Evil – From Global to Individual

In the book *A Course in Miracles* published by Arkana, it is argued that nothing real can be harmed and that nothing unreal exists. This builds on the idea that we create all that we experience in physical form, with the master design remaining unaffected, a blueprint as it were that remains eternally. It is as if we draw on a blackboard on which is already drawn the perfect picture. Whatever we draw can be wiped out, but always the original picture remains. Yet through the process of drawing, we learn to become better artists.

From the experiencing comes the growing and the knowing. We create many structures, forms and circumstances purely for the possibilities that they offer for learning. We overlay these on top of the eternal unchanging frame and when we are done with them they are eliminated, and only the original eternal frame remains.

I believe that many of the seemingly eternal mysteries that surround poverty, sickness and exploitation, can be better understood through realising the learning potential that exists within these painful life conditions suffered by millions of our fellow human beings. Learning potential not only for the individual sufferers, but also for all who see, experience, or come into contact with humanity's pain and suffering, directly or indirectly. Regrettably it seems to be the case that we learn more through pain than pleasure. Yet it is still difficult to reconcile a creative Universe with the appalling living conditions present in Africa and other parts of our world. How can we come to terms with the evil committed by individuals that is at the root of so much of the suffering evident within our world? For much, if not all, of the suffering experienced in Africa and elsewhere is man-made. Brought about through greed, corruption, exploitation and repression. Evils that leads to slavery, exploitation, starvation, cruelty, murder, torture and rape.

One of the horrors of the age in which we live can be seen in the fact that many, many women in the civilised Western world live their lives in fear of rape. This repugnant crime is viewed by all thinking people as unmitigated evil, for which surely there can be no claims for redemption of any kind.

Just this morning I heard a discussion on the radio during which a woman was giving voice to this real fear, which prevented her, as she saw it, from leading a normal life. She claimed that a rape occurred every three hours in Britain, and that this horrific fact was an ever-present worry for many women of all ages. If accurate, and I have no reason to doubt it, this is a frightening statistic.

Yet a detailed breakdown of this statistic shows that a woman has less than a 1% chance of being raped in her lifetime. Add to this the fact that over two-thirds of rapes are carried out in domestic circumstances by someone the victim knows, and this reduces considerably the fear that many women have that a fearsome stranger will rape them in appalling and horrific circumstances.

This is not to decry the fact that any rape is a violent, horrendous act. A crime of such horrific proportions that it is difficult, if not impossible, for a man to fully understand its impact on the unfortunate victims. Based on the media image of rape, tens of thousands of woman live lives that are restricted and hedged in by measures designed to protect them from its threat. Some go to extraordinary lengths to protect themselves from the possibility of this heinous act happening to them. Self-defence courses, locks and bars, self-imposed limitations on their freedom of movement and so on.

Rape is an evil crime that horrifies sane men and women everywhere. Yet if we follow through on the premise that we create all in our lives in the images that we hold in our minds, it can be seen that to spend our life in fear of an event that statistics indicate is unlikely to occur to the average female, is to project forward a thought image that may very well actualise the event. As the prophet Job lamented, 'Behold my fear has come upon me.'

Our fears then are an area of our thoughts that must be confronted if only for our own safety. For such fears are based on the premise that we exist in an inherently unsafe world from which we need protecting. Yet if we can learn to trust and view the world as an inherently safe place, and then go on to believe this at a deep level of our being, this imaged world will manifest in our life.

Yet how can we escape from the vicious circle that says: 'I must not let my guard down or I will be taken advantage of'? That is based on the belief that the world is an unsafe place and that we must always be vigilant and ensure that we are never unmindful of the multiple dangers that threaten us. How can we walk in trust in such a seemingly evil world? Yet this is precisely what we must do if we truly accept that we do indeed create all in our lives, and that nothing happens to us that we have not brought into our existence by giving it life and shape through our thoughts and beliefs.

One of the most important things to understand about the creative process ever present in life, is that it does not discriminate between positive and negative thoughts. If we think that we do not wish a thing to happen to us, the creative process only sees that which we visualise and proceeds to create this exactly in the image held. This then becomes our experience of life as we move forward and meet it in our future, our creation. The creative process does not recognise the negative aspect of our thoughts. Therefore, what we must always try to do is to think about what we want to happen to us, rather than what we do not want. The creative process is further boosted by the degree of energy that we attach to any particular thought. Fear carries within it the potential for great emotion. Fear and its opposite emotion love, are the major drives in life So if we add fear, or any other negative emotion (energy) to our thought creation then that which we think will be created faster than another thing to which perhaps we attach little importance or significance. Equally, if we endow our thought creations with love they will likewise become super charged.

A second important factor is that the first and most important Universal Law of life is that consciousness always seeks its highest potential. Seeks the greatest opportunities for us to grow, develop and become. We then at a superconscious level always follow this rule and manifest accordingly in physical form. It is for this reason that experiences happen to us that we would at a conscious level not choose to experience. That are challenging, perhaps painful, either physically or emotionally. That contain within them opportunities for us to experience, and through experience grow and become.

Those who are in pain, suffering perhaps from a debilitating disease or disorder, are engaged in an exercise of change. The most cursory examination of the life circumstances that are associated with such an experience demonstrates this. Life is literally turned upside down by such happenings. When in pain or suffering, howsoever caused, we are forced to re-evaluate our life. Reschedule our time; the changes required affect our home, our domestic circumstances, the routines practised by those close to us – the changes can be endless. Great upheaval, great change and potential for change. And this is the purpose of such life experiences. They jerk us out of the rut that we may have fallen into; we cannot ignore them. We must respond to them if only to alleviate our suffering. We must face them and either overcome them by responding positively; come to terms with them, or be destroyed by them. As always the choice is ours.

We live in a purposeful world, a world where all events have purpose for us. This means that all that occurs to us does so as the result of our choice and for a purpose that at a superconscious level we are aware of. This is a tough concept to accept for it means that the rape victim at an inner level of their being decided to experience the trauma of rape, and the perpetrator decided to experience it for a different purpose. They came together in a macabre horrific dance each drawn to the other; each providing for the other the potential for an experience that they had mutually chosen to explore. On the surface this proposition seems too ridiculous for words. So let's explore further.

If we take rape or any other serious violent assault as an isolated event, then it does seem inexplicable that any individual would choose to be violated in this way. Yet the event itself will occupy a very short period of time in a lifetime. I have no doubt that afterwards the event will dominate the thinking of the victim, particularly where excessive violence leads to the victim being injured. Even where it does not, the physical violation and humiliation will scar even the toughest person. Yet the event itself will occupy a relatively short time span. If it is considered in a total life context, then it becomes possible to look beyond the event to the possibilities that the event creates for both the victim and their assailant.

If the assailant does not escape justice, then the likelihood is that they will be imprisoned for a lengthy period. During the imprisonment they are likely to be isolated from other offenders, for even criminals abhor the crime of rape or other crimes that involve extreme gratuitous violence. The criminal will be made to feel an outcast from society. A pariah to be scorned and reviled by all civilised people. The criminal may as the result of this experience be forced to re-evaluate their life. The possibility exists that they will be forced ultimately to confront the violence within themselves. From this base they could realise that they should reform and reshape their life in line with the norms accepted as civilised behaviour. Of course it is by no means certain that this will occur. But the possibility is enhanced by the consequences of such acts.

If this does not occur, then the individual may continue to offend, may even descend further in a cycle of degradation. Like the alcoholic the bottom of the pit may have to be reached before the offender turns in disgust at the horror that they have become and says 'enough'. Repentance has no value unless it comes from a deep well of agony where the horror and self-disgust are such that the sufferer genuinely seeks a new start. Genuinely seeks to climb back up the scales of human behaviour until some degree of self-regard and self-respect is regained.

How different is the person who does not rape in person? Does not actually carry out the crime of rape, yet still is titillated by the stories of rape read about in the newspapers? Who purchases pornographic magazines that may be packed with stories of abuse and violence against women because these provide a sexual kick? May scour the internet in search of pornography? The difference surely is in the deed rather than the thought? The event gives the opportunity to confront the real horror of the thought in actuality removed from the fantasy that is created by magazines, videos or the internet. The event is surely merely but one step removed?

Christ stated unequivocally that the man who thinks adultery in his heart is as guilty as the man who actually commits adultery.

There was in his words little difference between the thought and the deed. Where the act is not carried out simply because of fear of the consequences, where is the difference? For thoughts are simply ideas awaiting manifestation and shape in physical form.

The act of rape forces every thinking, feeling man to look within himself, and confront that part of their sexuality that is based on violence and aggression rather than love and gentleness. The event, when read about with horror, forces every one to face the possibility of this horrific event happening to their loved ones. Their wife, companion, daughter, friend. It acts as a signpost to examine that which goes on within our own mind in this regard. Rape is never an isolated event. As with so much we see in society, rape forces us to look within ourselves, the act ripples out and has an effect far wider than the event itself. Thus, opportunities are created for all to change. The victim, the perpetrator, and society at large.

What then of the victim? Must she be considered simply as a sacrificial lamb on the altar of the need for change? Has her suffering purpose also? Can such personal violation and humiliation have any purpose? Hard questions indeed: how does the philosophy that all has purpose answer these most difficult of questions?

Rape is an act of violence not an act of sex, and should be considered in the same category as all other acts of violence. As Jill Saward the victim of the Ealing vicarage rape that took place over twenty years ago stated in an interview recently in the *Daily Telegraph*: 'Rape isn't like an act of sex. It is violence, it is power, it is humiliation, it is degradation.' Anthony Rice, a vicious criminal with convictions for both rape and murder, is reported to have told police after his arrest in 1989: 'People say rape is about sex. Of course sex comes into it. But really it is about power. I had to have power over her – sex is just an extension of it.'

Whether any act of violence, painful and traumatic though it may have been, continues to inflict pain and suffering once the physical scars and injuries have faded is always the choice of the victim. The result of all acts of violence have to be dealt with mentally, once the immediate physical scars have healed, with physical healing being the easiest to bring about. The mental scars will undoubtedly take much longer to heal, but the mental attitude adopted towards the violent act will ultimately determine the long-term recovery rate Those who choose to return to their lives without bitterness and ongoing despair give themselves a real chance of returning to a normal life. Those who constantly relive the traumatic events will sentence themselves to a life of continued depression, pain and unhappiness.

On the 8th of November 1987 there was a particularly nasty bomb attack in Enniskillen in Northern Ireland. The victims were attending a memorial service for the casualties of the two world wars. An old man, George Wilson, and his daughter Marie, a nurse, were standing together close to where the bomb exploded. The blast caught the girl and fatally injured her. As she lay dying in the rubble holding on to her father's hand, her last words were, 'Daddy, I love you.'

The pictures and the words of this courageous girl and her grieving father moved the nation. Yet we were moved even more when the next day her father said, 'I forgive the men who did this to my daughter.' He told the television interviewer that it was contrary to his Christian beliefs not to forgive. In his deep pain and suffering his belief held firm. He chose, and he expressed that choice in a deeply moving way. The nation wondered at his courage and his compassion.

The violence committed against George and Marie Wilson, that ended Marie's life, was like all such indiscriminate violence, senseless and seemingly without purpose. It was different from rape or any violent outrage only in its severity, in its outcome.

The victims had been brought face to face, as all victims are, with the ever-present violence that is inside all of us and in our society. They had suffered dreadfully as a result. Marie had died, but her dying words were ones that moved a nation. She died expressing her love, Christ-like in her approach to death. Her father, likewise, chose not to express his deep grief by contributing further hatred and violence to the world.

He broke the circle of violence by forgiving his daughter's killers. They were shamed as a result. Instead of hearing the usual boasts of the killer organisations on our television screens and in our newspapers, to this day there remains a resounding silence about who planted the sophisticated device that blew up with such devastation on that terrible day. A silence that says more than all the obscene boasts ever did. The death of the girl and the compassion of her father shamed the killers. They were shamed into silence. Her sacrifice was not in vain, her memory is sanctified by the manner of her death and her father's forgiveness.

Years ago when searching for truth I was confronted time and time again in my search by the ever-present reality of evil within our world. I struggled to come to terms with the fact of evil. How could a creative God allow evil to exist? It seemed to be a contradiction in terms. If God existed, then surely 'He' created all? It made no sense to speak of a God who only created good in life and a Devil who created evil. If God was, then he must create all, both good and evil. This was the puzzle; this the riddle. As I grew and explored further, I came to appreciate that our perception of our world is all. And our perception is limited by the boundaries of our experience. We live in a world of opposites and we know ourselves in relation to these. Good bad, night day, up down, sickness health, left right. We are able to orient ourselves by reference to these opposites. Without them growth, knowing and choice would be impossible.

We know the results of our actions by their outcomes and their effects. Our system of making judgements depends on this. Without opposites then our judgmental faculties would be greatly impaired, if not negated completely. Without evil then our ability to judge for ourselves what was good and what was bad would not exist. Evil enables us to recognise good using our inbuilt moral compass as a guide. The compass that always points in the direction of 'All that Is', the source from whence we came and to which ultimately, we shall all return.

We live in a world of equal, opposite and opposing forces. This is one of the Root Assumptions on which human form and life as we know it depend. The problem is that we tend to make judgements, not on factors such as growth, but on other more immediately subjective factors such as happiness, stability, safety and security. When these are confronted, or challenged, we override our ability to look objectively at an event to determine what, if anything, within it can be considered as beneficial to us. It is only by looking back at an event, when the pain and emotion that surrounded it have passed away, that we are able to make more objective judgements about what, if anything, we have learnt from it. That we can see that perhaps there was greater purpose in it than we realised when we were caught up in it.

Good and evil can be seen as the two halves that make a whole. We could not know one without the other. They provide us with a framework that as choosing beings we use to determine what it is that we want to experience in our lives. They provide us with choices. No man is an island: no event happens in isolation, the effects of any act ripple outwards and affects many people in many different ways.

The existence of evil does not deny the fact of an all-creative God. Nor does it confirm the existence of the Devil. It seems that the design of the system that enables us to grow is further exemplified. The violence that is everywhere present in our world is reflected in the violence that is inside us. It would not be right to condemn this violence until or unless we have successfully confronted the violence inside of us. We cannot expect to exist in a peaceful world until we know peace inside ourselves. If we can effect a change in ourselves, then we will have effected a change in the whole of mankind, for we are a part of mankind. A minuscule part perhaps, but none the less a part.

The lesson to be drawn from the forgiveness given to his daughter's killers by George Wilson in the Enniskillen disaster is clear for all to see. We make greater impact on life and our fellows when we can forgive. When we can break the cycle of violence and shame those who perpetrate violence in our society. It is easy to be vengeful, it is natural to seek retribution. It is much harder to forgive. But in the forgiveness is the growing and the learning, and perhaps it is this which must be faced and learnt, before we can truly confront the evil in our world and progress to becoming more than we are.

## Trust, Love and Spontaneity

Myriad imparted the following advice to me one cold February morning:

> *Trust, love, spontaneity; let these three be your guides. To plan overly is to define the future from the past. To create the unknown from the known. Rather be an explorer and let that which you think of as the unknown reveal itself to you as you move forward in a spirit of confidence, wonder and curiosity. The letting go of the old, the allowing to come into being of the new must be part of such a process. For the 'I' that exists now can only be known to you by how it has defined itself thus far in your life. Examine your life for it will speak volumes to you if you will only hear. Each aspect of your life is a symbol that quite defines the self that you have become. Examine these symbols, be honest with yourself and determine if what you see is what you want to see. Often you will see limitation and restraint in many areas as you judge and expect to be judged. We create always in the image of our beliefs and often these beliefs when writ large in the symbols of our life are unhealthy and unhelpful.*
>
> *Let there be a gentleness in your dealings with others and yourself. As you have quite come to appreciate love is not a weak vacillating thing. Rather it is the essence of life. Love*

*is firm, strong and resilient. It bends but does not break in the face of hostility and aggression. Love is constant, for without love nothing, literally nothing can exist.*

*Let such love then flow into your life without measure or constraint for you are right to parallel your thinking with the basic tenets of Christianity for Christ understood all that is being revealed to you. You are about truly ushering in a new age. But as you yourself have stressed, from that which is natural not from anything unnatural or supernatural. For God's creation is indeed perfect and you are part of that creation. The unnatural does not exist, cannot exist, for to do so would be to defy God's holy laws. The order and laws of God's creation, God's world is indeed perfect. The tools to right what you see as the wrongs of the world already exist, there is no need for external supernatural intervention. What we are about is bringing these neglected tools into play, using them to enable people to correct their own lives themselves. Then there is true, permanent and lasting correction. Change can never be imposed from without, it must always and ever be commenced from within. In such is the essence of true confession based.*

*So then allow the true Glory of God's creation to be revealed to you and to others, be not afraid to walk in the truth. Have trust and confidence that as you need help to sustain you when the going gets tough that such help will be available to you freely. You are not alone, no one is ever alone even when they quite believe that they are. You are most beloved as are all beings. You are the ones, this is the age, which has been chosen to usher in the new beginning. To become the creators rather than just the created.*

*Be trusting, loving and spontaneous then and approach life with a fine confidence and you shall enjoy all that God has to offer you.*

# Death

*He who does not understand death
does not understand life.*

## Preamble

On Tuesday 24th of January 2006, a retired doctor, Anne Turner, from Bath, a British woman with an incurable brain disease, committed assisted suicide in Switzerland, surrounded by her loving family. She died with the help of medics from the Dignitas clinic in Zurich the day before her 67th birthday.

Dr Turner was suffering from Progressive Supranuclear Palsy, or PSP, the degenerative disease which killed the actor Dudley Moore. She died at 12:35 GMT at a flat in Zurich after drinking a lethal dose of barbiturates. One death among the estimated 155,000 people who died that day throughout the world. Dr Turner died at a time of her own choosing, surrounded by her loving family. An event unusual in both its timing, and its circumstances.

In the opening section of this book I set out the four Universal Laws of life as revealed to me by Myriad. The third of these laws states unequivocally that:

> *Consciousness is of absolute duration; it had no beginning and will have no end.*

As conscious beings then our life will have no end. As life in physical form clearly ends in death, this assertion by Myriad posits consciousness both before birth and after death.

The closing act of any play is often the most important. It draws the threads of the play together. It enables the audience to make sense of the foregoing acts. Like a thriller novel, the answer to the questions posed in the early chapters is often to be found in the last chapter. So it is with life. Death draws the threads of life together – for life only becomes complete with death. It is only by coming to terms with the finiteness of physical form, that we can hope to make sense of life. Everyone must do this in their own way, for no one can tell another with certainty what follows death. The best that any author can do is to set out their findings into this most mysterious, yet fundamental, of subjects; can set out the evidence that may have led them to adopting a particular view. For whilst birth is a shared experience, with both mother and child participating in the advent of new life, death is faced alone. Even when surrounded by family and friends, each must face death alone. Likewise, each must decide for themselves whether they are prepared to accept the premise of a continued existence, or believe that only oblivion follows the ending of life.

I remember discussing this subject with a good friend of mine, many years ago, at a time when I was exploring various religious faiths. My friend was a Methodist minister,and, as such, had a firm Christian belief that life after death was indeed a reality. 'What if you are wrong?' I asked him. 'What if there is no life after death?'

'Well,' he replied. 'If I am wrong, and there is no life after death, then I am not going to be in a position to know much about it. If I am right, however, I will have a head start on those who do not believe in a continuing life!' A pragmatic response which matches Pascal's famous quotation:

> *If God does not exist, one will lose nothing by believing in him. While if he does exist, one will lose everything by not believing in him.*

For those who are prepared to make the effort and look, there is an enormous amount of material available purporting to set out what happens at the time of death and thereafter. The earliest accounts of life after death, worthy of serious consideration (apart from those in the Bible), commence with a study of the writings of Emanuel Swedenborg, 1688–1772. Swedenborg was an eminent scientist. He was the third son of the renowned, but controversial, bishop, Jesper Swedenborg. Emanuel Swedenborg had a prolific career as an inventor and scientist. At age fifty-six he entered into a psychological-spiritual crisis, experiencing first dreams, and later visions of a spiritual world where he claimed to talk with angels and spirits. Amongst other things, these spirits guided his interpretation of biblical scripture. Swedenborg's transition from scientist to mystic has fascinated people ever since it occurred – people such as Sir Arthur Conan Doyle and C.G. Jung, just to mention a couple. For Swedenborg, the human body was the external, while he saw the internal body as being of the Spirit.

Every religion sets out its tenets dealing with the subject of life after death. Indeed, the basis for many religions is death. In the final analysis no one can convince another of what follows death. Each must reach their own conclusions on the evidence available, and their own personal experiences. The true answer will only come to us in our final earthly moments.

In order to make sense of life we must come to terms with our mortality. If we believe in a continuing existence, then this will surely influence how we live our life. If we take the ends off life and see consciousness as an ongoing state, then life suddenly takes on a whole new meaning; what we do in our daily life suddenly takes on much greater significance. If, on the other hand, we believe that only oblivion awaits us, life may be viewed differently.

With the gradual demise of traditional religious belief, and biblical instruction, personal aims and purpose in much of the Western world has become random, directed in the main to material prosperity, health and personal beauty, with seemingly little or no attention given to deeper spiritual matters. Yet the concept of a continuing existence beyond physical form does not have to depend on a religious belief. It is perfectly possible to postulate a continuation of consciousness on a scientific basis. So what information is there to tell us what form such an existence might take? What can we learn from the various sources of information available to us, that will help us to effectively prepare for any existence that may follow on from physical life? That will enable us to manage the transition smoothly? How can we meet our life's purpose set out in the opening section of this book, of 'bridging the gap that exists between waking and dreaming'. Can we bridge these two states more effectively?

What can we learn from the communications claiming to come from those who have died? What have they to tell us? Why did they bother to communicate at all? By all accounts communication from beyond death is no easy task. Maurice Barbanell in *The Barbanell Report* describes it thus:

> *Have to slow my thoughts down to communicate this way;*
> *very painstaking.*

What information has been conveyed that can help us to better understand life? So much of the material that purports to come from those who have – in the euphemism – 'passed over' is trivial and mind numbingly boring. So many of the questions posed by those who attend spiritualist meetings are mundane and follow the form of seeking fortune telling from Auntie Florrie.

My investigation into the fascinating possibility of life after death has taken me to many places, over many years. I have travelled to Virginia Beach. To the headquarters of the Association of Research and Enlightenment (ARE), the spiritual home of Edgar

Cayce the 'Sleeping Prophet' (1877–1945). I have been to conferences and research organisations in Denver and high up in the Rocky mountains. I have travelled to Chicago and California; I have been to the headquarters of the Church in Los Angeles founded on the teachings of Ernest Holmes, the author of the excellent *Science of Mind* books. I have visited the Marble Collegiate Church in Manhattan, New York, that was for over fifty years home to Norman Vincent Peale (1898–1993), made famous through his *Power of Positive Thinking* books. I have explored Taoism the ancient philosophy based on the laws of nature, the importance of change and renewal and the intrinsic importance of energy, or chi.

I have been an avid reader of the many books that explore this most interesting of subjects. Many written by the psychic pioneers of the 19th and 20th centuries who devoted their lives to exploring the possibility of life after death.

Edgar Cayce spent time daily, for over forty years of his adult life, providing 'readings' to those who approached him for answers to problems they were experiencing in their life. Many of these led him to refer to past lives, and life experiences. Indeed, at one time he ceased giving the readings because of their reference to reincarnation, a reference which Cayce, as a fundamentalist Christian found very disturbing.

When providing his 'readings', Edgar Cayce would lie down on a couch, hands crossed over his stomach, and allow himself to enter a self-induced 'sleep' state. Then, in a normal voice, he would answer questions posed about any person that he was asked. These answers, which came to be called 'life readings' were written down by a stenographer, who kept one copy on file, and gave or sent another copy to the person who had originally requested the information.

Today, on file at the ARE at Virginia Beach, Virginia, USA are copies of more than 14,000 of Edgar Cayce's readings. These readings cover all aspects of life and death, of conditions experienced and endured, and the reasons behind many of them. The Cayce material represents the largest collection of psychic information ever obtained from a single source. These 'life readings' are available today on CD-ROM and can be purchased by contacting the ARE direct on their website.

In pursuit of material to back up or challenge the information on life after death I found in Jane Roberts' 'Seth' books, I have met with many 'Sethians' and questioned and discussed the validity of the 'Seth' material. I have attended Spiritualist churches and séances, together with reading books that purport to provide communications from those who have died, as well as listening to a large number of tape recordings of communications claiming to emanate from those who have died. I have on many occasions quizzed my own source of discarnate material, Myriad, on this most fascinating of subjects.

Research continues to be undertaken today to determine if the evidence purporting to come from discarnate entities justifies a belief in a continuing existence after death, or is explicable by other means. The Society for Psychical Research (SPR), an organisation founded in the UK in 1882 to examine, according to their founding manifesto:

> *without prejudice or prepossession and in a scientific spirit, those faculties of man, real or supposed, which appear to be inexplicable on any generally recognised hypothesis*

The SPR reported in their Journal (issue number 883, April 2006) an example of one such investigation that had been undertaken.

This investigation concerned the case of a chess match, that had taken place in the 1980s, between a living and a deceased

Grandmaster. The living Grandmaster, Victor Korchnoi, then third in the world rankings, was persuaded by a Dr Eisenbeiss, a Swiss amateur chess player, to participate in a chess match with the deceased Grandmaster. The automatic-writing medium who acted as a conduit between the two was a Mr Robert Rollans (1914–1993). Mr Rollans, it was claimed, had no knowledge of chess having never played the game. A resume of the match which was played at international championship level, and the circumstances of its intermediation by Mr Rollans, forms the introduction to newly disclosed material regarding this case.

During the course of the match, that took place over a number of years, a substantial body of information on the life of the discarnate Grandmaster – Hungarian Master Geza Maroczy (1870–1951) who was ranked third in the world in 1900, was elicited. This information has subsequently been successfully verified including unanticipated elements. An examination of the evaluation revealed that the information communicated about the life of the Grandmaster was 94% accurate. The match itself was won, after a hard struggle, by Korchnoi who commented that during the opening phases of the game Maroczy showed weaknesses. 'His play was old fashioned. He compensated for his faults however by a strong end game. In the end game the ability of a player shows up and my opponent played very well.' An examination of the records of chess matches played by the deceased Grandmaster Maroczy showed that a common feature of his game was a strong end game, when he had, on occasion, turned certain defeat into victory.

In order to determine if Maroczy was who he claimed to be, 39 questions containing numerous sub-questions were broken up to yield a total of 91 questions which were put to Maroczy about his life on earth. Many of these questions were of a very detailed nature requiring an intimate knowledge of the deceased Grandmaster's life. The answers to some of the questions were known only by Maroczy's living children, themselves no longer young, or through exhaustive research into the records of chess matches played many years previously. Of the questions posed, Maroczy answered 87.9% correctly, 1.1% semi-correctly, 3.3% incorrectly, with the remaining 7.7% unanswered. A very impressive result indeed.

The above case is just one recent example of the information available to anyone who sincerely seeks to find answers to the seemingly imponderable questions about death and the possibility of life after death. I have sought to explore material, from what ever credible source I could find. To determine if any pattern or commonality emerged from the material that would provide credible evidence on which to base a belief in life after death. I was not prepared at any time to accept as valid any single source, no matter how highly rated it was. If information claimed by one source could not be verified, or cross checked against other credible sources, then I rejected it. Make no mistake here, the object of the exercise was not to obtain information or evidence to convince anybody else of the certainty of life after death, but to obtain information and material that would satisfy me, driven by questions about my own mortality.

Hitherto, reference in my writings on this subject have been anecdotal, more in the format of recollections of information obtained, rather than conclusions reached. I have never attempted to convince any reader of the reality, or otherwise, of a continued conscious existence. However, I am now able to set out in the following chapters the conclusions that I have reached on this most fundamental of subjects.

## Death

*There is no separate individual specific point of death – life is in a state of becoming and death is a part of it.*

So Seth answered a question on death and dying in Jane Roberts' book, *Seth Speaks*.

*If the cells did not die, and were not replenished the physical image would not continue to exist. The death of physical tissues is merely part of the process of life... Consciousness is not dependent on physical tissue.*

Death then is not a one-off event. We are dying daily. Disease fighting white blood cells living only for a few hours, with stomach and colon cells having a lifespan of only a few days. Our skin cells exist for about a month, with our skeleton being completely regenerated every ten years. It has been estimated that we get through around 900 skins and about half a dozen skeletons in the average lifetime. The only part of us that has a full lifespan are nerve cells, including those that make up our brain. Barring accidents, these cells last as long as their owners.

Every time we visit the barber, or cut our nails, a part of us dies and is discarded. Yet we do not grieve for these parts of ourself. Yet when consciousness finally leaves our physical body it is an occasion for great mourning; rarely a cause for celebration. Death is a natural event, each of us will experience it at the end of our life. Yet rarely, if ever, is it viewed as a natural event. Often it is viewed as a tragedy.

Anyone who has viewed a corpse, particularly of a loved one, knows that the dead body is not the person that they knew. It looks like them, but is simply a flesh image of them. Like a television that has been switched off, something is missing. All the parts that enabled it to function remain, but it has lost the vital spark of life. The energy that made the body alive, that gave it its personality and individuality has gone. What remains is simply inanimate tissue. In all of the experiences of death I have come across, real, written and anecdotal, the first shock is the smallness of the body. Shakespeare's Mark Antony on seeing Caesar's dead body sums this up well:

> O mighty Caesar dost thou lie so low? Are all thy conquests, glories, triumphs, spoils shrunk to this little measure?

One of the problems of living in an increasingly secular age is the loss of the coping mechanism that religion provided to both the dying, and those left behind. In 1965, Geoffrey Gorer published the results of a nationwide survey he had carried out into death, grief and mourning in contemporary Britain. The body of the book *Death Grief and Mourning* analysed the replies given to a questionnaire by 359 men and women from every region and social class in Britain who had suffered a bereavement in the previous five years. Their replies demonstrated that the consolations of religious belief were only acceptable to a minority, and that for the majority the social ritual of mourning had completely disappeared. Gorer claimed that the whole subject of death had been smothered in embarrassment and, as such, often led to neurotic and unrealistic behaviour on the part of the bereaved. I have no doubt that forty years on from the publication of this book, the mechanisms in place for coping and understanding this life-ending event will, if anything, have become more secularised, and as a result more difficult for people to deal with.

In Geoffrey Gorer's book, he explained that the reason why the Christian clergy are so continuously involved in the disposal of the dead is that orthodox Christianity is dogmatic that the soul continues to exist after death. His survey showed that a quarter of the population stated firmly that they did not believe in a future life, and that a similar number is uncertain; of the remainder some 15% said that they believed in a future life but had little idea of what it would be like. The remainder voiced a series of unorthodox beliefs with no overtly religious content. This contrasted with a Mori poll carried out in 1993 that showed that up to 60% of the population of the UK believed in God. A belief in God must by its very nature presuppose a belief in an afterlife in some shape or form.

Death has become a taboo subject in our ego-focused contemporary Western society. Our ego violently resists any notion of its fallibility. It cannot conceive of a situation where it ceases to be, so our conscious mind rebels at any suggestion of our mortality. Death is associated with an event that is, largely, outside of our control. The concept of our ceasing to be is something very hard to imagine, so we recoil from thinking about it. We label any discussion of the subject as morbid and depressing.

Dying is the frontier where the unknowable confronts the scientific. Science is the study of what is; it is an objective study. Death is personal, and thus subjective, and the possibility of life outside of the physical, by its very nature is outside the framework of scientific study. Scientists recoil from the study of life after death; any such work is viewed by most scientists as working in the realm of fantasy. The world famous physicist, Stephen Hawkings, responding to an invitation to a discussion on Intelligent Design, is reported to have responded by saying that he was sorry he would not be able to attend, but he had a prior engagement with the Flat Earth Society!

This was not always the case, however. In the late 19th and early 20th centuries some brave scientists did involve themselves in investigatory work around the possibility of life after death, but they did so with some trepidation at the risk that such investigation posed to their careers and reputation. The period from 1850 through to 1920 was a very rich period for psychic research. In 1882 the group of scientists and academics who were later to form the Society for Psychical Research met for the first time as a group. They laid the groundwork for much of the serious research into death and life after death that is currently available to researchers in this subject today. The records of this early recorded research makes fascinating reading. A good place to start for any serious student is F.H.W. Myers' book, with the foreword by Aldous Huxley – *Human Personality and Its Survival of Bodily Death*. This book is considered as a classic in its field.

## Dying

Death is the severing of the connection between the mind and the body. If life after death is a reality, then it is clear that only the mind can survive, for we know that the physical body returns to the earth in one form or another.

The child becomes the adult; but to become an adult the child must first die. For in the child is the essence of the adult it will become, and in the adult remain traces of the child. For each age to come into being, the previous age must die. As such, the transition from babyhood to old age comes about. So it is with death. For any transition of consciousness must move us beyond the material physical world.

Sceptics argue that as hard physical evidence is not available that can be checked and verified under scientific, laboratory conditions, then life after physical death cannot be a proven scientific fact. Yet by definition hard physical evidence cannot be obtained from a non-physical state. The very questions posed are oxymoronic. It is an undisputed fact that there is much about our physical state of which science is ignorant. In broad terms we sleep for one third of our lifetime. In the average lifetime over twenty five years will be spent asleep. Think about that for a moment; one third of our life spent in a state that scientists are unable to completely explain or understand. What happens to our minds whilst we are asleep is a mystery to science. The knowledge we do possess about sleep is mainly related to our physiological, not our mental state.

Whilst scientists, and those who study the sleeping state, can provide evidence of the electrical activity of the brain, and the functioning of the heart and other organs of the body during periods of sleep, this is all that they can provide. No one can state precisely what the purpose of sleep is, or what happens to the mind during the time we are asleep. Scientists have provided us with studies of what happens to those who are deprived of sleep for long periods. The disorientation and other mind-altering states that occur. Yet this only tells us what happens if we do not sleep. It still does not explain the sleeping state, or that other more mysterious state 'dreaming'. What happens to our consciousness during this lengthy period each night? Where do our minds go? What are dreams? Why are some so vivid that they become nightmares waking sufferers up sweating and palpitating? Why are others so beautiful that they positively influence our mood upon waking?

Neuroscientists continue to debate the source of consciousness. Paul Broks in his excellent book *Into the Silent Land* states that:

> *Far from being the holy grail of neuroscience, the search for consciousness within the circuitry of an individual brain can lead only to fools' gold.*

It is without doubt that human beings, as all other living creatures, are greater than the sum total of their parts. Anybody viewing a corpse, whether of a human or an animal, cannot help but be struck by the absence of the life-force; something is undoubtedly missing. So before we categorically reject the possibility of life after death, we would be well advised to first study the evidence that exists for a continuing existence, with an open mind.

Considerable literature and other source material is available to the inquisitive about what actually happens at the point of death; literature that has built up over centuries. From Swedenborg in the 17th century to evidence available from present day. The Society for Psychical Research (SPR), based at 49, Marloes Road, Kensington, London W8 6LA has an extensive library of psychic material that has been built up over many years. Their website provides information about the society and its history. To anybody interested in exploring information that has been gathered over the past century, and more, this is a very useful research source.

There are also many recordings, freely available, of communications purporting to come from those who have died, or 'passed over'. A good source of information – and entertainment – for those who wish to satisfy themselves of the potentiality for living on, could be obtained by listening to some of these tapes available on: www.freewebs.com/afterlife/flint/flintrecordings.htm. This excellent website contains recordings made of sessions where the late famous direct voice medium Leslie Flint made contact with claimed discarnate spirits and recorded the resultant sessions.

One of my personal favourites is the recording of Ted Butler, whose earthy (no pun intended) reminiscences of his death and immediate experience in the life that followed are well worth listening to. Not because of the depth of the material given, but rather because of the matter of fact manner in which Ted tells his story. Ted Butler's recollections are echoed in many other recollections presented in these recordings and other sources. As such, they can be described as 'typical'.

Mr Butler, who died as a pedestrian in a road accident in 1923, recalled his death by stating:

> '...I was crossing the road, and before you could say Jack Robinson, something hit me. It was some lorry that I think

got out of control down the slope. It got me pinned against the wall and I was out.

'No memory of pain.'

'I just remember,' he continued, 'something coming towards me, and that's all. It all happened so sudden.'

Mrs Greene (an observer at the Flint session) interrupted to ask. 'How did you actually find yourself?'

'Well,' he replied. 'I don't know. All I know is that I saw a crowd of people all standing looking down at something. I 'ad a look with the crowd and saw someone who looked exactly like me!'

'At first I didn't realize it was me. I thought, that's a coincidence. That fellow looks the same as I do. It might be a twin brother. I didn't cotton on. Then I realised that my wife was there crying her eyes out. She didn't seem to realise I was standing beside her.'

'They put my body in an ambulance, and the wife got in, and some nurse. I got in and sat with my wife and she didn't seem to realise I was sitting there at all. Then gradually it came on me that that was me lying down there.'

'I went to the hospital. Of course they put me in the mortuary. I didn't like that at all. So I got out quick and went home. There was the wife, Mrs Mitchel next door, trying to comfort her. I think that was the worst time of the lot.'

'Then there was the funeral. Of course I went to that. I thought to meself, "All this fuss and expense for nothing, because here I was." I thought it's all very touching, but at the same time it all seemed so damn silly, because there I was.

Nobody took any notice.'

'The old parson was standing there reciting away. I thought, "He should know if anyone knows." So I went and stood beside him, and kept nudging him with me elbow in the side. He didn't take any notice at all. He just went on with his ritual.'

'Then there was the gravediggers. I knew one of them, old Tom Corbett. He was a case he was. I'd many a pint with him and a laugh. He filled in the hole, and the other bloke filled in the old coffin and the grave. I thought this is a fine how-d'you-do. I'm not staying down here with this lot, so I got out.'

'I must have hung around my house for weeks I should think. Once or twice I would go on the old trams. At first I was sort of all mixed up. But I used to have a laugh too sometimes. If the Corporation knew I was sitting in here not paying my fare, they would say something...'

Information on the circumstances that prevail immediately after death are not new. According to Swedenborg, a person who has just died continued to exist consciously in much the same way as before.

> The spirit of a man recently departed could easily be recognised by his friends.

Yet the spirit body was not the same, for a discarnate being had the ability to move, feel pain or joy, and travel in an instant over great distances.

Swedenborg elaborated:

> When a person arrives after death in the spiritual world...

*He seems himself to be alive as he was in the world, living in a similar house, room and bedroom, with similar clothes and with similar companions at home... The reason this happens to every person after death is so that death should not seem like death, but rather a continuation of life, so that the last act of natural life should become the first of spiritual life; and from this he should advance toward his goal... The reason the recently dead find this likeness in everything is that their minds remain exactly as they were in the world... The mind is the person himself, but he is then not a material person but a spiritual person; and because after death he is the same person, he is presented in accordance with the concepts in his mind with things similar to those he possessed at home in the world. But this (state) only lasts for a few days.*

Swedenborg's account, although centuries apart, compares directly with Ted Butler's recollections. Thought and mind, as would be expected, are of paramount importance in the world beyond the physical.

Swedenborg told how his old teacher – Pelham – who died on a Monday, spoke to him on the following Thursday. Pelham told him that he had attended his own funeral, saw his coffin, the funeral procession and the mourners who had attended his interment.

In the autobiography of the famous medium Leslie Flint *Voices in the Dark*, he recalls a spirit voice claiming to be that of Cosmo Lang stating:

*While you live on earth you are on the same wavelength, vibration or frequency as all around you and thus your physical senses perceive your surroundings as real and solid. But science has told you that nothing on earth is real or solid, but in reality open networks of electrical charges whirling around a central nucleus at a frequency that is the same as your own. When you die you will continue to live in your more subtle spiritual double which vibrates at a greater frequency than does your physical body... this body is on the same wavelength as the plane of being you will inhabit after death and for this reason everything in that plane will seem to you as real and as solid as once your earth surroundings seemed to be.*

In appearance, Swedenborg claimed that the spirit world was altogether similar to the material world, only more 'real'. The soul's preconceptions determining whether the spirit world was bright or dreary, dull or light. The mean spirited person finding himself in a somewhat miserable existence, whilst some who had embraced life to the full finding themselves in a happy, sunny life-exuding environment.

There are many books covering the subject of death, and after death experiences, far too many for me to attempt to refer to here. As such, I refer the reader to a few that I have found particularly erudite and worthy. One of the authors whose work I respect greatly is Paul Beard.

Paul Beard was the President of the College of Psychic Studies for sixteen years. He was the author of three books which have become classics in their field. These books carefully assess and analyse the evidence for and against the survival of the human soul after death. Having been a member of the Society for Psychical Research for many years, Paul Beard made a lifetime study of psychical research. Using his extensive knowledge and experience he reviewed the subject in a balanced way, quoting widely from many well-known writers and sources, such as the archives of the Society for Psychical Research. His books include:

*Survival of Death* (1966), Hodder & Stoughton, London. This is now available in a 1988 impression from Pilgrim Books.

A good assessment of this book was written in the Foreword by Leslie Weatherhead, who wrote:

> *Mr Beard offers evidence with a quality of analytical detachment, which, to my mind, is exactly what is so badly needed. In the end he regards the evidence as sufficiently conclusive to warrant belief in survival, but he examines every possible alternative interpretation of the phenomena and is never woolly, or afraid of where his investigations may lead. He concedes every possible claim that telepathy and clairvoyance may account for many alleged 'messages from the dead', but he finds a residue in the evidence for which the most intelligent and reasonable explanation is that of survival.*

In *Living On* Paul Beard (1980) 'A study of altering consciousness after death' George Allen & Unwin, London, the author presents some of the evidence for continuing life, analysing the material and making comparisons. He discusses the evidence available about the quality and meaning of life beyond death.

In *Hidden Man* Pilgrim Books, Paul Beard studies the contribution of discarnate teachers who seek to clarify something of the meaning and worth of the human journey through many lifetimes.

There is one other book which I would highly recommend. It is *The Barbanell Report* (1987) published by Pilgrim books. In this book, Maurice Barbanell the founder of the *Psychic News*, and its Editor for many years, communicated his experiences of life after death to Paul Beard, through the medium (channel) Marie Cherrie. This is a thoughtful and deeply reflective book, which avoids much of the trivia so often associated with the record of such communications.

The book, that was published in 1987, was edited and introduced by Paul Beard. In *The Barbanell Report,* Maurice

Barbanell, on the 24th of February 1982, communicating through Marie Cherrie said:

*There is no death, you will live after you die. Passing itself was easy, like going into another room, best description. Like going to sleep and waking up...*

This description of dying is a common one. In *Seth Speaks*, Seth states:

*You may or may not realise immediately that you are dead in physical terms. You will find yourself in another form, an image that will appear physical to you to a large degree, as long as you do not try to manipulate within the physical system with it.*

In Paul Beard's book *Living On*, he reports on the claimed after death observations of F.W.H Myers – the eminent scientist and researcher:

*Death is... a mere episode which we regard with a certain tenderness and not with any pain... there is contained in it a time of stillness, sinking gloriously into rest.*

And further, he reports on the claimed recollections of dying given by Sir Alvary Gascoigne, a former diplomat:

*Every part of me seemed to be switching off gently, and... I suddenly found I was floating above my body... Nothing in life comes up to the immense joy of dying... I told you that I had experienced a strange feeling of power that seemed to be drawing me out of my body during the last few days of my illness... I welcomed this in-rush of new life and let go very willingly. That was why I did not linger. You must be ready to receive the power that draws you quite painlessly out of your body. It is the most beautiful and glorious thing. I see so many are prolonging their life quite unnecessarily. Life commands; you agree and cooperate.*

A communicator claiming to be Oliver Lodge, the famous scientist and spiritual explorer, commented on the naturalness of the death experience after his own passing:

> *We have split up life into two parts far too drastically. We have drawn a line, and we must gradually erase that line. We have talked about the spiritual life, and the earth life or the physical life. The two are one and we must make them one again. There is no line, there is no line at all. Man has drawn a line and it must be erased, and it will take some time to erase it completely, but we must work towards that. We must do that in the same way that we must erase – what shall we call it? National boundaries, and racial ones. All these must go, and especially the boundary that we have, quite unnecessarily, erected between what we now call our two worlds, which are in reality one. It is only one world. There is only one world and we must take down these… barriers of illusion that compelled us to think there must be two, because through our limitations and ignorance we are unable to look over the self-erected barrier, or to look through it. It must come down. It is your work, it is our work.*

He argues that this is the most important of all the implications of survival, that the task which lies before men and women on earth, and those who have passed through the experience we call 'death' is a shared and common one; not separate and distinct.

Paul Beard in his book *Living On* states that the differences which arise in passing through the incident of death (appear to) fall into four main categories:

> *Some find it incomprehensible that it has happened and for some considerable time persist in believing themselves to be still on earth, and hence suffer a state of confusion.*

*Others, particularly those who have been ill, drift in and out of consciousness; their readjustment is gradual, and punctuated by sleep. The new arrival has to overcome gradually the weariness that was in the mind and feelings during the last days, and which sometimes remains. Periods of unconsciousness are part of the pattern of adjustment, enabling a more gradual and easy facing of the new experience bit by bit between each period of rest.*

*Many die without preconception of what, if anything, they will encounter. The mental furniture they carried about on earth, which some still cling on to, delays the process of adjustment.*

*Those who die by accident or violence (like Ted Butler) find it less easy, according to some writers, to adjust than do those who die naturally, although this may not always be the case.*

So the death experience is described as a perfectly natural happening that is much easier than being born. An event which according to Sir Alvary Gascoigne is to be welcomed as a wonderful experience.

How then do these experiences compare with the numerous near death experiences (NDE) frequently reported upon?

Dr Peter Fenwick, a neurophyschiatrist who is Britain's leading clinical authority on NDE, has received hundreds of letters from people of all ages and in all walks of life detailing their NDE. In his book, *The Truth in the Light*, co-authored by Elizabeth Fenwick, he reports on the experiences of many of those who have claimed to have undergone close shaves with death. These are the recorded experiences of people who have 'died' for a short period before being resuscitated and returning to life. The participants all report similar experiences of leaving their body, which frequently they report being able to view from a distance, and travelling at great speed along a tunnel towards a bright light where the are met by relatives, or beings of light, before returning with a rush to the physical body.

A typical report would describe feelings of overwhelming peace and joy with any feelings of pain dropping away. This would be followed by the person leaving his or her body; slowly rising out of it and floating weightless until they are able to look down on their physical body lying inert beneath them. They would then proceed into a dark tunnel which they pass through without any physical effort. At the end of the tunnel they see a very bright light which grows larger and larger as they approach it. At the end of the tunnel they meet either a being of light, or relatives that they recognise who have previously died. Those who have undergone NDE often report a barrier which in some way bars their path, preventing them from proceeding further; a point which they instinctively know that they cannot go beyond. Often people want to stay; more than anything they want to stay. But in every case they recognise, however reluctantly, that this is not possible. Sometimes they make the decision to go back, sometimes it seems that it is made for them. Invariably, they report returning to their body in a rush. A description not dissimilar to the feeling of rapidly falling that can wake us with a start, shortly after we have dropped off to sleep. The spirit that claimed to be Cosmo Lang recorded as speaking in Leslie Flint's autobiography *Voices in the Dark* stated:

> *Sometimes the astral body is projected from the physical sheath during a person's lifetime. Those who had the experience of finding themselves out of their body can see their other body lying inert on a bed or a couch or even sitting in a chair.*

For most people the NDE, or out-of-body experience, has a most profound effect upon them. Many are quoted as saying that they have lost any fear of death and that their life has taken on a whole new significance as a result of the experience they have undergone. There are, it seems, many similarities in these reports when they are compared with the immediate afterlife experiences of the discarnate spirits recorded through psychic research. The similarities between the two are so marked than any serious seeker after truth cannot fail to be impressed by them. On their own, each NDE or discarnate spirit report can be challenged. When compared, however, their similarities require considerable effort in any attempt to explain them away.

I end this chapter with the claimed words of 'Mrs Willett' recorded by the automatist Geraldine Cummins in her book *Swan on a Black Sea*:

> *There comes to me from the earth such a feeling of oppression, of worrying, of anxiety, of fear of death, and all is derived from non-belief. If they could but realise half the glory, even a fragment of the peace of this life I now experience. Oh! If I could make them accept it, there might at last be some rationality. Rationalists are irrational, and it makes such a confusion, creates so much fear, when death, that deliverer approaches.*

## Life After Death

In *Seth Speaks* Seth states:

> *There is an order of personalities, an honorary guard so to speak who are ever ready to lend assistance [to those who have recently died or passed over]. This honorary guard is made up of people both living and dead. Those who are living in your system of reality perform these activities in an 'out-of-body' experience whilst the physical body sleeps. They are familiar with the projection of consciousness, with the sensations involved, and they help orientate those who will not be returning to the physical body...*

And further:

> *This is not incidentally necessarily any kind of sombre endeavour, nor are the after death environments sombre at all. To the contrary, they are generally far more intense and joyful than the reality you now know.*

The 'honorary guard' Seth refers to is echoed in many writings and taped recollections. Those who pass over often recall being met by friends or relatives who have predeceased them. A welcome party as it were.

Paul Beard names the early environment experienced

immediately after death as the 'Summerland'. This environment is described in his book *Living On*:

> ...*There are things... of the same kind as you see on earth, only somehow different. They are real, but you have a sense that they are only temporary, that they just belong to that first waking stage... you begin to realise that all the things around you are really thought forms, and that it is arranged like that so as to make the transition easy from material life to spiritual life.*

In answer to the question: Where is this mysterious place that we go to after death? I can do no more than point the reader back to the opening section of this book where 'dark matter' and 'dark energy' were discussed. There is it seems a great deal of non-physical matter in our Universe. Matter without mass, that can exist within the same space as known matter and which can pass freely through the material of which the earth comprises.

In *Seth Speaks* we are told of the conscious state which exists immediately after death:

> *The inner portion of you (that survives death) does not suddenly change its methods of perception nor its characteristics after physical death.*

We are its seems the same personality after death as immediately before it. We do not suddenly change miraculously into something we were not before. As the old saying tells us, 'As above, so below.'

One of the characters referred to in *Living On* reinforces this:

> *You must remember that your surroundings hereafter are limited by your mental and spiritual development up to date. You are the same as you were because this is your conception of*

*yourself that you hold in your mind. Mind controls all things.*
*The present margins of the mental consciousness limit the*
*present capacity for perception.*

Emanuel Swedenborg in 1760, when he was seventy two years
of age, reported that the first state of man after death is like his
state in the world because his life, or focus, is still external. He
therefore possesses a similar face, speech and disposition; so that
he thinks he is still in the world. Because thought creates directly
in the image held in the mind then the 'thought' creation in the
immediate after death environment reflects this earthly image.

Maurice Barbanell in *The Barbanell Report* said:

> I*t is a strange thing this reality. You've got to realise constantly*
> *that you'll only see what you want to see, and so you have got*
> *to make a conscious effort to broaden the field, and sometimes*
> *you are seduced by seeing what you want to see… So much*
> *depends on what you want to see. Difficult to keep*
> *readjusting. Mother's reality not my reality. It is like speaking*
> *to people with different points of view, only the points of view*
> *are reflected around them. And so they have reality. Can be*
> *confusing. I am groping towards my own reality, can't be sure*
> *that I have achieved it yet. I know how easy it is to see what*
> *you expect to see. Comfortable trap, but still a trap.*

Barbanell's description is a very common one in his assertion that
after death 'you'll only see what you want to see'. Nothing it
seems is hidden in this state; thoughts are visible. What you are
inwardly is literally what appears to others. Thoughts are visible
with communication being via thought, not words; very
disconcerting indeed.

Barbanell commented:

> *Need a lot of will power and discipline over here.*

*Concentration not always easy. Over here concentration needed. Think it is because I'm a beginner. Can't afford to let my attention wander. Think of keeping your thoughts disciplined all of the time. Don't realise how undisciplined I was in my thinking.*

Those who deny the fact of their death may remain in the earth environment until such time as they can be reached and made to understand the reality of their new state. In fact, it seems that the pull of earth and familiar surroundings can be such as to draw the spirit back time and time again to familiar places, or places, where significant events happened to them. Even where these events were of a violent or unpleasant nature. The spirit it seems acts as if it were suffering from compulsive obsessive disorder. It returns again to the place where a significant memory imprint remains. This may account for stories of ghosts or haunting.

Neville Randell in his book *Life after Death* tells the story of 'Mr Higgins' a Painter and Decorator who died falling off a ladder and decided to return to see his wife thus:

*Sometimes, soon after death, either while still tied to this world, or soon after arriving in the next, people seem to get an overwhelming urge to visit those they loved best and have got to leave behind. Always they are warned it will be little comfort to them or their families. Almost always they go. So it was with Alfred Higgins.*

*'The next thing I knew I was standing in our kitchen, and I was watching my wife. She was standing over the sink peeling some potatoes. I thought I wonder if she knows I'm here, and I called her name. She didn't say nothing. She didn't hear me. My friend (guide) says:*

' *"She won't hear you, you know."*

' "Well I don't know. What could I do?"

' "Nothing you could do," he says. "But she may sense your presence. You never know. Let's just wait a little while."

'Then he says to me:

' "Concentrate your thought on her. Just think hard. Think as hard as you can. Think her name."

'I did. And all of a sudden she stood up and looked. She dropped the knife and potato she was peeling, and she looked round. Proper bewildered she looked, almost scared.'

'I was rather sorry in a way that I'd scared her. I realised it must have been me trying to get at her. She just flew out of that kitchen. She opened the door, and then sort of shut it again, and then she sat down, put her head on the table and started to cry. I felt awful about this. I thought, "Oh dear, this is terrible."

' "Don't worry," he said. "She senses. She knows in herself, she doesn't understand yet, but she knows in herself that you're near her." '

'Summerland' seems generally to be a place of great peace. An environment that gives the spirit time to recover from the travails of life. A time to adjust to the new form in which the spirit finds itself. It is non-judgemental except in so much as the spirit experiences only that which it is able to perceive. As was said 'mind is all'. So the state of mind will determine the environment experienced. If the mind holds patterns of a rigid Heaven and Hell form, then this will be that which is experienced. If the mind is violent and aggressive, then this is likely to be the environment created and experienced by the spirit. So 'Summerland' can be 'Shadowland' or even

'Winterland'. It seems that after death, perception really is all.

Once the spirit has adjusted to its new surroundings a period of life review – 'the judgement' of the religious – can take place. This seems to consist of a life review where the spirit re-experiences life events both from their own perception, and the perception of others who were affected by the events. In this re-experiencing the spirit feels the pain experienced by others that was caused by their own actions, and thus comes to better understand how their life and actions affected and helped or harmed others.

In Paul Beard's book *Living On*, W.T. Stead refers to this judgement thus:

> *At first there is nothing done but what is helpful and comforting – later there is a refining process to be gone through… On being established here, in the real world, each one is interviewed by one of the Advanced Spirits' Instructors and the whole record of earth is discussed and analysed. Reason, motive and result. The full and detailed record contains everything, there is nothing overlooked, and this is the time for paying the bill. Each is interviewed alone, and there is a minute analysis of all events, acts and thoughts. Then there is the making good to be gone through, the sum total to be paid… For all our thoughtlessness and our unkind acts and words – all that have had direct results must be paid for.*

As Paul Beard comments, communicators clearly find difficulty in conveying the experience of judgments in all of its depths, for it is the ultimate personal and individual experience.

In *Living On* an account of the judgement of 'Pauchard' is set out:

> *Every one of us, no matter who he may be, has at the bottom*

*of his being a layer of dregs of which he is not aware. I did not know how true that was until I got here. 'Purgatory' is not a fancy, it is a reality. We are good people you and I, and when coming here I expected to find only glory and delight, but after the first feeling of liberation has passed we are brought... directly face to face with the various departments of our 'I'. I assure you it is then – and only then – that one learns what self-knowledge means and it is not difficult to draw the conclusions. You cannot even imagine all the revelations that result from such objective encounters with our 'I' when seen... under different aspects. There are some very unpleasant moments to be passed through, I can assure you.*

In *Seth Speaks* Seth states, regarding this period of self-examination:

*You examine the fabric of the existence you have left, and you learn to understand how your experiences were the result of your own thoughts and emotions, and how these affected others. Until this examination is through you are not yet aware of the larger portions of your own identity. When you realise the significance and meaning of the life you have just left, then you are ready for conscious knowledge of your other existences.*

Life after death is often described in terms of tiers, layers or spheres, where each level must be worked through before it can be left behind. These spheres are best described as states of being, with differentiation between them best thought of as being similar to the separation of colours in a rainbow, with one colour merging smoothly and overlapping another. They are not movements in space, however, for the spirit world is described as devoid of space or time. Rather, it is a question of density rather than distance. Movements in being, from one state to another more rarefied state. The best description I can find is where earth matter being solid, like ice, changes to a more fluid state – water – before changing again into steam. Each state consisting of the same substance, but each in a different state of being.

It seems it is possible for the newly arrived spirit to travel 'down' to lower levels, denser levels, but not to ascend to 'higher' levels until their development is of such a state as to allow this. The 'higher' levels being of a too rarefied form for the unaccompanied spirit to cope with.

Many upon passing over after death are content to remain for long periods in 'Summerland' with its comforts. However, eventually the time arrives when the spirit is encouraged to move on. One described it thus:

> It's most peculiar. It seems as if you can go on and on. And then when you get browned off, or fed up, or think you know all there is to know of where you are, then you can sort of – just sort of go into a kind of sleep or something, and then go into a different sphere…

> No one's content for long. You give them everything that they want. You give them all the things they thought they needed. And after a time it palls on them, and they want a bit more of something else. They find that it isn't what they thought it was going to be. I thought I'd be content with all the things that I had (in Summerland), but I soon began to realise that although in a way I was doing things for others I wasn't doing enough. I was finding that these things didn't mean as much to me as they did before, and that there was something else I had to strive for. I had to find out what it was.

> You'll exhaust this place or this sphere, or this condition of life in which you are now. Eventually you'll realise that there is nothing more that you can learn here, or nothing more that's necessary to keep you here, and you'll find the urge and the need to extend your experience. And you'll pass into a different existence in a higher sphere or place where you'll be

*able to appreciate and learn and experience all sorts of things
that you couldn't possibly experience on this.*

The Rev Drayton Thomas, who died in 1953; who in his time
on earth was an exhaustive physical researcher introducing
Woods (the medium) to psychic investigations, reported on what
he had been told.

*'Have you visited any of the higher planes?' asked Woods.*

*'Well,' Drayton Thomas replied, 'there are laws which no one
can avoid. The point is, you are allowed to go on as far as you
have merited within yourself by your life, by your
development. But you cannot go into a higher sphere until you
are ready to enter into that state.'*

*'Of course one can go to many spheres below that particular
sphere of life in which you find yourself. But you cannot enter
into a higher condition until you yourself have merited it...'
'I would never dream of attempting to go to a condition or
sphere of life to which I was unsuited, to which I was unfitted,
for which I was not ready. I would go down into the lower
spheres because I could give a service... I could help those of a
lesser development. It is not possible for me to go into a higher
state of being. For one thing I would not be happy there. You
probably think it would be wonderful to have the experience
and one would actually be happy. But you wouldn't.'*

*'In a sense I suppose it is comparable in your world too. A
man can only be happy in an environment to which he is best
fitted, and to go into one which is a much more developed state
of being, although it may sound on the surface to be a
wonderful experience, one knows instinctively it is the law.
That you could not get peace or rest because you would not fit
in. You would be unsettled. You can only reach a given point
when you develop towards it.'*

Advanced spirits in the really high spheres, it seems, are too far removed to describe them to us directly. Any reports that do reach us are based on rumours or snippets of information which reach the inhabitants of the spheres still in contact with earth.

As George Hopkins, a Sussex farmer, stated in his communications to Woods:

> I've come to the conclusion that there are all these different spheres, or states of being. And as one progresses from one to another, things which once were vital or important gradually disappear according to your outlook and understanding... I think that it's feasible that on the higher spheres certain aspects of life change so considerably that it would hardly be recognisable to some as life in the same sense.
>
> I've been told – I don't know this – but I've been told that the very highly advanced souls – it is not necessary – in fact they don't feel the need to have bodies! Of course that's something I can't understand. But they say that when you become very highly advanced, you cease to have the need for a body, and you cease to exist in shape. Of course I don't understand that at all. It baffles me. But no doubt if I ever reach that stage it may be that I shall understand it.

Paul Beard's book *Living On*, referred to earlier, sets out his understanding, after years of research, of the various levels, or spheres of existence that are known. These he defines as:

- Summerland – the land of reception and illusion.
- The First Heaven.
- The Second Death.
- The Second Heaven.
- The Third Heaven.

After 'the judgement' it seems that the spirit passes into the

First Heaven. This is followed by the Second Death which Beard describes as the death of the 'personal self'. This death occurs through the spirit ceasing to identify itself with the personality that it once was. Where it becomes able to observe its previous personality with some detachment. As he describes it:

*What is meant by our personal self? It is the sum of all the memories of the experiences, thoughts and feelings which made up his sense of himself as a particular identity during his past life on earth, which continues to live on as the same familiar person after death.*

The Second Death can be described as the breaking, or shedding, of this image. In this casting off of what was the personality, comes the finding of the true identity; the being behind the mask of the personality. So a loosening process comes about, a gradual letting go of the persona. The movement from being a personal individual to becoming a being of spirit. Yet this change does not bring with it a loss of personal consciousness, rather a greater awareness of the greater beingness that has lived before, lives now and will live again. In Christian terms, it is the losing of oneself in order to find oneself. It is the transformation from the chrysalis to the butterfly.

As Paul Beard puts it:

*In the words of the discarnate teacher: 'Men will lose all the shells of unwanted matter accumulated around them... of a soul kind... and will become spiritual...'*

And further:

*'...that Second Death, so marvellous and yet so terrible an experience. For in this life we cling with all our might to Self... And then... crown and climax of all our striving,*

*comes utter relinquishment – such is the marvel and miracle of*
*the human soul and spirit…'*

Following the Second Death the spirit passes into the Second
Heaven.

In Paul Beard's book *Living On* the transition is described as:

> *…not separation, but a feeling of complete serenity and peace*
> *with no concern for anything, or awareness of people around*
> *you… you are supported by something that is almost*
> *unidentifiable, you have lost your own identity without any*
> *concern or anxiety about it. It is a true spiritual release…*
> *Then you become aware… of what I can only describe as a*
> *harmonic reverberation around you, a beautiful ecstasy… You*
> *feel this divine, ecstatic unified joy that you just don't know*
> *what is happening to you.*

No being is forced to pass through these states. Each proceeds at
their own pace, at their own ability to develop and absorb, or
experience the changes in circumstances. There is no compulsion
or compunction indicated, just an inevitable drawing on, an
inevitability of destination as it were. Some, at the lower spheres
or levels, return to physical form quickly without passing
through the 'Second Death or proceeding to higher levels. Some
it seems require further physical existences to develop their
understanding to a level where they can proceed further after
passing over, for reincarnation is often referred to as a fact.

Only after passing into the Second Heaven does it seem that
awareness of previous lives becomes possible. In *Seth Speaks*, Seth
states that:

> *Until this examination is through you are not yet aware of the*
> *larger portions of your own identity. When you realise the*
> *significance and meaning of the life you have just left, then*

*you are ready for conscious knowledge of your other existences.*

It seems that there must be movement beyond the recent past life personality before an awareness of other lives becomes possible. Each past life must be seen in context in order that previous existences can become relevant. Seth postulates that the 'greater being' consists of the totality of all past lives, each being a facet of the greater whole as it were. Only when this state has been reached can a being consider the possibility of reincarnating again dependent upon perceived needs of further development and learning.

In Paul Beard's book *Living On* this period of self-examination is further elaborated:

> *There are times when we have to be set apart, to undergo a retreat, in order to understand more of our development. During this retreat I was shown not only my earth life, but the whole course of my evolution... Once you have conquered and risen above the small self, you can go through the test... You can learn so much from it and yet feel no pain, because you see how each mistake was turned to your advantage in spite of yourself, by the light of the Divinity working within you as far as you would allow it to.*

> *You are able to see the line of gold which has persisted through every thing, and you think only of that. You store in your aura all the lessons that you think will be helpful to you in future intercourse with other people or in any work you may be given to do.*

So the idea of reincarnation, of living again and again. The concept that so disturbed Edgar Cayce: 'The Sleeping Prophet' – the famous American psychic of the last century, that he gave up his readings for a period of time because the idea of living again was so diametrically opposed to his fundamentalist Christian beliefs, has great validity.

Reincarnation provides possible answers to so many of the unanswerable questions of life. It makes sense of the lives of those who die young with their promise unfilled. It suggests answers to the seeming unfairness of life for those who are born disabled or in poverty. It provides a pattern against which the Universal Laws of life can be met. So what does the study of reincarnation tell us?

## Reincarnation

The theory of reincarnation is very old indeed. It is found in the Jewish Cabbala; it was held by Plato, Pythagorus, and the later Platonists, it may even be found in the New Testament with comments by Jesus, in both Mark (9:12) and Matthew (17:11), relating to Elijah being reborn as John the Baptist. It is a tenet of faith in many Eastern religions, with more people believing in it than not. Christianity, which in the main denies the concept of reincarnation, posits that we are judged on how we lived during one lifetime. This proposition fails to answer the question as to what happens to infants who die young, or whose lives are cut short violently. How are these poor ones judged? One of the advantages of reincarnation is surely that those who died violently, or who die young without having the opportunity to reach maturity, are able to be reborn again to live out a full lifespan.

Transmigration, the passing of the soul at death into a new body or new form of being: transmigration and reincarnation, or the rebirth of a soul in a new body, are roughly synonymous. Resurrection, especially the Christian doctrine of resurrection, is the rising again to life of the physical body after death, this is not reincarnation.

There are echoes of the information reported on in the previous chapter in the beliefs held by Plato who maintained that the soul is eternal, pre-existent, and wholly spiritual. He believed that after entering the body, the soul becomes contaminated through association with bodily passions. Delivery from the body occurring only after the soul has passed through a series of transmigrations. If the soul has been of good character in its several existences, it is allowed to return to a state of pure being. If, however, its character has deteriorated in its transmigrations, it ends in 'Tartarus', the place of eternal damnation.

The idea of reincarnation was never adopted into orthodox Judaism or Christianity. Among Jews, it seems that only the mystical Cabbalists adopted it as part of their system of philosophy. Early Christians who adopted reincarnational doctrines were at risk of being declared heretics by the Church. In Eastern religious thought and philosophy, reincarnation appears first in doctrinal form in the Indian religious and philosophical collection of the Upanishads. It is one of the major tenets of the three major Eastern religions: Hinduism; Buddhism; and Jainism. According to modern Hinduism, the state in which the soul is reborn is predetermined by the good or bad deeds (*karma*) done in former lives, release from the karmic cycle being achieved only after atonement for bad deeds, and a recognition that the individual soul and the universal soul are identical. Buddhism specifically rejects the existence of the individual soul. However, its definition of the cause-and-effect chain of rebirths is virtually indistinguishable from the Hindu doctrine of reincarnation.

The Dalai Lama, the spiritual leader of Tibetan Buddhism, is believed by his followers to be a reincarnation of the Buddha. When he dies, his soul is thought to enter the body of a newborn boy, who, after being identified by traditional tests, becomes the new Dalai Lama. By tradition, much searching precedes the identification of the child who will attain this significant world role.

The leading researcher into claimed reincarnational memories, in the Western hemisphere, is Ian Stevenson, M.D., Director of the Division of Personality Studies at the University of Virginia Charlottesville, Virginia. He is the leading scientist who has studied the claimed survival of the personality after death for over forty years. In 1966, his book *Twenty Cases – Suggestive of Reincarnation* was published. He has since published a number of major books and scholarly articles dealing with the subject of reincarnation. His work has taken him across the world to India, Ceylon, Brazil, Alaska and the Lebanon investigating and reporting on claimed reincarnational memories mainly held by children.

In his book *Twenty Cases – Suggestive of Reincarnation* he reports that he has records of six hundred cases of possible reincarnation, of which he personally has investigated one third. In the concluding remarks in this book he states:

> *In 1960 I concluded my review of cases suggestive of reincarnation without opting firmly for any one theory as explanatory of all the cases. I still hold to this general position (in 1974). We may find some cases we can best explain as due to fraud, cryptomnesia (according to this theory the child investigated would somehow have known a person or some other source having the information he later 'remembered') or extrasensory perception with personation (perhaps mixed with telepathy or retrocognition). For other cases we may favour survivalist explanations such as possession or reincarnation… I believe, however, that the evidence favouring reincarnation as a hypothesis for the cases of this type has increased since I published my review (in 1966). This increase has come from several different kinds of observations and cases, but chiefly from the observations of the behaviour of the children claiming the memories, and the study of cases with specific or idiosyncratic skills and with congenital birthmarks and deformities.*

Bishop Hugh Montifiore in his book *The Paranormal, a Bishop*

*Investigates*, writes of an interview he conducted with Professor Stevenson whilst researching his book. In this interview Bishop Montifiore asked Professor Stevenson:

*'One of the things that puzzles me is how a person who has died exists before reincarnation. I mean do you think of a bare soul, a kind of ground of being, or an astral body that is affected by the previous physical body to which it belonged, or again is this an area about which you really don't want to say anything?'*

*Professor Stevenson replied: 'Well, I don't think that we can avoid saying something about it. Some of the subjects whose cases we have studied say something about another existence between death and presumably rebirth in some other planes of existence (possible references to Summerland, etc.), and some of them recount events that they have observed in the family that they have left…'*

Stevenson, whose work in the main has been in studying young children who had evidenced memories of a previous existence, when asked why their memories of a presumed past life tended to fade with age replied:

*…the reason may be the same as the reason why we forget memories of our infancy and early childhood… I think the memories of early childhood get covered… I think that the memories of the events may simply become layered underneath the earliest memories… The memories of previous lives may be a defect*

(this in answer to a question as to why so few people have memories of an earlier life)

*it is not necessarily a gift. The children (with such memories) are often in a state of considerable turmoil, with a sense of being loyal to two different families. A feeling of being isolated, being different. A stranger in their own family, I don't think it is a gift at all.*

A discarnate entity, reported on in Paul Beard's book *Living On*, refers to the pattern of reincarnation experienced through many lifetimes thus:

*Perhaps the most important change which has come over me in the period since I left the earth is the deepening of the realisation and confirmation of the serialised life which we all lead... There is a definite continuing thread. One meets old friends, tried companions, and former teachers. From conversations and communions with them, and through listening to their stories, the missing portions of one's own experiences return to memory and the pattern is built up anew.*

This entity continues:

*As the chief actor in my own particular drama I had become, as it were, so immersed in the last act or chapter that the incidents, tragedies, lessons of the previous scenes had tended to grow misty. But now I am beginning slowly and laboriously to piece together the scenes into a whole, into a serialised effort at living.*

Albert Pauchard in the same book is reported as saying of this state:

*First I saw Albert Pauchard... just as if he were outside of me... I realised that the I who was observing thus was not 'Albert Pauchard'. At that instant I gradually recognised who I was. I did not see this real I, but realised it by an inner warmth which kept on intensifying and increasing in light... I understood then that our 'personality' is only the 'shadow' of our I. A shadow which always moves towards perfection –*

*through the lives on earth and the lives in Heaven… And which forms itself according to the outline of the one who had given it existence. The outline of the real I.*

Maurice Barbanell in *The Barbanell Report* observed:

*I have some awareness of past lives, still not clear. Each time (of passing) has a different awareness. Think it is easier to pass when you are primitive. You don't know what is happening, don't question; when more evolved, it is more complicated. The more simple the soul the more acceptance. More soul evolves, more questions to be answered, more awareness and need to understand. Understand now why some guides speak in riddles; even explaining is difficult, different concepts at work.*

Barbanell goes on:

*I know that I had to come back and do what I did because of religious intolerance (in a former time). That now I had to stick with truth without the trappings of religion. I think this is why I was so anti-religion when I was around last time. I was so aware on a subconscious level that I was not to be trapped again in this vicious circle (of organised religion).*

Paul Beard in *Living On* comments:

*that it is interesting that those spirits whose after death recollections are closest to earth, do not mention reincarnation.*

It seems that very unevolved beings, with scant spiritual understanding are likely to reincarnate very quickly. Remaining close to earth's vibrational level after death allows them to return quickly, thus enabling them to learn more from the physical stage of development. More evolved beings appear to benefit more from longer periods of reflection between incarnations.

Reincarnation also seems to make greater sense of both inherited strengths and weaknesses. The concept of reincarnation can give meaning to disabilities and other deeply held personal characteristics, not in a karmic sense, a debt to be repaid, but rather as a determination to experience, or meet some personal soul desire, as a development need or opportunity.

In answer to the question: Why do we not remember past lives? The answer from Seth is that each incarnation is complete within itself. That the memory of past lives would prevent us from experiencing anew and, thus, would hinder our potential for development in each incarnation.

Seth in *Seth Speaks* contributes significantly to the reincarnation debate by stating:

> *You do not understand your own multi-dimensional reality...*
> *you live many existences at one time... Time is not a series of*
> *moments... there is an assumption that all knowledge comes*
> *from the senses. That all information comes from without, that*
> *nothing comes from within... lives are lived simultaneously,*
> *each within its own focus... these creative periods represent*
> *what you call reincarnational lives. They all exist basically at*
> *one time... These plays (lives) seem to be taking place one*
> *before the other, and so these communications seem to intensify*
> *the false idea that time is a series of moments passing in a*
> *single line from some inconceivable beginning to some*
> *inconceivable end... Progress has nothing to do with time...*
> *But with psychic and spiritual focus... Each play is entirely*
> *different from any other. It is not correct therefore to suppose*
> *that your actions in this life are <u>caused</u> by a previous existence,*
> *or that you are being punished for crimes in a past one. Your*
> *lives are simultaneous.*

Seth reinforces the Universal Law that: 'Consciousness always spontaneously seeks the path that leads to its greatest growth or becomingness' by stating in *Seth Speaks*:

> *Your own multi-dimensional personality is so endowed that it can have all these experiences and still retain its identity. You are the multi-dimensional self who has these existences, who creates and takes part in these plays... It is only because you focus in this particular role now that you identify your entire being with it... Consciousness is in a state of becoming... Your multi-dimensional self is also then in a state of becoming... Each actor has an inner guide line... and there are periods set and allowed for within the play itself in which each actor retires in order to refresh himself. In these (periods) he is informed through the inner senses of his other roles, and he realises that he is far more than the self appearing in any given play.*

He goes on to claim that we have at all times an inner awareness of our greater self. A realisation of this enables us to solve problems in life more easily, as well as tackle new challenges more successfully.

Seth further states in *Seth Speaks* that reincarnation is not the only avenue open to us after death, that other opportunities are available and adopted by some:

> *There are unlimited varieties of experience open to you after death, all possible, but some less probable than others according to your development. Very generally now, there are three main areas, though exceptions and extraordinary cases can take other roads.*

> *You may decide upon reincarnation. You may decide to focus on your past life... or you may enter another system of probability entirely... Now some individuals, some personalities, prefer a life organisation bound about past, present and future in a seemingly logical structure, and these*

*persons usually choose reincarnation. Some simply find the physical system not to their liking, and in such a way take leave of it, this cannot be done however until the reincarnational cycle, once chosen, is completed... some finished with reincarnation may choose to re-enter the cycle acting as teachers or leaders.*

Neither, it seems, is the process of reincarnating a simple one of deciding that it would be nice to experience physical form again. Many issues need to be taken into account in deciding the most appropriate life that will provide the greatest opportunity for progression. In *Seth Speaks* Seth elaborates:

*When most people think of reincarnation, they think in terms of one life progression in which the soul perfects itself in each succeeding life. This is a gross simplification. It seems that choices are involved in determining which aspect of being will benefit most from reincarnating. Where intellectual ability may have been high in one incarnation, emotional development might be preferred in another. The suppression of one aspect of being may then create the desire for it in another. The true value of the suppressed aspect being fully appreciated in this way... At the end of the reincarnational cycle you understand quite thoroughly that you, the basic identity, the inner core of your being is more than the sum of your reincarnational personalities.*

And further that:

*Throughout your reincarnational existences you expand your consciousness, your ideas, your perceptions, your values... you grow spiritually as you learn to step aside from conceptions and dogma.*

Geraldine Cummings, in her book *Swan on a Black Sea* refers to each as being part of a Group Soul. This Group Soul often consists of those who appear in each lifetime as relatives or close friends. Such Group Souls it seems cooperate in carrying out specific broad humanity advancing, and personal developmental tasks, during each lifetime. In her book she states:

*The human being's soul belongs to, or is derived from a Group Soul, which is inspired by one spirit. If we make progress in the after death, we become more and more aware of this Group Soul. It is more than a brotherhood, it is organic, an organised psychic structure. Its spirit is the bond that holds together a number of souls. The spirit might be described as a thought of God, or as the light from above – the creative light from above... As we evolve in the hereafter, we individual units enter into the memories and experiences of other lives that are derived from the earthly and other existences of the souls that preceded and that are of our Group. It is not therefore necessary to reincarnate, as Buddhists and Theosophists, I believe, claim, hundreds of times on earth.*

The arguments for life after death and for reincarnation are powerful indeed. They make sense of what, at times in life, may appear senseless and of little value. If our pain and suffering has value beyond that which may immediately be apparent to us, then through this perhaps it can be ennobled, and borne with greater strength, and perhaps even some joy.

If, in addition, they hold out the promise of meeting loved ones who have predeceased us, then death indeed can be an event to be anticipated with pleasure. The realisation that attending a funeral also is the one we mourn, is also reassuring in its own way. Looked at in this way a funeral can be a time not only for reflection, but also of celebration. A time for silently wishing the unseen observer well in their journey ever onward.

But more than this is the concept of eternal development, of progress and growth being made irrespective of how mean or short the life. Of being part of a greater whole, with death merely a transition from one state of being to another, not the extinguishment that many suppose; this is a seductive proposition indeed.

The concept of a continuing life provides the form and structure which at times may be lacking in day to day life, with each day remorselessly following its predecessor. The acceptance of an inner self that survives physical death, that is provided with the opportunity to rest and review the life just lived. That decides how best to develop further before deciding, choosing and being reborn. Such a concept can indeed make life meaningful, irrespective of our specific life circumstances or station. Life can, after all, have great purpose and meaning.

There are many I am sure who will read this and reject the concept of living on, or of reincarnating. How often I have heard the words, 'Well, you only live once.' How often I have been tempted to reply, 'Well, maybe, maybe not.' But I have chosen not do so because of how deep the subject of living on; of living more than one life, can be to those who have not considered it. Dealing with one life is more than many can cope with without the complexity that can come from accepting the notion of life after death and reincarnation. Yet I find the concept somehow reassuring, not because it proposes that life does not end with death. In some ways the concept of oblivion takes off the pressure to conform, or try to improve and become more than we are. Leaves us with only our conscience to guide us. The acceptance of a continuing life brings with it great responsibility; means that what we do in, and with, life really matters.

The suggestion of a future life review is not one to be feared, however the realisation of such a possibility means that the way in which I live my life, the way in which I conduct myself, particularly in my relationships and my dealings with other people becomes of paramount importance. Against the background of a continuing existence, relationships take on a much greater meaning than I may, in earlier times, have appreciated. The realisation that at some future point the 'I' of my being could be looking back at my life, and determining whether what I did was done honestly, in accordance with the principles that I hold about life, and in full consideration of the impact that my decisions, and the way in which I conducted myself affected others. Without doubt such a realisation – such a 'taking the ends off life' – changes the whole perspective of life in every respect.

In many ways I am thrown back to the opening section of this book and forced to review the 'Purposes of Life' set out therein. For if these are indeed the purposes of my life, and the life of all others, then it would be wise to make a start in meeting them in every area of life, and, through my writing, encourage others to do likewise.

In *Seth Speaks* Seth states that our soul is:

> ...*energy concentrated to a degree quite unbelievable to you... within it are personality potentials beyond your understanding. You are but one manifestation of your soul. You do yourself a disservice to imagine that your present self is your entire personality. Or insist that your identity be maintained unchanged through an endless eternity.*

It seems then that in accordance with Universal Law we are constantly being drawn onward on our journey to return to the source of our being. As our development as beings progresses, so we see more and know more. For this is the purpose of Universal Law as a re-examination of the four Universal Laws shows:

1.  Consciousness always seeks its highest potential.

2.  Energy constantly transforms.

3.  Consciousness is of absolute duration; it had no beginning and will have no end.

4.  Consciousness always spontaneously seeks the path that leads to its greatest growth or becomingness.

Each of these Laws is met through the concept of reincarnation. Each makes sense only against the background of living and experiencing a variety of lives, with each incarnation adding to our innate knowledge of how life works. Each allowing us to develop further as multi-faceted 'whole' beings.

An acceptance of the reality of reincarnation has enormous implications for how we live our life and the value that we place on our life experiences. What we do today matters, no aspect of it being unimportant; our relationships, our families, our work all come together to make up who and what we are today. Whether the inner us is 'bright and shining' or 'dull and grey' it seems is always our choice. The creative energy of the Universe is equally available to all. Whether a belief in a continuing existence is accepted or not is for each person to decide; as my Methodist Minister friend stated: 'If I am wrong, and there is no life after death, then I am not going to be in a position to know much about it. If I am right however, I will have a head start on those who do not believe in a continuing life.' A good note, I think, on which to end this section of the book.

## Conclusion

On the introductory page of the Life section of this book are the words:

> *Between stimulus and response there is a space. In that space lies our freedom and our power to choose our response. In our response lies our growth and our happiness.*

I first read these words in an introduction that Stephen Covey, the well-known leadership teacher and author, had written for a book whose author, Alex Pattakos had been a student of Viktor Frankl's. Covey had not penned the words himself, but remembered them from a book that he had picked up while on holiday in Hawaii; regrettably he was unable to trace their originator. Covey stated that these words graphically illustrated the three values that Viktor Frankl continually taught throughout his lifetime: the Creative value; the Experiential value; and the Attitudinal value.

The truth of these values adequately sum up the outcome of my years of searching. For it is not what happens after death that is important, fascinating though this may be, it is what happens in life. All of my searching has been directed to finding the truths that work throughout life. That hold fast no matter what the circumstances. Truths that act as an anchor when coping with pain, tragedy, suffering, grief and death. Truths that have within them the attributes to enable us to grow in dignity and stature as human beings, both individually and collectively. Truths that when acted upon have the potential to raise us above mere creaturehood.

The power of choice is present in the space between stimulus and response. No one can take this from us. No matter how powerful or mighty. No matter what the circumstances we find ourselves in; the freedom to choose our response cannot be taken from us, for this is the ultimate freedom that all people have no matter their race, colour, creed or life circumstance.

The fundamental questions that led me to commence my searching all those years ago still remain. They will remain until the last human draws breath. The answers which satisfy me, upon which I can rest my weight as it were, are now clearer for me. They may not be the same answers as my readers will reach. They do not encapsulate the whole of life's truth, I would be amazed if they did. For as St Paul wrote in Corinthians:

*For now we see through a glass darkly…*

There will always be a haziness to the conclusions we reach about life. For what we are studying we are experiencing. We can never in physical form truly detach ourselves from life and stand back to reach a finite unchanging judgement. Life will always be a moving target.

The uniqueness of each person's life is part of that which makes life so special. We are not robots nor machines programmed to follow specific actions in order to produce predictable results. Each of us is different, each of us unique, and each must seek and find their own truth. In this book, I have merely sought to provide pointers to possible answers to the fundamental questions posed by life. For this is all any author can do. I welcome disagreement, for disagreement presupposes the evaluation and rejection of the conclusions I have reached and the formation of alternative views. If my writing is no more than food for thought or 'grist to the mill', then it will have served its purpose.

Without doubt there is a purpose to life and that purpose is growth and development that brings with it an ever-expanding awareness of consciousness and our place in the Universe. The truth is that we can never learn more than we are capable of understanding. The expansion of conscious brings with it the ability to see more and understand more. It can be likened to climbing a mountain. An exercise requiring skill, ingenuity, endurance, perseverance, resolution and not a little effort. Yet one which brings with it clear rewards. Rewards of satisfaction and a growth in self-esteem. A growing belief in one's own powers of determination and durability and, beyond all, the ability to see so much more because of the vantage point that one has reached.

No one can admire the views possible in life unless they too have made the effort to climb the mountain. Pictures will never do it justice. We can describe what we have seen to others, but it will merely be that, a description and not the real thing. So it is with personal growth and development as beings. To know more we must actively seek to know more; we must test what we learn to satisfy ourself of its validity, for we must never accept the truth of another, always we should seek to find our own truth.

The growth I refer to throughout this book is not an intellectual thing given only to the most intelligent. It is a growth that is open to all seekers after truth. It is not to be found in public acclaim or in large bank balances. Rather, it is to be found in quiet places, in reflection, in small kindnesses to others and most of all in love for one's fellow man. Those who know me will attest to the fact that I am not the most loving of people when it comes to my fellow man. I am impatient and at times ultra critical. But I try, for I know that my personal growth will be enhanced exponentially by practising and learning this most difficult of personal skills. Do not misunderstand me here when I speak of love, I do not mean soppy, fluffy love but tough love. Love which on occasions means moving both yourself and another out of the comfort zone that so many 'do gooders' reside in. Love which, if the Bible is to be believed, was practised by Christ and exemplified in his crucifixion.

We do indeed possess the power of creation; we are an integral portion of 'All That Is'; the power that creates and sustains our known Universe. The words that I would like to see on my tombstone, if ever I were to have such a thing, are 'Thought creates all'. Not some thought, not occasional creation, but all thought bringing into being the whole of creation. The creation that makes up the whole of my life and your life, without exception. This the most pertinent of truths which when once universally accepted will transform humanity and bring about changes of which we can now only dream about.

I will end by quoting Myriad who at Stonehenge told me that:

> *Your purpose is to reactivate the memory of the earth.*
> *Through reactivating and focusing your own energy*
> *And the memory of your wholeness and connectedness to all.*
> *It is not necessary to do anything except be.*
> *You are merely about a most instantaneous recognition*
> *Of the great joy of yourself.*
> *And if you allow yourself to do such a thing*
> *And do not push and try most hard.*
> *Then you will find that you have quite got it.*

Dennis D. Hunt
*June 2006*

# Bibliography

Paul Beard *Survival of Death,* Hodder and Stoughton.
Paul Beard *Living On,* George Allen and Unwick.
Paul Beard *Hidden Man,* Pilgrim Books.
Paul Boks *Into The Silent Land,* Atlantic Monthly Press.
Marie Cherrie *The Barbanell Report,* Pilgrim Books.
Geraldine Cummins *Swan on a Black Sea,* Pilgrim Trust.
Dr Peter & E. Fenwick *The Truth in the Light,* Berkeley
Publishing Group.
Lesley Flint *Voices in the Dark,* Macmillan.
Viktor Frankl *Man's Search For Meaning,* Random House.
Viktor Frankl *The Doctor and the Soul,* Souvenir Press Ltd.
Viktor Frankl *The Will to Meaning,* Plume Books.
Geoffrey Gore *Death Grief and Mourning,* Cresset.
Dr E. Holmes *The Science of Mind,* Dodd, Mead and Company.
C. S. Lewis *Merely Christianity,* Harper San Fransisco.
Abraham Maslow *Motivation and Personality,* Longman.
Hugh Montifiore *The Paranormal – A Bishop Investigates,* Upfront
Publishing.
F.W.H. Myers *Human Personality and its Survival of Bodily Death,*
Hampton Roads Publishing Company.
Norman Vincent Peale *The Power of Positive Thinking,* Fawcett
Books.
Neville Randell *Life After Death,* Corgi.
Jane Roberts *Seth Speaks,* Prentice Hall Press.
Jane Roberts *The Seth Material,* Prentice Hall Press.

Jane Roberts *The Nature of Personal Reality,* Prentice Hall Press.
Jane Roberts *The Individual and the Nature of Mass Events,* Prentice Hall Press.
Michael Ruse *Can a Darwinian be a Christian?* Cambridge University Press.
Ian Stevenson *Twenty Cases – Suggestive of Reincarnation,* Virginia.
Thomas Sugrue *The Story of Edgar Cayce,* ARE Press.
Emanuel Swedenborg *Conversations with Angels,* Chrysalis Books.
Signe Toksvig *Emanuel Swedenborg,* Swedenborg Foundation.
Yatri *Unknown Man,* Fireside.
A Course in Miracles, Arkana.

## Websites of Interest

Society for Psychic Research:
www.spr.ac.uk

College of Psychic Studies:
www.collegepsychicstudies.co.uk

Lesley Flint recordings:
www.freewebs.com/afterlife/flint/flintrecordings.htm

Edgar Cayce:
www.edgarcayce.org

Jane Roberts – Seth:
www.sethcenter.com

Viktor Frank:
www.logotherapy.univie.ac